Space, Place, and Children's Reading Development

Bloomsbury Perspectives on Children's Literature

Bloomsbury Perspectives on Children's Literature seeks to expand the range and quality of research in children's literature through publishing innovative monographs by leading and rising scholars in the field. With an emphasis on cross and inter-disciplinary studies, this series takes literary approaches as a starting point, drawing on the particular capacity for children's literature to open out into other disciplines.

Series Editor
Dr Lisa Sainsbury, Director of the National Centre for Research in Children's Literature, Roehampton University, UK.

Editorial Board
Professor M. O. Grenby (Newcastle University, UK), Dr Marah Gubar (University of Pittsburgh, USA), Dr Vanessa Joosen (Tilburg University, The Netherlands).

Titles in the Series
Adulthood in Children's Literature, Vanessa Joosen
The Courage to Imagine: The Child Hero in Children's Literature, Roni Natov
Ethics in British Children's Literature: Unexamined Life,
Lisa Sainsbury
Fashioning Alice: The Career of Lewis Carroll's Icon, 1860–1901, Kiera Vaclavik
From Tongue to Text: A New Reading of Children's Poetry, Debbie Pullinger
Literature's Children: The Critical Child and the Art of Idealisation, Louise Joy
Rereading Childhood Books: A Poetics, Alison Waller
Irish Children's Literature and the Poetics of Memory, Rebecca Long
British Children's Literature and Material Culture, Jane Suzanne Carroll

Forthcoming Titles
Activist Authors and British Child Readers of Colour, Karen Sands-O'Connor
The Dark Matter of Children's "Fantastika" Literature, Chloé Germaine Buckley
British Children's Literature in Japanese Culture, Catherine Butler

Space, Place, and Children's Reading Development

Mapping the Connections

Margaret Mackey

BLOOMSBURY ACADEMIC
LONDON • NEW YORK • OXFORD • NEW DELHI • SYDNEY

BLOOMSBURY ACADEMIC
Bloomsbury Publishing Plc
50 Bedford Square, London, WC1B 3DP, UK
1385 Broadway, New York, NY 10018, USA
29 Earlsfort Terrace, Dublin 2, Ireland

BLOOMSBURY, BLOOMSBURY ACADEMIC and the Diana logo are trademarks of Bloomsbury Publishing Plc

First published in Great Britain 2022
Paperback edition published 2024

Copyright © Margaret Mackey, 2022

Margaret Mackey has asserted her right under the Copyright, Designs and Patents Act, 1988, to be identified as Author of this work.

For legal purposes the Acknowledgments on pp. xiv–xv constitute an extension of this copyright page.

Cover design by Rebecca Heselton
Cover image © Zoonar GmbH/Alamy Stock Photo

This work is published open access subject to a Creative Commons Attribution-NonCommercial-NoDerivatives 4.0 International licence (CC BY-NC-ND 4.0, https://creativecommons.org/licenses/by-nc-nd/4.0/). You may re-use, distribute, and reproduce this work in any medium for non-commercial purposes, provided you give attribution to the copyright holder and the publisher and provide a link to the Creative Commons licence.

Bloomsbury Publishing Plc does not have any control over, or responsibility for, any third-party websites referred to or in this book. All internet addresses given in this book were correct at the time of going to press. The author and publisher regret any inconvenience caused if addresses have changed or sites have ceased to exist, but can accept no responsibility for any such changes.

A catalogue record for this book is available from the British Library.

Library of Congress Cataloging-in-Publication Data
Names: Mackey, Margaret, author.
Title: Space, place, and children's reading development :
mapping the connections / Margaret Mackey.
Description: London, UK ; New York, NY : Bloomsbury Academic, 2022. |
Series: Bloomsbury perspectives on children's literature
Identifiers: LCCN 2021058938 | ISBN 9781350275959 (hardback) |
ISBN 9781350275997 (paperback) | ISBN 9781350275966 (ebook) |
ISBN 9781350275973 (epub) | ISBN 9781350275980
Subjects: LCSH: Reading, Psychology of. | Literacy–Social aspects. |
Place attachment–Psychological aspects. | Maps–Psychological aspects.
Classification: LCC BF456.R2 M23 2022 | DDC 372.4–dc23/eng/20220406
LC record available at https://lccn.loc.gov/2021058938

ISBN: HB: 978-1-3502-7595-9
PB: 978-1-3502-7599-7
ePDF: 978-1-3502-7596-6
eBook: 978-1-3502-7597-3

Series: Bloomsbury Perspectives on Children's Literature

Typeset by Newgen KnowledgeWorks Pvt. Ltd., Chennai, India

To find out more about our authors and books visit www.bloomsbury.com and sign up for our newsletters.

*This book is dedicated to
Annabelle, Gabriel, Eleanor, and Lucy,
my reading buddies and my great delight —
Lots of love, Granny*

Contents

List of Figures		xi
List of Tables		xiii
Acknowledgments		xiv
1	Introduction	1
	The Role of the Maps	3
	The Project	4
	What Follows	6
2	The Mapmakers and the Maps	10
	The Participants	10
	The Maps and Their Makers	12
	The Urban Maps	13
	Images of Home	15
	Park Areas	19
	Abstract	21
	Fiction-Oriented Maps	23
	Preliminary Patterns	27
3	Compass and Key	28
	Where Is North?	28
	Preliminary Questions	28
	Key Terms	32
	(Im)materiality	33
	The Life Space and the Reading Space	34
	Movement	35
	The Subjunctive and the Deictic	40
	Agency	43
	Autotopography	44
	Managing the Interface	46

GEOGRAPHIC SPACES

The First Place

4	Home and Away: Stability, Disruption, and Agency	50
	Security, Fear, and Fantasy: Amy	53
	Stability and Specificity: Riya	57
	Change and Growth: Liang	61
	A Double Identity: Laura	64
	A Seamless Transition: Lily	67
	Purposes of Reading	70
	Reading Spaces	72

Social Spaces

5	Family Matters: Relationships and the Development of Reading Spaces	74
	Strategies of Access Management: Suleman	75
	A Relational World of Reading: Amani	81
	The Social Face of a Reading Life: Halia	84
	Reading and Relationships	86
	Life Spaces and Reading Spaces	89

Domestic Spaces

6	The Home Range: Rehearsals and Repertoire	91
	Life on the Geographical Home Range	91
	Rehearsing a Repertoire with the Body	94
	Building a Repertoire from a Textual Home Range	100
	Cartoon Watching	104
	The Textual Home Range as Glocal	106

TEXTUAL SPACES

Border Country

7	Fundamental Scenes of the Reading Space: The Forest	110
	The Forest of the Reading Space	119
	The Cultural Forest	121
	Border Country	123

A Shared Fictional World

8	The Many Reading Spaces of Harry Potter	126
	The Readers	129
	Growing with Harry Potter: Matt	133
	The Portals	137

PSYCHOLOGICAL SPACES

Interior Worlds

9	Diversity Inside and Out	144
	Varieties of Visualization—and the Nonvisualizers	146
	Specific Visuals	146
	Transient Visuals	149
	Make-do Visuals	150
	Culturally Specific Images	152
	Transfer from Films/TV/Other Books	154
	Just Knowing	156
	Visualization and Readers	157
	The Bigger Picture	160

LITERARY SPACES

Ongoing Worlds

10	Opening a Lifelong Reading Space	164
	Ongoing Reading Spaces	165
	Living in Other Worlds: Rahina	166
	Exploring and Imagining: Roman	174
	Merging Many Worlds: Ying Yu	180
	Lifelong Reading Spaces	184

LIFE SPACES AND READING SPACES

Conclusions

11	Reading Minds in Motion	194
	Drawing Conclusions	195
	Reading as Reflection	196

Reading in Motion	199
Learning How to *Be* in Space	201
Counterpoint	203
Moving Around and Between Versions	205
Complicating the Straight-Line Arrow	209
References	215
Index	221

Figures

1.1	Moving through the territory	8
2.1	Laura's maps (the reach of the map on top is global)	14
2.2	Liang's map: a small town in Eastern China	15
2.3	Two of Lily's three maps: a Chinese and an Ontario neighborhood	16
2.4	Halia's first Canadian house	17
2.5	Amy's grandmother's kitchen (camera angle near top right)	18
2.6	Floor plan of Riya's childhood home in India	19
2.7	Amani's generic park	20
2.8	Roman's map and montage of photographs from a local ravine	22
2.9	Rahina's abstract map of a lifetime's reading	22
2.10	Matt's chosen map for the landscape of Hogwarts	24
2.11	Ying Yu's mix of real and fictional landscapes (edited to remove two stock images)	25
2.12	Suleman's mix of covers and cartoons (partial representation with personal photographs removed)	26
4.1	Amy's grandmother's kitchen	53
4.2	Riya's floor plan	57
4.3	Riya's image for reading *Tinkle*, precisely located in her home floor plan	58
4.4	Liang's map of her early home	61
4.5	Image of Liang's model princess	62
4.6	Laura's broad geographic framework, paired with the close-up perspective on her neighborhood in Hong Kong	65
4.7	Lily's trio of maps	68
4.8	Image of *You Mo San Guo* book cover	69
5.1	Suleman's map of cartoons important to his literate life	76
5.2	Suleman's most-read monthly magazine, *Naunehal* by Hamdard	78
5.3	Amani's generic park and the fountain at the entrance to her favorite park	82
5.4	Halia's living room, where she did her Arabic reading	85

6.1	Liang's urban home range outside the motorcycle shop, which is behind the trees; Matt's suburban soccer pitch with the trees behind	93
6.2	The toy room in Grammie's house where the fabric squares lived and the games of house and school took place	97
7.1	The few trees behind Halia's house that fueled her mental schema of a forest	112
7.2	Ying Yu's atmospheric forest images	113
7.3	A view of the tree-lined walk toward West Highland Creek	115
7.4	Matt's "forest" behind his school's soccer pitch	116
8.1	Roman's image of the cycle path between the pylons—the transition zone to the ravine	132
8.2	Matt's map including images of the school soccer pitch and the Rocky Mountains, both of which he incorporated into his mental setting	135
9.1	Halia's little stand of trees	150
9.2	Ying Yu's beach—Beihai Beach in China	153
9.3	Some of Ying Yu's ideas of a castle	153
9.4	Ying Yu's oceanic imagery	155
9.5	Simplified neurocognitive model of reading literary books	160
10.1	The initial screen of Rahina's map	168
10.2	Rahina's imagined mosque	169
10.3	Rahina's imaginary flight over Europe	172
10.4	The overview image of Roman's map	175
10.5	The first scene in the ravine	177
10.6	The third ravine image	178
10.7	The final image from the ravine	179
10.8	The home screen of Ying Yu's map (edited to remove two stock images)	181
10.9	A Chinese supermarket in Edmonton	182
10.10	An image of the Great Wall of China	183
11.1	Cartoon version of *Journey to the West*, as placed on Liang's map	206
11.2	Revisiting the straight-line account of reading	209

Tables

2.1	Participants, Listed Alphabetically	11
2.2	Descriptors of the Participant Pool	12
6.1	Home Range Discernible in Participants' Accounts of Their Childhood	94
9.1	Habits of Visual Imagery as Described by Participants	147

Acknowledgments

This project ran over a span of eight years, from early 2014 to the end of 2021, though the main data collection took place in 2017–18. Its trajectory wound through personal and family illnesses, my retirement from the University of Alberta, and an assortment of Covid-19 crises and lockdowns. Along the way, many, many people contributed to its achievement, and I thank them all, even though I cannot name every person to whom I am indebted in this brief note.

My primary and heartfelt gratitude goes to the twelve undergraduates who produced the digital maps that energize this study. Their enthusiasm and care, their thoughtfulness, creativity, and good humor, their fascinating and idiosyncratic memories, all made this project a true pleasure.

Profound thanks also to many graduate students in the School of Library and Information Studies at the University of Alberta. My biggest regret in this whole project is that I did not gain ethical approval to make use of the fascinating maps some of these students produced as part of a software assessment job. The virtuosity of expression and the depths of the emotional core of these creations persuaded me that literacy maps provide an eloquent new way of thinking about childhood reading. Never was a pilot project more exciting.

Other SLIS graduate students worked with the participants in 2017 and 2018, and I thank them also for their flexibility, their attention to detail, and their many intelligent contributions to the project. It is always a pleasure to work with SLIS students; their highly relevant skill set, their kindness, and their inbuilt curiosity make them ideal research assistants.

I will cluster all these students together in alphabetical order—a significant thank you to each of you: Christine Adams, Andrea Budac, Céline Gareau-Brennan, Lucinda Johnston, Alliah Krahn, Kyla Lee, Elizabeth Linville, Robert McClure, Samantha Nugent, Natasha Nunn, Rachel Osolen, Jennifer Plecash, Amanda Poitras, Deborah Schamuhn Kirk, Darcie Smith, and Megan Spaner. I especially appreciate the work of Robin Wells, who took on the complex job of serving as project manager with grace and skill.

I am also exceedingly grateful to Andrew Theobald and Erik Christiansen for their many contributions to the mapping exercise; their help was technical and, at the same time, constructive and imaginative. Matt Cheung later offered very productive and timely assistance as well. Thanks also to the teams in Technology in Education and the Research Innovation Space in Education (RISE)—and to the Faculty of Education at the University of Alberta more broadly for making this kind of support available.

Other invaluable assistance (in alphabetical order again) came from Bethany Arsenault, the world's most tenacious permissions tracker; Elliot Damasah who enhanced the map images to publishable quality; Judy Dunlop, indexer extraordinaire;

and Lori Purvis, who was an enormous help with all the final editing work. I would also like to thank the finance people at the University of Alberta, and especially those in the Dean's office in the Faculty of Education; everybody produced prompt and cheerful assistance whenever asked, despite the ongoing and surreal pressures caused by a combination of Covid and cuts.

The Social Sciences and Humanities Research Council of Canada (SSHRC) funded this project generously, and also looked out for my well-being when I became ill in the early stages of the study, rather than adding to the pressure to get it completed. I appreciate the kindness of individual staff members, and I thank SSHRC collectively for their ongoing support of my work over several decades. It has made all the difference.

The pilot work was sponsored by a RISE Catalyst Grant from the Faculty of Education in the University of Alberta. I am grateful for that early support, and I appreciate the "research imagination" that put RISE in place.

My colleagues in the School of Library and Information Studies at the University of Alberta have always been stalwart allies, and I especially thank Sophia Sherman and Aman Powar-Grewal for their administrative support. As ever, I am fortunate in my friends, and I am particularly grateful to Ingrid Johnston and Heide Blackmore for being early readers of this manuscript. Jill McClay, Anna Altmann, and Roberta Seelinger Trites have also been big-time supporters. There are so many more I should mention, but I hope that a blanket thank-you to very many people in the Children's Literature Association and the United Kingdom Literacy Association is at least a start.

Bloomsbury Academic made me very welcome, and I particularly thank Lisa Sainsbury and Lucy Brown for all their help.

I thank Arthur Jacobs for informal consent to use his diagram (Figure 9.5) and Cambridge University Press for official permission. The diagram is reproduced with permission of The Licensor through PLSclear. I am also very grateful to Charles Mize and Kiersten Elder for their very gracious consent to publish their beautiful Hogwarts map (Figure 2.10) that Matt selected for his own use after a thoroughgoing exercise of quality control assessment.

Finally, as ever, a huge thank-you to my family. It would be impossible for me to exaggerate the significance of the love and support they give me. The past eight years have been difficult and complicated in many ways, but they are my joy and my ever-renewable energy source. To my dear husband, to my wonderful daughters, to my terrific sons-in-law, and to my four magnificent grandchildren, to whom this book is dedicated, my most profound thanks, and lots of love!

1

Introduction

Imagine you are opening a printed book—any book, this book if you like. Its clean pages, with the black marks in their neat rows, embody orderliness. The words are marshaled and tidy, aligned and controlled.

But we do not lay down our interpretations in tidy rows of sequential words. Our minds seize on the uncluttered black marks and create profusion and multiplicity and contradiction in many highly active ways. Reading is not orderly. Even one reader's processes, patterns, and conclusions proliferate in plural, personal, and very messy ways that expand and shift beyond any possibility of description. Once we start to explore the possibilities of variation in any set of multiple readers, the potential for contradiction and confusion increases exponentially. My first task in addressing the challenge of this book, therefore, is to concede its limitations before I even begin. I will not capture anything approaching the full scope, the idiosyncratic range of reference and the personal nuances of even a single reading event. Nevertheless, I find it useful to approach a discussion of reading from an initial perspective of messiness.

In this book, twelve undergraduate readers offer insight into how their literate lives developed. To ground their observations, in many senses of that verb, they create and discuss a digital map of a landscape (real or fictional) that was important to their reading youth. Digital affordances permit them to layer connections and associations onto this map as they choose. We meet twice for an interview that veers on a conversation, once when the maps are partially developed and once on completion; these discussions last between one and two hours each time. The participants in this study are diverse in many ways: nationality, cultural background, ethnicity, academic discipline, and readerly tastes and behaviors. The focus on the map permits glimpses of the situated children who became readers with a broad range of experiences and interests. The number is small but the messiness is maximal. By starting from a significant landscape, these participants supply a context for their reading lives that suggests many intriguing perspectives on the act of reading.

Readers have minds full of traces of personal experiences. Those minds are embodied; those bodies are emplaced. Karen Coats reminds us, "human beings are more than embodied; we are also *storied*" (2019: 367). Each reader brings a distinctive experiential, cultural, and intertextual repertoire to bear on a text. How to address these plural backgrounds in meaningful and productive ways is a problem probably impossible to solve, but it is important to keep trying, rather than occluding multiplicity in the name of simplicity and elegance. Lisa McNally quotes Hélène Cixous's musing on the "beforehand of a book" in terms of its writing (McNally, 2014: 31). What happens when we open our awareness to "the beforehand" of a reading experience? Clearly the challenges of volume and variety prevent us from ever coming to terms with this notion in its full and diverse complexity, but much that affects the quality of a reading happens *before* and it is important not to ignore it, simply to make things more convenient.

This book investigates the habitat of young readers, as perceived and presented by themselves. The maps provide settings in which they learned important lessons about moving through the world. I start from the personal environment and move toward the intellectual and emotional transfiguration of reading. The maps permit us to explore how readers may represent the miscellaneous ingredients of that wider world while retaining some focus on how these elements feed into the interpretive activities of reading.

The twelve undergraduate students whose reading stories are presented here are aged between eighteen and twenty-five, recruited from across my large university in Western Canada. My project is funded by the Social Sciences and Humanities Research Council of Canada and authorized by the Research Ethics Board at the University of Alberta.

In 2017, my team of research assistants posted sign-up invitations across campus. A dozen undergraduates from a wide variety of national and disciplinary backgrounds successfully committed to the time-consuming process of designing these maps (encouraged by a relatively generous honorarium that acknowledged the value of their time and creative contribution). My team and I mounted the maps on the screen-capturing software Screencast-O-Matic (https://screencast-o-matic.com), which we also used to record the interviews. Each participant met with me and a graduate assistant in a designated research space in the Faculty of Education. We sat in front of a screen featuring their map; the participant controlled the cursor to point out highlights or shift to new images online. The only visual recording was of the screen, and that screen recording also captured the audio of the interview; thus, the record connects the visual and audio information being addressed in any given moment. The graduate assistant in attendance at each session later transcribed the interview. These audiovisual records, the maps themselves and the transcripts of all twenty-four interviews form the core data set. I have lightly edited participant responses for ease of reading.

This book is organized around a concept of starting with diversity and variety and exploring what can be learned from dwelling in the messiness. I am alert to what patterns can indicate, but I am not working toward any singular account. Ethnographer and philosopher Annemarie Mol says, "The point is not to fight until a single pattern holds, but to add on ever more layers and enrich the repertoire" (2010: 261). I hope to deepen the questions that may productively be asked about the experience of reading; in Mol's terms again, "tell cases, draw contrasts, articulate silent layers, turn questions upside down, focus on the unexpected, add to one's sensitivities, propose new terms and shift stories from one context to another" (2010: 262). Even as I set this expansionary aim, I remind myself and my readers from the outset that refining childhood experience into the expression of a map already entails some tidying up of life, some reduction of what Wohlwend, Buchholz, and Medina call, "the productive affordances of blurring and muddying," some marshaling and organizing of the "mess [that] often becomes learning in the chaotic relationships among play, making, and children's collective imaginaries" (2018: 143). Nevertheless, these maps help us to add to our sensitivities about the complex and often randomly accumulated matrix out of which reading develops.

Part of the diversity that marks this book is based in what the participants choose to read today. Many of them lament that being a student has reduced their time and energy for private reading, but what they do engage with when they can reflects a very broad range of tastes and priorities. Some read fiction, some wish they were reading fiction, some start a fictional text and abandon it partway through. Some read nonfiction that appeals to them, and the scope of their engagement runs from ancient Chinese fortune telling, to ecologically harmonious ways of inhabiting the earth, to Tumblr diaries, to how to set up as a young entrepreneur. Some make viewing a priority, with reading very much an afterthought.

In the face of this great diversity, I shift the range of my own initial thinking from a relatively literary focus to a more diffuse concept of literacy, with literary reading as one major subtopic. All these kinds of reading involve ways of connecting with the world.

The Role of the Maps

In 2007, I published a book about adult readers and media users and made metaphorical use of the idea of mapping in the title (*Mapping Recreational Literacies: Contemporary Adults at Play*). This time around, actual maps provide the major data source for the whole project. In this section, I recount the history of this project.

The idea of the mapping exercise arose from an earlier project, in which I made an intense study of the reading materials of my own youth (Mackey, 2016). Although my initial focus was on the range of texts I encountered in my childhood, I soon registered the significant import of my setting, my "first place," as defined by Australian writer David Malouf (1985: 3). As part of that study, I experimented with the potential of using apps to explore my local geography as it affected my developing literacy. The process was fascinating and frustrating in equal measure. I am not technologically sophisticated enough to produce my own apps, so I recruited talented students to help out. Logan Gilmour and Cody Steinke brought skill and imagination to bear on the creation of two prototypes: PlaySpaces and SchoolWalk. Unfortunately, I did not have the budget to follow through past the prototype stage to a more secure development, but the experience of organizing my thoughts in the form of two displays of digital topography was exciting and informative. I discovered that playing with representations of the landscape of my youth provided a new language for thinking about my life as a reader and was a source of delight in its own right.

Might a technologically simpler creation of a digital map, rather than a full-blown app, prompt other readers to productive exploration of the landscapes within which they became literate?

My own proxy experience with the development of PlaySpaces and SchoolWalk took place between 2010 and 2014. During this time span, available map programming options became more intuitive and user-friendly. In 2014 and 2015, I organized pilot work with graduate students from the School of Library and Information Studies (SLIS) at the University of Alberta. Funded by the Faculty of Education, I hired them to test different mapping programs through the exercise of delineating some significant landscapes of their own literary past.

The exciting quality of the maps these graduate students produced confirmed that such maps offered a forum for instigating many kinds of intriguing discussion. Because my relationship with these students was employer–employee rather than researcher–participant, my Research Ethics Board declined the full review process; I could look at their maps but not publish them as part of my own project. I regret that I cannot display and analyze these powerful documents. The imaginative and eloquent mapmaking of these SLIS students undoubtedly confirmed the potential for a landscape project to create a focal point for very fruitful conversation. My debt to these students is very great. We established that programs ThingLink (https://www.thinglink.com) and ArcGis StoryMaps (https://storymaps.arcgis.com) offered user-friendly possibilities, with our existing technical support. Participants were welcome to use other options and some chose to do so.

At this point, I shift my perspective from this past-tense account of historic events. From here on, I make every effort to reserve the use of the past tense for participants' descriptions of childhood events and attitudes. In the process of wrestling with my enormous dataset, I discover that even as subtle a marker as tense choice can give too strong an impression of "over and done with" and I focus instead on being as open-ended as possible. Reading is not a finite event that concludes in a definitive way when the book is shut for the last time. Traces of our textual encounters may linger in lifelong ways.

The Project

Delayed by illness, I finally launch the recruitment process in 2017. Nineteen undergraduates sign up. I accept every volunteer (my major selection criterion is that they are interested in this kind of thinking, though I am sure the financial incentive is not irrelevant). Eventually twelve participants complete both maps and interviews. The seven who drop out along the way generally cite pressures of time.

The briefing for the participants is very broad. A brief paraphrase of my verbal explanation to potential recruits might read:

> Create a map of a landscape (real or fictional) that was significant to you at some point in your youth as you became a reader. Augment your map with

layers of explanations and examples in any way you like. Feel free to call for help with technological issues or with background research into materials you may remember but perhaps not very clearly.

This open-ended approach makes room for an extensive range of responses, and the variety of the maps themselves testifies to a great diversity of readerly priorities even in a very small sample population. Interviews take place between late 2017 and mid-2018, supported by a second team of SLIS students.

A limitation of this project is that participants for the most part draw on a single landscape, a single aspect of their literate past, and usually a finite time period. Some do produce more than one map (declaring that it is impossible to work with just one), and, of course, the interview process allows me to invite them to think more laterally and also more longitudinally. But the overall focus of the maps is necessarily more singular than the unruly real-life work and play of ongoing development and mutation, as readers build competence and confidence through the structures and the happenstance disruptions of ordinary life. Their daily lives and their reading lives are complex beyond anything that can be articulated, even drawing on the multiple affordances of a digital map.

Creating these maps jogs participants' memories, but the exercise is also limited by what the creators can actually recall, and what they can represent. In the first interview, I frequently invite participants to invest time and energy into research on titles of books, movies, and games they have enjoyed if it would help them think usefully about these materials. I tell them to recruit the research assistants for technical help in assembling their maps. I make parts of the interviews relatively conversational, hoping to open up further associations in these complex and tacit networks of memories and ideas. I also ask explicit questions about their internal reading processes, many of which they are clearly articulating for the first time ever. Nevertheless, this project is limited by the boundaries not only of memory but also of what is *askable*, and what is *sayable* and *showable* about reading. Much remains inchoate.

Another complicated limitation is the effect of nostalgia. As undergraduate university students, these participants have all made a formal transition to a more adult life (though it is clear that the degree to which their lives remain relatively sheltered is highly variable, for a range of culture-related and financial reasons). Looking back on childhood reading is an exercise that can make people wistful. I acknowledge this element as a potential drawback, but if it is handled with care, nostalgia about reading can also be mined for considerations of affect. I do not claim to have succeeded in this subtle enterprise, but I do try to make the most of the affectionate way many of these readers look back at their childhood geographies and their early texts. I regularly remind them that they need not answer any question they find too personal, but they are frank and fascinating in their willingness to reflect on their childhoods, and I have done my best to reflect my huge gratitude to them by being as respectful as possible in presenting their observations. This project does not measure or evaluate people's reading choices; it simply displays them, as far as possible, in the reader's own terms.

What Follows

In Chapter 2, I introduce the twelve readers and offer a first glimpse of their maps. The number is small, but the diversity is great, both in demographic terms and also in relation to the landscapes they choose to identify as significant.

Chapter 3 supplies a compass, a description of the overall direction of the work, and a set of key terms that help me to clarify my findings. The order of operations in the development of this chapter follows the asynchronous process that occurs when a key to a map is created and used: The mapmakers survey a landscape and spot landmarks that they indicate on their map by creating an icon of some kind. Before they publish this map, they develop a key to explain the markings. Readers of the map, on the other hand, look to the key first. Similarly, I collect these maps and interview their creators, then begin to interpret my findings. Certain significant terms offer effective paths to thinking constructively about the data, so I gradually assemble a working list of key vocabulary. Readers of this study, however, need not follow this meandering and reflexive route; I supply the terms from the outset.

The remainder of the book presents my findings. I have organized the chapters into an artificially coherent order, again for thinking purposes. In effect, I begin with the outside world of these readers, their geographies, and work toward a better understanding of the reading mind. The geographic section introduces the idea of the home space and also includes consideration of social spaces and domestic spaces, each allocated a chapter.

At this point, I shift gears and investigate textual spaces presented by these readers. I investigate the ways in which many of them extrapolate from the real trees in their lives to imagine a literary forest, and move from this generic operation to their most significant common text set: the Harry Potter series. In these two chapters, participants describe specific examples of drawing on life experience to illuminate reading experience. In contrast to these elements of commonality, I next look more closely at psychological spaces inside the reading mind, and investigate what these very diverse readers have to say on the topic of mental imagery. Finally, I address the issue of literary spaces and explore the impact of reading as articulated by very different readers. Some chapters provide an extended focus on particular readers; others draw from the general pool. Every participant is featured at length somewhere in the book.

Starting with the geographic space, Chapter 4 looks at the impact of childhood homes. I take the age of twelve as a rough cutoff line for childhood (drawing in part on comments from the participants). Chapter 4 investigates two readers who lived in stable circumstances until the age of twelve (Amy and Riya). It explores the experiences of two who moved in mid-childhood (Liang and Laura). Finally, it turns to Lily, who provides an outlier example of what constitutes formative change. Chapter 5 introduces the important topic of how other people may influence literary growth; Suleman, Amani, and Halia illuminate some important questions about social influences on reading. Chapter 6 presents the concept of the "home range," a child's space of autonomous movement. It explores the implications of two early sources of relatively independent learning and growth. The first is the kind of self-determined play that occurs within a social and geographic home range, a physical space that parents consider safe, where children are allowed some freedom to exert control over their own actions. Such a space fosters a sense of agency and a developing capacity to invest agency into worlds of make-believe, which will come to include written fiction. The second example involves what I label a "textual home range," a domestic repertoire of texts that parents consider suitable for the young to explore, more or less on their own. Here, the primary focus is on the television cartoon, and many participants are represented, as we begin the segue to focusing on textual forms.

With Chapter 7, I shift more completely to the textual space. Eight of the twelve participants make significant reference to the common literary trope of the forest. The importance of a topos of this nature to the development of reading competence is discussed with reference to all these eight readers, as they present examples of the mental crossover from life to reading. Chapter 8 then addresses different approaches to the text-set most commonly mentioned: the books and films about Harry Potter. Ten of the twelve participants raise the topics of Harry and Hogwarts in very diverse ways. Matt features prominently in both these chapters, especially in Chapter 8, as the reader most invested in the Potter world, who also articulates a complex scenario of reading about forests.

Chapter 9 introduces issues of diversity in psychological spaces, through an exploration of the fine-grained processes of developing mental imagery (or not). All twelve participants make an appearance in this chapter. Chapter 10 addresses literary spaces and investigates the larger arc of an ongoing mental space created by a reading life. Rahina, Roman, and Ying Yu provide the main examples here, with cameo appearances from several other participants. Finally, Chapter 11 revisits all these spaces and explores how our understanding of reading can be enhanced by this extensive cross-disciplinary navigation of twelve individual maps.

Figure 1.1 structures this approach. In the face of great proliferation and variety, I introduce a form of organization, leading from the external world "through" the pages of books, as readers donate life to the words, "into" the minds of the readers themselves. The straight one-way arrow in this graphic representation is entirely hypothetical and stylized. In reality, my path from the beginning to the end of this study is traced through an assortment of meandering routes with many detours and dead ends.

Even as I create this graphic organizer, I agonize over its blatant artificiality and try to come up with something less simplistic. In the end, I decide that alternatives that add complexity to the dynamic (e.g., a two-way arrow, or a circular effect) create even greater distortions. This singular, unidirectional line represents neither the recursiveness of reading nor the multiplicity of routes I took back and forth through the data. It does a somewhat better job of representing the ruthless one-way-ness of life, I suppose, but its real purpose is to offer a structure—misleadingly firm, but nevertheless useful—to guide readers through the complex accumulation of information provided by the lively thinking articulated in this study.

1. Introduction

2. The mapmakers

3. Compass and key

GEOGRAPHIC SPACES   from the outside world
    The first place
4. Childhood stability and disruption
    The social space
5. Reading and relationships
    The domestic space
6. The home range and agency

TEXTUAL SPACES
    Border country
7. The forest
    A shared fictional world
8. Harry Potter

PSYCHOLOGICAL SPACES
    Interior worlds
9. Diverse approaches to mental imagery

LITERARY SPACES
    Ongoing worlds
10. The arc of the lifelong reading space   to the reading mind

LIFE SPACES AND READING SPACES
    Conclusions
11. Reading minds in motion

Figure 1.1 Moving through the territory.

Late in this project, I discover Janice Radway's reflections on reader-response theory and its impact on literary studies. Radway offers some oblique support for the forward nature of my arrow, in the following terms:

> And most readers, of course, as every librarian, English teacher, and literature professor knows, willfully engage texts from their own ground, wandering about within them sometimes aimlessly, sometimes hell-bent on a purpose. They raid them, remake them, perform them in contemporary and ethnocentric dress, as Michel de Certeau has reminded us. In effect, they write them anew, even if only in mobilizing a single image, phrase, figure, or vignette in future speech, conversation, or written form. Is there a way to understand the vitality and ongoingness, the forward trajectory and unsecured nature of the social process without capturing it and fixing it as a tiny, delicate insect caught in amber? (2008: 339)

In starting with the readers, in their home territory and their own words, I hope to capture at least some fraction of the vital, ongoing, forward, and unsecured nature of how they encounter different kinds of reading. Texts, at least initially, appear in this scenario as something to be moved *through*, in a forward direction. The texts are not themselves neutral or passive, but the focus of our conversation is on the forward movement.

The risks of methodological promiscuity are very great in the approach I use here. My own conviction is that the maps are so divergent by nature that applying the orthodox procedures of coding the transcripts and extracting common themes actually entails an even bigger risk of distorting the data. I am well aware that not every reader of this work will approve of this assessment. As a general statement of principle, I suggest that a dozen readers will not provide any kind of definitive answers, but that their thoughtful presentations of the landscapes of their reading youth hold considerable potential to add intriguing and productive nuance to the kinds of questions we ask. They also provide solid testimonials to the many ways in which readers are profoundly diverse—a finding to which many reading researchers and teachers pay lip service without appreciating the depth and significance of the differences.

Obviously, my debt to these mapmakers will never be repaid by a simple honorarium, even a generous one. Any one of these reflections on a reading childhood enriches our sense of the creative intertwining of life and reading. The complex tapestry created by closely investigating the diversity and the common patterns in all the various perspectives so thoughtfully offered by these young people is illuminating and intriguing.

2

The Mapmakers and the Maps

Learning to make sense of representations and to bring them to life inside the head is not a one and done exercise completed as the toddler moves from board books and concept books to more elaborate fiction and information in picture-book format. It is a process that, at a minimum, continues throughout childhood and, for most people, lasts (at least in spurts) throughout a reading lifetime. This project invites readers to explore at least some of the settings in which their early literary development occurred. By means of an oblique approach involving the specifics of a known landscape, I hope to induce readers to articulate some relatively shadowy and implicit elements of their youthful literate experience.

For a variety of reasons, both principled and practical, this project features young people aged between eighteen and twenty-five. I have conducted research with this age range on two previous occasions (Mackey, 2007, 2011) and found the work both enjoyable and productive. People in early adulthood have relatively fresh access to childhood memories, but they are far enough away from childhood to be reflective, and they are old enough to articulate abstract observations and questions. Additionally, for a researcher based on a university campus, they are plentiful to hand and are legally entitled to sign their own consent forms without involving parents or teachers, decidedly a convenience factor. As I have done before, I distributed recruitment posters across campus, rather than drawing on a more homogeneous single-class or single-discipline grouping. The result is the assembly of a diverse participant pool. By design, they are all of similar age and they are all involved in university education; women preponderate by a ratio of nine to three. In most other ways, the group represents a broad range of reader identities and many perspectives on life in contemporary Canada. I regret that no Indigenous participants followed up on the recruitment call. The intense focus on the land represented in an Indigenous perspective would have contributed constructively to this project. Nevertheless, the demographic and disciplinary range of this group offers a rich diversity.

The Participants

Table 2.1 outlines the public facts about the participants in this project. All names are pseudonyms.

Table 2.1 Participants, Listed Alphabetically

Name	Age	Background	Discipline
Amani	21	Canadian	Elementary education
Amy	20	Canadian (Irish/German heritage)	Environmental sciences
Halia	19	Iraqi-Canadian (born in Iran)	Education—biology/English
Laura	18	Hong Kong Chinese-Canadian	Food and nutrition
Liang	22	Chinese-Canadian	Fine Arts—painting
Lily	23	Chinese-Canadian	Civil engineering
Matt	23	Canadian (Dutch heritage)	Industrial design
Rahina	24	Canadian (Somali parents)*	Education—English
Riya	21	Indian	Psychology
Roman	21	Canadian (French/Ukrainian heritage)	Industrial design
Suleman	19	Pakistani	Engineering
Ying Yu	22	Canadian (Chinese parents)*	Electrical engineering

*Second-generation Canadian.

The participants in this project come from a number of countries and cultures. I offer here the information volunteered during the interviews. Four are immigrants to Canada, and I have awarded them a hyphen. Two more are Canadian-born daughters of immigrants (second-generation in Canadian terminology); each maintains a close relationship with the diasporic community of her parents' country of origin and I have added an asterisk to mark this connection. Two are international students, undecided about whether they will stay in Canada after graduation. The remaining four grew up in the Edmonton region; three of them specify a European heritage (without indicating when their families arrived in Canada) and the fourth does not self-identify except for being local.

Responding to a campus-wide recruitment poster campaign, these individuals represent a variety of disciplinary backgrounds: ten different academic departments and four separate faculties (five if you count the crossover field of psychology as a science). The tables and lists provide more detail about the factors of diversity represented in this small group. Four have personal experience of immigrating, and two moved to Canada to study. Rahina, the Canadian of Somali descent, is the child of immigrants and lived in Somalia herself for a while; she describes her daily life as tightly connected to the activities and customs of the Somali community in Edmonton. Ying Yu was born in Edmonton of Chinese parents, with strong Chinese links, making regular lengthy visits to China (see Table 2.2).

It is also important to note the other heritage involved in all these interviews. Rather than rendering my own white perspective as an invisible norm, I include the background information that I am an Anglo-Canadian from many generations back, with ancestors from all four countries of the British Isles along with a dash of Huguenot, and two and a half centuries of residence in Nova Scotia. It is a

Table 2.2 Descriptors of the Participant Pool

	Background Summary
Canadian	6 (1 Somali heritage, 1 Chinese heritage, 1 Dutch heritage, 1 French/Ukrainian heritage, 1 Irish/German heritage, 1 no further information)
Chinese-Canadian	3 (immigrants)
Iraqi-Canadian	1 (immigrant)
Indian	1 (international student)
Pakistani	1 (international student)
Undergraduate Discipline Summary (faculty added where not clear)	
All branches of engineering	3
All branches of education	3
Industrial design (Arts)	2
Psychology (Arts/Science)	1
Fine Arts—painting (Arts)	1
Environmental sciences (ALES*)	1
Food and nutrition (ALES*)	1
*ALES: Agricultural, Life, and Environmental Sciences	
Age Summary	
24	1
23	2
22	2
21	3
20	1
19	2
18	1

commentary on the dynamic and polyglot nature of contemporary life in Western Canada that it is possible that I am the only participant in the interviews whose family spoke English as a mother tongue for more than a generation or two prior to our encounters.

The Maps and Their Makers

A preliminary look at the maps confirms the open-ended nature of the challenge that faces me as I look for ways to represent this diverse set of readers. Throughout the course of this book, I will group participants in different categories as it suits my local purpose. To start with, I work from the basis of surface similarity between content of the maps themselves, in order to introduce the mappers whose thinking and execution ground this project in a variety of ways. The maps presented here are the initial screenshots supplied by participants before any layering of links has begun.

The Urban Maps

Three participants (by coincidence or not, all child immigrants from China, though their disciplinary divergence is pronounced) produce town or city maps and focus on their local neighborhoods. Laura presents a broad range of landscapes based on a global map; Liang concentrates on her hometown in China; and Lily offers three visuals: a Google Earth image of her Chinese hometown, Zheng Zhou; a parallel image of Scarborough, Ontario, where she first moved; and (later, in our second meeting) a floor plan of her Chinese apartment.

Laura

Laura, an eighteen-year-old student, studying food and nutrition, immigrated to Canada at the age of nine; her initial map shows the area in Hong Kong where she first remembers living in an apartment complex. She zooms in to present a close-up street map as she speaks. Both perspectives are shown in Figure 2.1. The apartment is on the side of a mountain and the complex features a clubroom with a swimming pool, and a parking lot where the children also played. Laura's map also presents many travels: she zooms out from the initial setting to include trips to the Hong Kong Disneyland, to another Hong Kong amusement park ("the best ever") called Ocean Park, to Thailand, to Taiwan, to Singapore, and later to Toronto and Vancouver, with a recent holiday in New York also in the mix. One such trip made a mark on her because she stayed in a house for the first time in her apartment-dwelling life, having previously encountered them only in fiction—in books and on television. She has one sister, older by about two years.

Laura moved to Edmonton from Vancouver at the start of her undergraduate education and is living on her own for the first time. She is very aware of multiple perspectives in her head, and she draws on a dual repertoire.

Liang

Liang is twenty-two, and a fine arts student with a painting major. She has moved around a great deal, both within China and within Canada. Until the age of about nine (Grade 4), she lived in a small town in Eastern China. Her family then moved to a large city near Shanghai (leaving her grandparents in the small town) and thence to Canada when she was fourteen—to Winnipeg, Toronto, Calgary, Camrose, and Edmonton. Her early childhood was spent in the area she mapped (Figure 2.2), where her parents ran a motorcycle store. She recalls playing among the discarded boxes the motorcycles were shipped in. She mentions no siblings.

From the beginning, Liang had considerable access to Western texts. Her childhood included a number of television programs in Chinese, and she estimates that about 40 percent of this material was Western in origin. She also read Western fairy tales (Brothers Grimm, Andersen) and says her default with such stories was to picture white characters who speak Chinese. She also watched cartoon versions of four masterpieces of Chinese literature. Once she moved to Canada, however, she lost access to most

14 Space, Place, and Children's Reading Development

Figure 2.1 Laura's maps (the reach of the map on top is global).

Chinese material, and her childhood repertoire of Western material was too babyish to be helpful to her. *High School Musical* and *Hannah Montana* helped her understand the new culture she had entered.

Today Liang considers herself as a postmodern rather than a culturally national thinker. She believes her fine arts ethos is more Western than Chinese, though it very much depends on what she wants to say. She has nowhere she considers home.

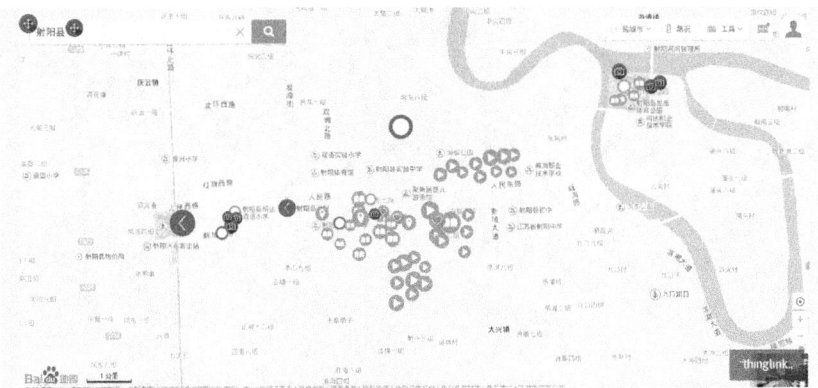

Figure 2.2 Liang's map: a small town in Eastern China.

Lily

Lily, a civil engineering student, age twenty-three, first offers a Google Earth image of her Chinese neighborhood in Zheng Zhou. Her second image is of Scarborough, Ontario, to which she moved at the age of eleven and where she stayed for about a year. Lily says the two neighborhoods resemble each other very strongly.

According to Lily, the move from Zheng Zhou to Scarborough was not very difficult for her. Her family's life in China would be thoroughly recognizable to a downtown Scarborough dweller, and she points to explicit similarities in the two maps (Figure 2.3): "Everything was pretty much the same. I went to school and I ate food and I went to the store and I hung out with friends." In downtown Scarborough, just as in Zheng Zhou, she could walk to parks and shops; she recognized the urban experience as familiar. "I don't think I even knew I was in a different culture, besides the language, of course." She ascribes some of this ease of transfer to her mother reading her many Western stories to her when they lived in China.

For Lily, the more disruptive upheaval came when her family moved from Scarborough to Edmonton, and the key difference is that they moved to the suburbs where a car or school bus was necessary for almost every activity. To this day, Lily feels more comfortable in a downtown setting. She was an only child until after her arrival in Canada, and she comments on the difference between her young sister's suburban experience and her memories of her own more independent childhood. She has almost never encountered a book that mirrors her experience as a relatively untroubled immigrant; what she found resonant were urban stories like *Harriet the Spy*, which was "relatable because she walked everywhere and she walked to school."

Images of Home

Three participants provide images based on a particular dwelling. Halia, who emigrated from Iraq to Canada at the age of about six, offers a representation of the first house she occupied in Canada. Amy, who grew up on an acreage outside the Edmonton area,

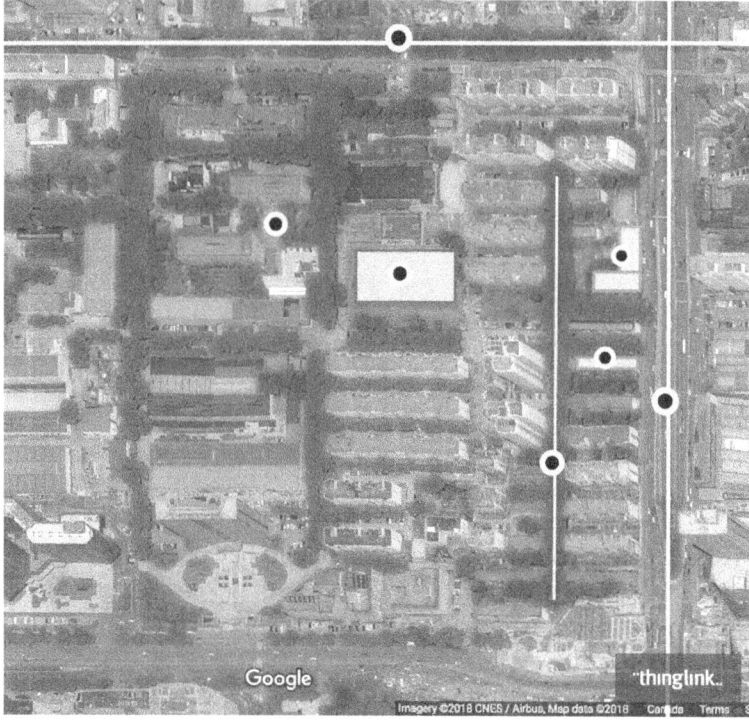

Figure 2.3 Two of Lily's three maps: a Chinese and an Ontario neighborhood.

Figure 2.4 Halia's first Canadian house.

presents a three-dimensional walk-through of her grandmother's house in the city, where she spent much of her childhood. Riya, an international student, sketches a detailed floor plan of her childhood home in India.

Halia

Halia is a secondary education student, age nineteen, majoring in biology and minoring in English. She was born in Iran and moved to Iraq in early life. From Iraq, she moved to Canada at the age of six or seven. She was an only child when she immigrated, meeting her father for the first time when he arrived to take her mother and her to Canada. She now has a younger brother and two younger sisters.

On her arrival in Edmonton, Halia briefly lived in an apartment, but her family moved to a house like the one pictured in Figure 2.4, very soon after their arrival. She lived in this house through her elementary and junior high years, moving elsewhere in Edmonton during the first year of high school. This is an image she generated to resemble the building as closely as possible. One reason for providing the image of the house, she says, is because "I didn't have the chance to go out as much because of my parents' situation; we had just moved in, we were getting accustomed to the place, we didn't know where to go and my parents didn't know anyone else so I didn't go to

Figure 2.5 Amy's grandmother's kitchen (camera angle near top right).

a lot of friends' houses." The interior of this house was her main environment outside of school.

Halia reads in both Arabic and English, and is conversant in Persian. As a child, she associated her Arabic reading with locations in Iraq, but when reading in English, she would assume she was in Canada and would try to envision a Canadian setting. I ask, "And at that point you had a shallower Canadian repertoire?" And she replies, "For sure." The implications of this limited Canadian background are discussed in more detail in Chapter 9.

Amy

Amy, age twenty, has lived all her life in the Edmonton area and is studying environmental sciences. She mentions both Irish and German ancestors, and her heritage possibly includes other nationalities as well. Her map presents a three-dimensional walk-through of her grandmother's home (Figure 2.5), developed from a program she found online called Homestyler (https://www.homestyler.com). Her grandmother died when Amy was about twelve years old, but she has detailed recollections of this house because "Grammie" looked after Amy and her younger brother for much of the time; Amy, on her own, also regularly slept over. Amy strongly associates her memories of this house with a large variety of activities, literary and otherwise. For example, for many years Amy kept a special journal there; even her mother did not know of its existence.

The interior of this house is particularly significant for Amy because she was phobic about windows looking out onto the street. Perhaps as a consequence of this indoor focus, she invests a great deal of mapmaking energy in rendering internal details as precisely and accurately as possible. For example, there is a newspaper on the kitchen

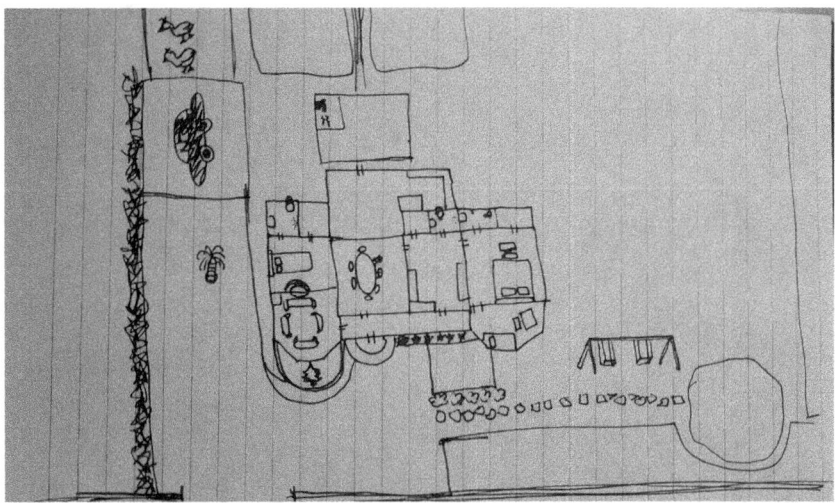

Figure 2.6 Floor plan of Riya's childhood home in India.

table because her grandma read her newspapers and magazines at that spot. The wallpaper is as close to identical as she could find on the Homestyler site.

Riya

Riya is a psychology student, age twenty-one, with one brother a year younger. She came to Canada as an international student at the age of eighteen, and has returned to India only once since that time. Her floor plan of her home in India is hand-drawn on lined paper; the digitized version presents many details (Figure 2.6). She identifies the locations where the books were kept, where she and her brother played on her dad's computer, where they watched television and even the room where she read Archie comics. Her childhood reading was largely British or American, and she talks at some length about Enid Blyton. She read very little Indian material, except for a comic called *Tinkle*, which she enjoyed for the familiarity of its representations; she is eloquent about what a different reading experience it afforded. To this day, however, she is neutral about where a book is set and does not particularly hunt out Indian fiction or other materials. She feels very much at home in the West.

Riya left this home when she was about twelve, when her parents divorced, and she then lived in other parts of India before departing for Canada.

Park Areas

Two participants, who both grew up in Edmonton, offer images of park areas within the city. Amani's map refers to four different urban parks, though her main visual offers a more generic image. Three of the parks she cites are local neighborhood playgrounds and the fourth is a more elaborate civic space in the river valley. Roman

Figure 2.7 Amani's generic park.

spent much of his childhood playing in a neighborhood ravine and he creates a montage of black and white photographs of that area, overlaid with a map of the main trails through the ravine.

Amani

Amani is a student in elementary education, age twenty-one. She grew up in a number of Edmonton neighborhoods with a younger sister and a younger brother. Wherever she lived, a common feature of her life was the neighborhood park. Figure 2.7 does not exactly represent any of them. Amani says, "I didn't want to make four parks, so I just kind of set one generic park image, which is the picture we have here. You have your bench and you have your trees and the grass."

Three of the parks she outlines in her expanded map are small local ones, but she also features scenes from a larger park in the river valley that she names as her favorite. Visiting this bigger park entailed a family outing. Some of its specific features are significant: she includes links to the paddleboat rentals and the playground because she spent time with each, and she also registers the fountain at the entrance as a marker of arrival.

Amani speaks of many small parks in Edmonton beyond the four she specifically mapped. She also refers with enthusiasm to the four years when her family home included a private backyard. This yard augmented the parks rather than replacing them in the lives of Amani and her siblings. The sense of privacy and ownership afforded different kinds of play.

Amani and her friends in junior high explored other parks during their lunch breaks. Amani would research the city maps in the telephone book for new destinations, and they would set out to explore. Edmonton contains many parks and playgrounds, and Amani's relationship to her hometown is, in many ways, filtered through her sense of access to these small but significant green spaces.

Roman

Roman, a twenty-one-year-old student, majoring in industrial design, also grew up in Edmonton, with one brother less than two years older. His family heritage is French and Ukrainian.

A feature of Edmonton's geography is that the city's river is fed by a number of creeks that snake through ravines into the river valley. Many of these ravines have been left relatively undisturbed, as is the case with the one in Roman's neighborhood (though it is now much more built up and radically less wild than it was in his youth). He spent much of his childhood in this ravine, playing with his brother and sometimes with his friends. He speaks eloquently of how the ravine nourished his imagination, equipping him both with scenery and also with emotional insight to bring to his fiction reading. When I press him, he is very clear that the experience of the ravine came first and was something he brought to his reading, rather than the other way around. He did not impose any experience of fiction on his time in the ravine, though he readily played fiction-based games elsewhere. He does, however, list a number of titles that he brought to life in his mind by way of his experiences in the ravine.

Roman deliberately chooses to take black and white analogue photographs to compose his map (Figure 2.8). He says,

> I wanted to shoot black and white because the quality of the photos aren't super-detailed and the contrasts are a bit grey and muddled, and so I think that more accurately represents my emotions with it. Because this was never just visual. There's all these other feelings and senses, so I felt like something that was super-digital and high [resolution] would take away from the other kind of emotions that were going on at that time. And I think all of the senses play in to how I read.

Abstract

I give participants free rein to shape their maps in any way that seems useful to them, and Rahina's response is to "map out" her reading past on an abstract background. Many of her links contain an illustration, but the balance of information is verbal.

Rahina

Rahina is a twenty-four-year-old Somali-Canadian, born in Canada of immigrant parents. She is studying secondary education with a major in English. She has lived in Toronto for ten years and in Edmonton for fourteen years, during which spans she spent periods of nearly a year apiece in Somalia and Kenya. She is acute on the different

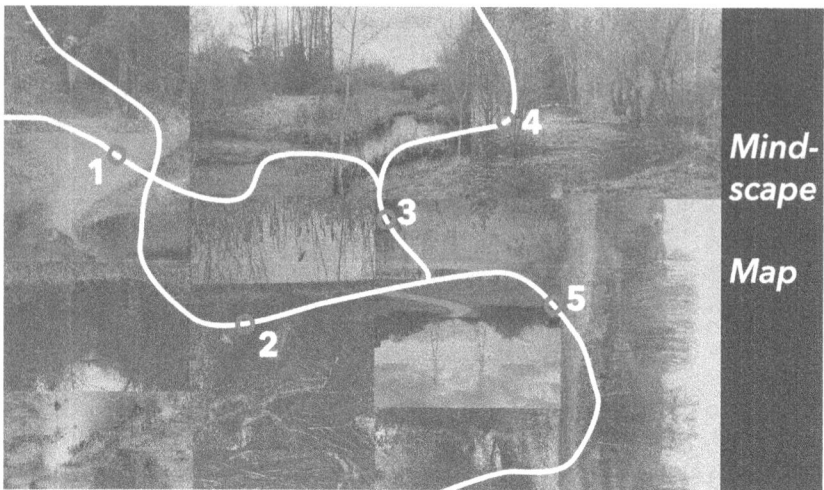

Figure 2.8 Roman's map and montage of photographs from a local ravine.

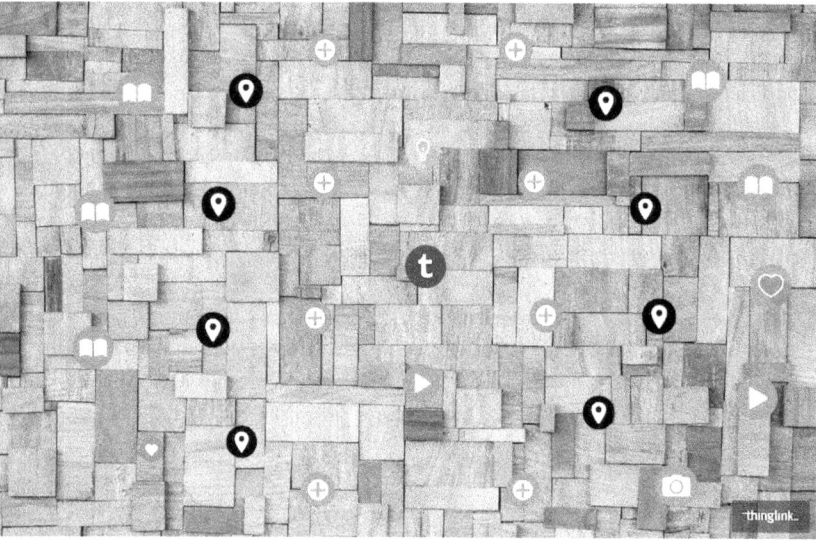

Figure 2.9 Rahina's abstract map of a lifetime's reading.

experiences: "I feel, in the West intellectually more comfortable, but in Africa I feel visibly and religiously more comfortable, so I'm literally torn in between. So if you ask me where to live, I don't know."

Rahina chooses an abstract organizer for her map (Figure 2.9), in part to be able to articulate such complexity: "You told me to do landscapes, but then I realized that landscapes were just a small part of reading and literacy. So what I did is, like, everything as having to do with literacy from when I was five to right, right now when I was twenty-five years old." She has a clear mental key:

> The blue [containing a book shape] indicates books, all these blue ones, and the green ones [containing a cross] indicate landscapes. The three middle ones are more like outliers, and then the hearts are things that are consistent, things that I do every single day. For example, this heart would indicate—you have to touch it, I guess—oh, there, libraries!

Rahina is the oldest of ten children, living in a very conservative household with many domestic responsibilities. The ability to go into her room, shut her door, and read has been a lifeline to her, and she says that much of her experience of mainstream life in the West has come vicariously through her books.

Fiction-Oriented Maps

I also give participants the option of creating a map of a fictional landscape important to them in their youth. My initial reasoning is that today's young people are much less likely to be permitted to roam as freely as I did in my own youth. I want to make room for readers whose broadest universes were textual. Although some of my participants do refer to being constrained in their outdoor activities, nobody turns to a fictional map to express their childhood relationship to literacy because of any lack of outdoor experience. Instead, the three participants who produce text-related landscapes offer diverse explanations for this choice.

Matt

Matt, an industrial design student, age twenty-three, grew up in a dormitory town on the outskirts of Edmonton with one older sister. His family background is Dutch. He combs the internet to find a map of the Hogwarts landscape from the Harry Potter books that satisfies his own sense of author J. K. Rowling's geography. He highlights different areas of this map and adds supplementary images from his own life and from other texts to illuminate how he brought this landscape to life in his mind (Figure 2.10).

Matt's interpretation of the license to work with a fictional map correlates closely with how I had anticipated such an option might work, although he does not fit my stereotype of the housebound child in any way. He describes a careful approach to his reading, conscientiously matching his mental imagery as well as he can to the specifications on the page. Once he creates a satisfactory rendition of a setting, he will "borrow" elements of it when needed, so he does not always compose his mental landscape from scratch. For example, he built Hogwarts in his mind, and if he encounters the need for a Great Hall in another story, he simply imports the version he has already created.

24   Space, Place, and Children's Reading Development

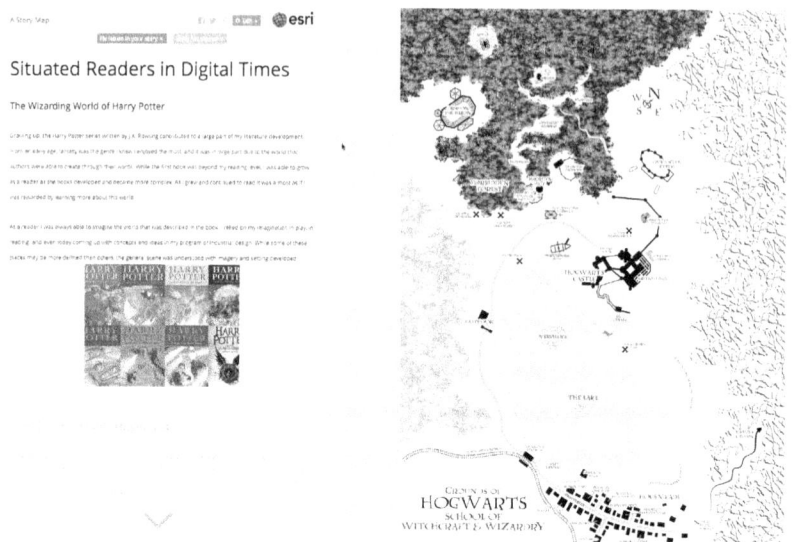

Figure 2.10 Matt's chosen map for the landscape of Hogwarts © J. K. Rowling (original map Mize and Elder n.d.).

Ying Yu

Ying Yu, age twenty-two, is studying electrical engineering. She was born in Canada of Chinese parents and grew up in Edmonton. She speaks Cantonese to her parents and English to her siblings (one older sister and two very much younger brothers). She has visited China every couple of years throughout her life and harbors a wish to work there for a while after she graduates. But she does not want to live permanently in China; she plans to end up in Canada.

Ying Yu's reading shifts in response to the text. She enjoys fantasy and has a taste for mythical creatures, or magical powers. I ask her if her mythical creatures feel Chinese to her, and she answers in relation to a book about dragons: "Every time I imagine the dragon, it's red. Yeah, it has a lot of scales and long whiskers, so it's kind of similar to the Chinese dragons." But Ying Yu is also a fan of Disney movies, and she selects and blends mental imagery for her reading from her Chinese and/or her Western repertoire according to what feels appropriate for the text.

Ying Yu's opening screen (Figure 2.11) includes a mix of actual and fictional settings. She includes Google Earth images of her Edmonton neighborhoods (she moved frequently throughout her childhood) and street scene photographs of areas particularly familiar to her, for example, in Edmonton's Chinatown. Some of her images include a specific fiction, such as *Hannah Montana*. Others represent a kind of visual building block: for example, the castle or fortress, based on a kind of generic medieval image, nuanced by flashes of the Great Wall of China and also by the animated movie *Shrek*. Much of her discussion about how she reads features hybridity, and this quality is reflected in her screen of images.

Figure 2.11 Ying Yu's mix of real and fictional landscapes (edited to remove two stock images).

Suleman

Suleman is a nineteen-year-old engineering student from Pakistan. His opening screen includes more information than I have provided in Figure 2.12. He adds an assortment of family photographs but asks me to omit any that include his mother's face. Additionally, I choose not to display a photograph of Suleman with a number of other young men, his cousins, on the grounds that I am unsure about my ethical clearance for such a picture. Seeing the actual images is not necessary to gain an understanding that Suleman's map is more conceptual than geographical, mixing his reading and viewing experience with moments from his daily life, mostly in the shape of formal group photographs.

Suleman, an international student at the University of Alberta, has lived in Edmonton for only a few months when I first talk to him. He describes his childhood as very sheltered; he is an only child, and he and his parents did most things together throughout his youth. He likes the family togetherness, and says it contributed to his ability to gain admission to a foreign university. He was accepted by more than one university, but he has cousins in Edmonton, and his parents preferred to send him to a location with family. The cousins have been very helpful in acclimating him to Western life.

Figure 2.12 Suleman's mix of covers and cartoons (partial representation with personal photographs removed).

By his own account, the child Suleman was a conscript to reading rather than a volunteer. He claims that he read, on purpose, a total of "four, maybe three novels" in his youth. One was *Black Beauty*, and one was *A Walk to Remember* by Nicholas Sparks, and he thinks there was another Sparks title in the set. Otherwise, he read school novels only. This little burst of voluntary reading happened quite quickly; his friend recommended the titles: "All I read were in a month's span because I was getting into reading, and then my exams started, and then my habit broke, totally."

Suleman "got the internet" in Grade 10, but his computer time was limited, both by parental order and by the restrictions of his data package. In fact, much of his discussion of his literate life involves restrictions. As we talk further, however, he begins to recall more reading experiences from his youth: a monthly children's magazine in Urdu, and Pakistan's first superhero comic, also in Urdu. He was also a reader, in English, of *Encarta*, the multimodal, digital encyclopedia. Without a doubt, his main textual passion was for television cartoons, and he negotiated hard with his strict parents and some more lenient relations to be able to watch dozens of them. The left-hand image in Figure 2.12 displays reading material and the right-hand image incorporates animated cartoon figures.

Preliminary Patterns

This initial presentation of the twelve maps, with a very preliminary introduction to the readers who created them, can do little more than tantalize. At a minimum, I hope I have conveyed something of the range and variety of the participants in this project. It would be perfectly feasible (if not necessarily useful) to follow this introduction with twelve separate chapters exploring this diversity in very great detail. Instead of this linear approach, I explore points of overlap and points of illuminating contrast. In my initial pass, I have clustered the individuals by means of a conceptual grouping of map content, but there are very many more ways of comparing and contrasting these participants and their approaches to reading and thinking. I look at what the maps tell us about issues of landscape, emotions, and evocative atmospheres; I analyze what participants say about the impact of moving house, and also their observations on spending childhood in a single place; I investigate the impact of the unavoidable Harry Potter texts as they affected the lives of different readers; and I explicitly discuss the significance of private approaches to the mental work of reading, such as the tendency to visualize or to shun optical detail. Throughout this process, readers are differentially grouped; each participant's representations are analyzed in greater detail in the chapter where it makes most sense to present them (though most maps could relevantly be located in a number of different contexts). By the end of the book, I hope it will be clear that such collective patterns are transient and used mainly for purposes of highlighting aspects of reading. I am not aiming for any artificial tidying of readers into permanent categories; the book ends, as it begins, with the inherent messiness of reading.

3

Compass and Key

Where Is North?

Working with the "beforehand" of reading is an intriguing and useful principle, but if it just amounts to a list of different kinds of memories, its utility is limited (though its interest is not). At the same time, trying to match up themes and create artificial patterns out of twelve very distinct examples is a route to a false sense of orderliness. As I work many times through these maps and transcripts, noting multiple points of stubborn individuality, I gradually develop an alternative analytical approach. As I read the transcripts, I am also reading very widely in a variety of disciplinary backgrounds, pursuing questions raised by the participants in different ways. I am a librarian, and the concept of key terms is very familiar to me. Perhaps controlling the vocabulary with which I discuss these very different cases can equip me to manage this disparate data set.

What I offer now is a key, with some grounding of my choice of language in ways that offer connections across disciplines. To begin with, I set the context of the issue itself, where readers come from and why it matters. My exploration of this topic draws on many other scholars; in order to keep track of the broad diversity of perspectives bearing on the idea of reading as placed, I provide a brief disciplinary tag for each.

Preliminary Questions

Educator Maxine Greene, describing how each of us, in infancy, faces the initial challenge of understanding the world through a process of *locating* ourselves, outlines some of the territory I hope to explore:

> We are first cast into the world as embodied beings trying to understand. From particular situated locations, we open ourselves to fields of perception. Doing so, we begin to inhabit varied and always incomplete multiverses of forms, contours, structures, colors, and shadows. We become present to them as consciousnesses in the midst of them, not as outside observers; and so we see aspects and profiles but never totalities. We reach out into the world—touching, listening, watching what presents itself to us from our prereflective landscapes, primordial landscapes …

Because we have the capacity to configure what lies around us, we bring patterns and structures into existence in the landscape. Before we enter into the life of language, before we thematize and know, we have already begun to organize our lived experiences, perceptually and imaginatively. (1995: 73)

Greene's account is innately plural and such plurality is reflected in this project. My initial research plan draws on some basic empirical principles in that participants engage in comparatively similar endeavors as a starting point. The activity of personal mapmaking is so open-ended, however, that forcing forms of comparison risks producing a completely artificial and unproductive outcome. Yet just listing differences rapidly becomes sterile.

My focus in this work lies in this question: what can we learn about processes of private reading from the individual specifics presented in these diverse and inherently personal maps? Most of the reading described by the participants in this project is contemporary narrative fiction and that literature will be the primary topic for consideration. These young women and men also mention other kinds of reading, which are of interest in their own right and which throw our common assumptions about literature into relief in useful ways. But before we move into this fascinating territory, I begin with a much broader question.

Where are we when we read? Our bodies are always emplaced, and that place is always particular. But our minds are *somewhere else*, regularly when we read fiction, and frequently when we read many other kinds of text. How does this cognitive miracle occur?

The link between that real world *where* and that imaginatively engaged *somewhere else* is complex. An able-bodied person exists temporally in a spatial world of three dimensions, with an open-ended power of movement and agency constrained by physical limits and numerous social and cultural arrangements. In the most material sense, a book also has three dimensions but any particular page or screen is flat and immobile, marked with abstract symbols. Yet, when the person picks up and reads the book, a mental leap, whose energies and limits we do not truly understand, infuses those flat pages with life, with motion, with powers of decision and of action. This distillation of mind into text occurs to a greater or lesser extent with both fiction and much nonfictional material. Scholars writing about literary reading describe this achievement with depth and subtlety, so I will initially rely on them for a maximal account of what children's literature specialist Alison Waller calls "one of the most enigmatic qualities of the reading act, whereby printed text is decoded and transposed into mental images" (2019: 78). Her careful vocabulary only hints at the lively profusion of this cognitive event. Our minds move *into* that world created out of a blend of private personal experience and the invitation shaped by the words on the page.

Philosopher Jean-Paul Sartre reminds us that *ignition* of these words into life in the mind is not automatic:

The hundred thousand words aligned in a book can be read one by one so that the meaning of the work does not emerge. Nothing is accomplished if the reader does not put himself [*sic*] from the very beginning and almost without a guide at the height of this silence; if, in short, he does not invent it and does not then place there, and hold on to, the words and sentences which he awakens. (1978: 30)

How we *awaken* the words on the page is both a general and a very personal process. Most capable readers will recognize Sartre's account of how a reader must enable meaning to come to life, but the descriptions of that process from two very experienced readers are profoundly different.

Author Francis Spufford, reading narrative fiction in his childhood, provides a paradigmatic example of a straightforward transfer of visual information into fictional settings, talking about his local city of Newcastle:

For a long time, just as I set any wild scene in Keele woods, whenever I read a story set somewhere urban, I borrowed Newcastle in my mind's eye as the setting. Newcastle figured as London, as Paris; tweaked with columns, it was Rome, with a few pointy bits on the roofs it was Chinese. Later, when I read *To Kill a Mockingbird*, I made it into the Deep South … I upped the temperature and let the rooflines sag. I put Maycomb town jail in the arcade by the town hall where they sold the eclairs. Scout and Jem Finch lived where Woolworth's stood, and Boo Radley's house was the hairdresser's a few doors along, with a verandah slapped on the front and yellow grass set growing between the paving stones. (2002: 78)

Spufford's account of how he transferred settings and his description of his very particular realization of Maycomb using raw materials from Newcastle manifests many elements of the scenario I had in mind when I began this project. Some participants in this project do indeed make use of local scenery in similar ways, although nobody describes such a wholehearted and singular basis for their readerly imaginations as we see in the transmutation of Newcastle. In fact, although Spufford might seem to be describing a universal strategy, he is really speaking for readers who want or need a visual background consisting of some specified details. As a young reader, I never made such transfers myself, for two reasons: my preferred reading stance did not call for a detailed visual background; and, even if it had, I was a colonial reader who did not trust my own outsider setting to stand in for the real places in my books. It simply did not seem to me to be the kind of important place where significant events would take place. I did transfer my emotional understanding of the world to my books, but the physical setting remained underdetermined and ineluctably elsewhere for me. Similarly, some of my participants enact Spufford's approach only in fragmented ways, or not at all.

As a reader myself, I resonate much more significantly with critic Helen Vendler's account of close reading of a poem; I find her description also helps me articulate my own experiences with narrative fiction. She says,

I think of close readers as people who want to read from the point of view of someone who composes with words. It's a view from the inside, not from the outside. The phrase *close reading* sounds as if you're looking at the text with a microscope from outside, but I would rather think of a close reader as someone who goes inside a room and describes the architecture. You speak from inside the poem as someone looking to see how the roof articulates with the walls and how the wall articulates with the floor. And where are the crossbeams that hold it up, and where are the windows that let light through? (Cole, 1996: 189–90)

Spufford speaks of somebody seeing a space in some visual detail as a necessary part of his reading life. Vendler talks about going inside a room and figuring out how the words work together to create a virtual space. She says elsewhere in the interview with Cole (1996: 178) that she is not a visual reader; and it seems from her description that what she sees (and possibly also hears) from the inside of this space are the words and lines that make it work. Each response is a valid form of reading that, in each case, has manifestly served the reader well. But they do not seem to have much in common.

Critic Sven Birkerts provides a profound and vividly articulate account of the act of reading fiction from an introspective point of view, one that is neutral on the visuals but clear on the necessity of a space for characters to move within. He describes reading *Catcher in the Rye*:

Salinger, via Holden, posits a world. Holden's world. And the reader who would hear more about it is forced to open up a subjective space large enough to contain it. The opening of that space is the crucial move, for it requires the provisional loosening of whatever fixed attitudes and preconceptions we may have. In that space, two versions of reality will be stirred together—the reader's and the author's. A hybrid life will start up. Not the author's life, not fully the character's, and not quite our own though all of these must be present for the mysterious catalysis of reading. (1994: 92–3)

In that internal space, says Birkerts,

We create the textures of [Holden's] reality with what we have learned from our own. But we don't disappear, either. Our awareness, our sense of life, gets filtered into the character, where it becomes strangely detached from us. The novel, in a manner of speaking, *smelts* its reader, extracting responsive emotions and apprehensions, and then showing them forth in an aesthetic frame. (1994: 93, emphasis added)

A great deal of literary attention focuses on how the abstractions on the page are marshaled and organized to evoke the phenomenon of activation in the mind. The heart of such study is the text and what it does, rather than the infinitely plural worlds of readers. In this book, however, I approach the enigma of vivification from the other side, from the world of readers and the environments that influence them as they learn to enliven the written word inside their heads. Geographic and social awareness and literary understanding are co-emergent and entwined in the minds of the readers— and these minds are specifically located. As Christopher Preston, an environmental philosopher, suggests, "organisms that know things about the world are situated beings cognitively grounded in the worlds from which they speak"; and "the physical realities of the environments in which beliefs are formed are relevant to the ways people know" (2003: xi). He says,

> Epistemologists have found that just as one cannot tell the whole story about knowing minds by isolating them from any connection to their brains, so one cannot tell the whole story about knowing brains by isolating them from any connection to the bodies and the environment in which they operate. Knowledge claims emerge from wider contexts than just the mind or the biological brain. This apparent need to look at the wider contexts in which knowledge gets made might helpfully be called the need to *richly situate knowledge*. (2003: 26)

The project outlined in this book represents an exploration of how particular readers draw on their own store of richly situated knowledge, in order to animate their private reading experiences. Our immediate environment in babyhood and early childhood fosters the development of our initial schemas and scripts about the world, and it is these personalized and local cognitive and affective tools (themselves in development) that we bring to our earliest efforts to make sense of text. Even babies looking at a bright and simplified image of a teddy bear in an early concept book are making connections with the visual and tactile attributes and the emotional significance of the teddies around them—and adapting their schema of "teddy" to include the idea that it may be represented in two dimensions.

Key Terms

In the next sections I outline some of the key terms that shaped my analysis. These terms arise out of the findings of this study and out of a broad range of interdisciplinary, even eclectic background reading. The risks of indulging in scholarly tourism through a variety of different disciplines are very real; on the other hand, to ignore provocative and potentially instructive cross-links because of a hardline standard of disciplinary purity also seems like a mistake. In my researches, I focus on materials that illuminate the act of reading in a variety of ways. As far as possible, I abide by the terms established by Marcus Hartner, a literary scholar interested in the inherently interdisciplinary field of cognitive literary studies. His "basic heuristic guidelines" include "the principles of *coherence, moderation*, and *autonomy*" (2017: 18). Coherence means that scholars visiting from another discipline should only deal with established scientific theorizing and not ignore "potential conceptual conflicts" (2017: 25). Borrowed terms and concepts should provide goodness of fit rather than skimming over potential contradictions. Moderation means that such borrowers trade only in "established, well-corroborated theories and concepts" (2017: 26), rather than drawing on controversial or speculative or experimental ideas that have yet to be fully established. Autonomy means that scholars dipping into other disciplines need to remember the powers of their home discipline. In the case of literary cognitive studies, Hartner lays out the issue of autonomy as follows:

During the development of adequate approaches, scholars should by all means look beyond the borders of their discipline for inspiration. Yet the incorporation of scientific concepts into literary analysis should ideally be free from false scientific pretence and avoid broad-sweeping reductionist claims that naively equate lower-level phenomena such as mirror neurons with higher-level phenomena like empathy.

Given that a literary text is not a naturally occurring phenomenon but a cultural artefact and a work of art, the research methods developed for its study can also differ from scientific procedures because literary scholarship may be interested in what could be called non-scientific aspects of reading … Whereas scientific approaches thus generally aim at gaining conclusive insight into the workings of the mind, the prime concern of many scholars in literary studies still lies within the reading of individual texts. (2017: 28–9)

Hartner's three principles support a modest and prudent approach to interdisciplinary work that speaks to my own combination of personal diffidence (and my natural wish not to be found naive), plus a strong conviction that there is much to be learned by opening the gates between ways of working. To the best of my ability, I adhere to these guidelines as I explore insights made possible through a wide range of perspectives.

The key terms I list below are largely simple and familiar words, but they offer at least a partial set of handgrips for further exploration:

- (im)materiality
- the life space and the reading space
- movement
- the subjunctive and the deictic
- agency
- autotopography

(Im)materiality

People who achieve the abstract ability to decode and interpret written symbols are situated in real contexts. Their real-life setting frames how they develop an awareness of the world that they then bring to the challenge of interpretation, and they infuse their reading with the oxygen of their felt understanding of that world. Each reader brings that intangible individual consciousness to bear on the material and objective marks on the page. The processes involve what educator Cathy Burnett et al. call "(im)materiality" (2014: 90), a concept they elaborate as follows: "the varied and multiple ways in which the physical and representational may inter-weave as individuals make meaning from texts. We explore how the material constantly conjures the immaterial which in turn relies on material experience for its salience. It is this reflexive and recursive relationship between the material and immaterial that we refer to as (im)materiality" (2014: 92). The entire nature of the mapmaking project is (im)material in this sense, as participants create representations of actual and fictional worlds and discuss how they intermingled.

Simone Murray explores print culture studies within an (im)material framework of "the dual dimensions of *text* (i.e., the words that are perceptible by readers) and *object* (the three-dimensional thing that can be bought, sold, archived or burnt)" (2021: 4). It is useful to conceive of reading studies as equally shape-shifting in nature.

Three participants offer explicit descriptions on factors of (im)materiality in their reading.

Matt describes the impact of the physical text on the mental event. He dislikes the experience of reading on a screen, saying, "Even just reading articles online, it's draining. Whereas I can flip through pages in a book, actually having it there and being able to control how light and dark it is just by tilting it towards the sun or not. I definitely think I read better like that." Other (im)material factors also fed into his reading; for example, a pretend game of Quidditch, which entails hanging onto an imaginary broom while running on real-life ground, provided a feeling of moving in Harry Potter's world.

As with Matt's preference for a paper book rather than a screen, Amy's experience of the Harry Potter series was affected by material ingredients. She read the first six titles of the series in paperback (her pronounced preference). But then she had to wait for the seventh to be published, and she impatiently bought and read the hardback edition when it first appeared. The difference made by the physical qualities of the hardback invaded her reading experience and interfered with her immersion in the known world of the immaterial story. Her reading of Book 7 was also altered by her (im)material experience of seeing the first movie in the series before she read the final book. Recently, Amy's aunt gave her an e-reader, and she tried to adapt to it but eventually gave it away; its particular set of (im)material affordances interferes with her immersion in a story.

Ying Yu's exposure to the self-published series of Morgan Rice was affected by the fact that she read the novels on her phone. It was lighter to hold than a book; she could easily look up any unfamiliar word; and she always had it with her, making it easy for her to read a bit further. Furthermore, Ying Yu describes herself as something of a germophobe and says she would have been distracted by worries about her book getting dirty, whereas a phone may readily be wiped clean. At the same time as she was attending to these material considerations, Ying Yu was creating mental castles for these stories out of a blend of images of the Great Wall of China, references from *Shrek*, and a large variety of other sources.

The Life Space and the Reading Space

To organize my reflections about the significant diversity represented in this project, I find two concepts essential: the *life space* (*where we are* when we read) and the *reading space* (the *somewhere else*). A reading space opens when a person meets a text. As I have discussed elsewhere (Mackey, 2021b), the reading space comprises the intangible creation of a virtual mental arena in which the encounter between an interpreter and a set of words plays out. The example I explore in that article, Rumer Godden's *The Story of Holly and Ivy*, is a literary text, carefully shaped and designed to evoke a set of complex responses that draw on material and immaterial conditions of living and reading. This example and most of the materials discussed by participants in this study invoke the conventions of mainstream Western narrative fiction. But at the other end of the literary scale, a set of IKEA instructions, calls on its reader to make links between the representation on the page and the three-dimensional things in the box, while holding a concept of the finished item in mind as a point of achieved coherence. The reading space, so to speak, holds the plan of action while the life space is cluttered (literally) with the nuts and bolts of the project. I certainly do not propose that the story and the instruction leaflet are equivalent, but I do suggest that even the most utilitarian forms of reading open a mental space. Different participants offer a small set of examples that represent materials other than mainstream narrative, and I discuss them briefly where appropriate. A reading space does not necessarily require a story for it to be set in place, and/or set in motion.

The reading space also incorporates and makes room for tangible ingredients of the reading experience—the printed page itself or its screen counterpart, other texts, life knowledge, myriad forms of institutional scaffolding, and much more. The life space entails daily practices and environments, including the juxtaposition of available texts, and the interpretive experience that makes usable information out of ordinary living. Both spaces are effectively (im)material.

Without using this vocabulary, Lesley Bartlett, an educational anthropologist, observes that participating in a reading space may affect how we subsequently relate to a life space. Learning literacy, she says, involves more than the capacity to decode; it develops new ways of looking at the world. Schooling entails participating in relationships and networks as well as acquiring a literacy toolkit (2008: 737). How these participants use literacy, in Bartlett's words, is "filtered through their specific cultural definitions of education, their social networks, and their positioning in larger social structures" (2008: 351). Thus, Liang goes online to pursue information about ancient Chinese fortune-telling, joining a social network where wisdom is imparted by those steeped in this history and also weaving an element of her own Chinese culture into the persona she presents to the world. Suleman discovers a world of business acumen that appears to be open to the novice; he reads with purpose as part of his project of creating online business sites. Rahina relies on fiction reading and her own writing to sustain a sense of personal autonomy in the face of many domestic demands. The life spaces of all the participants are inflected by the kinds of reading spaces they choose to sustain in the midst of their daily activities (in addition to the obligatory reading spaces they manage as students).

We do not necessarily attend consciously to the interaction of these miscellaneous forces of material and immaterial input as we read. But neither can we simply wish away the impact of all the conditions of our engagement with a text.

Movement

There are many conceptions of space as still and peaceful, but geographer Doreen Massey effectively reconceptualizes the idea of space as full of motion. Rejecting the idea of space as "that causally closed sphere of the nothing-doing" (2005: 41), she develops a dynamic account of space as "the dimension of multiple trajectories, a simultaneity of stories-so-far" (2005: 24). The reading space and the life space as I propose to use these terms are both full of activity and motion.

Similarly, the maps that comprise the main data in this study are full of implications of movement. Like a book, a map, even a digital map with links and the potential for virtual movement, presents a comparatively orderly face to the world. It is an object, something we consider inherently static by its very nature. But as these participants map key landscapes from their literate childhoods, and, even more as they describe their maps in the interviews, they compress action and movement into representations of the sites where such activity took place; it can be argued that they create what cognitive scientist Lawrence Barsalou calls "action-environment interfaces" (2003: 522). Barsalou makes a case that the human conceptual system is based on "situated simulation" rather than an encyclopedia or database of attributes and hierarchies. Following this approach, throughout this study, I attend to the "verbs" that are hidden in the "nouns" of the maps and transcripts. What these participants describe, over and over again, are not simply locations, they are *located actions* and/or *located potential for action*. Literary scholar Terence Cave says, "both perception and imagination are always mobile; static representations are not the currency of cognition" (2016: 120). Movement is certainly part of the currency of these maps. In charting the personal hinterland each reader brings to bear on selected texts, they also incorporate some of the charge of energy that brings a reading to life. Educators Cathy Burnett and Guy Merchant expound a process of looking for "openings and possibilities rather than stability" and focusing on "those moments in which movement, interest, curiosity, concern, ordinariness, or enthusiasm is generated" (2021: 357). The potential of such moments comes across clearly in the accounts I present here.

A single example that highlights the varied and dynamic behavior of readers arises out of the concept of mental imagery, a topic I address in more detail in Chapter 9. It is common to think of a mental image as a picture in the mind, a concept with some inherently static qualities. Philosopher Gregory Currie, however, suggests, "With visual imagery, we do not see things; we simulate the experience of seeing them" (1995: 26). He expands on this idea of simulating in the following terms:

> According to simulationism, imagery simulates visual experience, not the object of visual experience. A visual experience is the experience of seeing something: glancing at it with perhaps less than complete attention, attending to one part and then to another part. It is never the experience of attending perfectly and simultaneously to every visible property of the object, no matter how minute. We need not postulate a sequence of indeterminate and fluctuating images— merely the simulation of acts of selective visual attending. (1995: 36)

Emily Troscianko, who works in cognitive and medical humanities, calls this approach enactive, rather than simulationist, and confirms Currie's account: "I don't have a mental image of the cat I'm imagining, but I perform the same kind of exploratory behaviours as when I see one, with weaker forms of sensory feedback provided from memory." Thus, "imagining isn't about building up a picture in the head, but is a form of ongoing exploration just as is seeing" (2013: 185).

Thinking of a mental image as an experience of seeing rather than a thing seen is a good example of reading "in action" in all senses of that term. In this project, the participants map their life spaces as they impinge on their reading spaces, and sometimes refer to how their reading spaces affect their life spaces in return. Movement is constitutive of life in both spaces. There are conventional terms that invoke reading as a form of stasis: "drop everything and read," "stop what you're doing and read this." As I investigate the information these readers articulated and also offered more tacitly, I develop a new and more dynamic personal schema of the act of reading. We stop, we sit down, we pick up a book, and our minds just keep moving—through a virtual rather than an actual world. To an outside spectator, we appear to occupy a "causally closed sphere of the nothing-doing" (Massey, 2005: 41), but our neurons remain active, creating simulated rather than actual movement, engaging multiple areas of the brain in fostering a sense of virtual activity. Neuroscientist Vittorio Gallese provides a clear account of this transfer of life experience into our capacity to simulate:

> The activation of embodied simulation is the recall of the background bodily knowledge we acquire during our factual relation to the world of inanimate objects and of other sentient beings. We also recruit this knowledge when remembering past experiences, when planning future actions, when engaging in fictional experiences, and when comprehending linguistic descriptions of facts, actions, and events ... Indeed, also when we read or listen to narratives, we literally embody them by activating part of our sensory-motor system. (2021: 379)

The life space implies movement; as urban theorist Kevin Lynch notes about the urban landscape, "People observe the city *while moving through it*, and along these paths the other environmental elements are arranged and related" (1960: 47, emphasis added). We situate ourselves in our rich settings as we move around and through them. Preston further suggests that "the way in which we move around diverse environments with our bodies is in itself *cognitively* significant" (2003: 130).

Literary theorist Frederic Jameson, reflecting on Lynch's work on how people understand cities, confirms the importance of movement but reminds us that much of our initial take on the world we move through is highly provisional:

> Lynch's model does not yet in fact really correspond to what will become map-making. Rather, Lynch's subjects are clearly involved in pre-cartographic operations whose results traditionally are described as itineraries rather than as maps; diagrams organized around the still subject-centred or existential journey of the traveller, along which various significant key features are marked—oases, mountain ranges, rivers, monuments and the like. (2000: 230)

We learn how to make sense on the fly in the way that Jameson describes within the terms provided by our local neighborhoods. That same skill of tentativeness flashes into action as we start to read a new text.

Terence Cave argues that reading evokes a sense of movement; I suggest that such mental movement necessarily also entails a sense of space. Cave says,

For an attentive reader, written language does its very efficient work as kinesic proxy. It provides enough information to allow the reader to enter the ecology of the storyworld and thereby rehearse an imagined event—not a picture (or movie) in the mind, but a complex echo of real-world movements, voices, gestures, postures. I would be inclined to call this a mental representation or simulation, but the word itself doesn't matter. What matters is that something of this kind happens, or we wouldn't bother to read at all. (2016: 121)

Modern languages professor Derek Schilling supplies a fascinating account of readers in motion, as it were, creating a provisional setting for their stories. It is not difficult to read his account as a description of how we initially create a reading space, using ingredients that arise both in the text and in relevant corners of a life space. His discussion arises in relation to the idea of literary cartography, of the mental mapping of a fiction; he is eloquent on its tentativeness:

Mapmaking in a literary-critical context capitalizes on a readerly impulse that in most interpretive encounters with the fictional text remains latent, failing to resolve into a graphic representation of any sort. Readers use discursive cues routinely to ascertain the shape, scale, and axiological status of the story world, and, aided as they are by extended passages of description and what Umberto Eco calls a readerly "encyclopedia," may generate more or less precise mental images of place. A world begins to coalesce alongside and around the characters that populate it. Yet at this stage in the literary encounter, the experience remains immersive and projective, pre-schematic at all events. (2014: 215)

Like Jameson's traveler, Schilling's reader is also creating a world on the fly, adding details as they seem necessary or appealing, but not really pausing to consolidate these details into a clearly specified setting in the initial stages of interpretation. "Discursive cues" help to establish this setting and they are augmented by an "encyclopedia" accumulated from experience in life spaces. But note how tentative Schilling's own language is: this space-making capacity is latent, projective, and pre-schematic. Settling into the story, this reader will worry about sorting out the representative details later—and some readers are not terribly invested in ever returning to consolidate their initial and fleeting mental imagery.

Literary scholar Renate Brosch, drawing on what we know about the cognitive processes of reading, distinguishes between "default" and "vivid" forms of mental imagery. The default process, to which almost every reader resorts at least some of the time, is swift and provisional, and her account reinforces Schilling's description of tentativeness. In our default form of reading, visualization "hovers on the threshold of consciousness and cannot be fully remembered once the reading is completed." It is "continuous, fluid, transient, and indistinct" (2017: 256–7). She observes,

This optical poverty is not a lack but an advantage for the reading mind. It means that mental images during reading are polyvalent to an extent that real ones are not. Their indeterminacy allows constant transformation. Because visual indeterminacy ensures the adaptability of images to information received at a later stage, it is an enabling capacity, not a constraint … Phenomenologically, readers do not register a lack or a deficit in experiencing the story world. (2017: 258)

Both Schilling and Brosch evoke a reader in motion, processing swiftly and fleetingly, not worrying about creating a permanent mental image, either because they realize they may encounter further information that requires them to change it, or, more fundamentally, because they may never feel any need to fill in the missing details unless and until an author calls on them to pay more careful attention. Brosch contrasts this kind of reading with a more visually vivid and detailed form of realization that some readers value more than others. I return to these issues in Chapter 9.

Brosch and Schilling implicitly describe a form of forward momentum that is an integral component of reading, especially in the early stages of a story, with the reader making whatever temporary decisions about mental imagery that are helpful to keep the process in motion. This kind of movement is inherent to the whole idea of reading, and I stress it so strongly because it is important to register that the activities of a child's life do not come to a halt as they meet a composition, a static structure, a *text*. A child's life is active and so is that child's reading process; indeed, as Sartre indicates, the child who cannot sustain momentum really cannot yet be described as a reader.

Psychologist Keith Oatley's elegant evocation of the simulation provides an activist frame for thinking about reader behavior:

We don't just respond to fiction (as might be implied by the idea of reader response) or receive it (as might be implied by reception studies), or appreciate it (as in art appreciation), or seek its correct interpretation (as seems sometimes to be suggested by the New Critics). We create our own version of the piece of fiction, our own dream, our own enactment. We run a simulation on our own minds. As partners with the writer, we create a version based on our own experience of how the world appears on the surface and of how we might understand its deeper properties. (2011: 18)

Oatley rejects the language of passivity and his central statement revolves around the highly active verb, run. The concept of simulating incorporates action and it also entails the potential for provisional thinking and adjusting of parameters, in short for readerly agency.

I would move a step beyond "running the simulation" (which implies a potential for a constant repetition of the same simulated event) and add one final element: anthropologist Tim Ingold's invocation of improvising. In his discussion of how makers follow the flow of their materials, he says, "To improvise is to follow the ways of the world, as they open up, rather than to recover a chain of connections from an end point to a starting point, on a route already travelled" (2011: 216). A reader assesses the grain of the story and improvises an entry into that story, simulating the actions and interactions of characters and enacting their agency in the context of a space created (on the fly by some readers, in more careful detail by others) to make room for that agency.

This kind of cognitive effort is not static, nor is the setting thus developed fixed and complete, as is the case with a painting or an object. As literary theorist Wolfgang Iser reminds us,

> The whole text can never be perceived at any one time ... The "object" of the text can only be imagined by way of different consecutive phases of reading ... The relation between text and reader is therefore quite different from that between object and observer: instead of a subject-object relationship, there is a moving viewpoint which travels along *inside* that which it has to apprehend. This mode of grasping an object is unique to literature. (1978: 108–9)

Iser's account of reading is constituted both by the time of the movement through the text and by the space of that "*inside.*"

Literary scholar G. Gabrielle Starr talks about our daily bias toward motion and how we convert that energy and understanding when we read. She singles out poetry for special attention, saying, "Motor imagery appears particularly important for encounters with poetry" (2015: 248). She says that the understanding of metrical writing "involves motor processes in other ways, for it is necessary to keep track of the timing of spoken words and syllables" (2015: 249). She quotes theorist William Empson on the need to get the "muscular image" of poetry in order to understand it.

> For silent reading, however, rhythm is dependent on motor imagery and motor processes at base. That is, even when readers engage in varying levels of imagery in response to description (whether that representation draws on the senses of vision, sound, taste, touch, or smell), and even if they eschew the reproduction of any sensory scene, they engage images of sound and motion whenever they follow the rhythmic path that is meter or whenever they mimic the sounds they read or "speak" these sounds in silence as they read. (Starr 2015: 249)

Prose authors also establish a rhythm to their sentences, and this kind of active engagement, conscious or otherwise, with the sound and cadence and motion of words is an aspect of reading that does not always receive due attention. The rhythms established on the page may help to create a sonic space, which, for some readers, may matter more than the visual space developed through explicit descriptions.

The Subjunctive and the Deictic

How do we get from here to there, from the quotidian world that surrounds us to the imagined space of a textual fiction? Two grammatical descriptions capture the linguistic invitation that enables readerly processes of entering, and then being inside and moving through a narrative space constructed by language. These grammatical constructs express the dynamics of that *entering*, that active handing over of our selves into worlds created by language.

Psychologist Jerome Bruner talks about inhabiting the fiction through the subjunctive mode, "trafficking in human possibilities rather than in settled certainties"

(1986: 26). Readers move into that zone of human possibilities when they align themselves with a narrative perspective in which outcomes are not yet settled. The subjunctive deals with mental states relating to future potential. Readers hope, believe, and fear along with the characters; they align themselves with characters' senses of agency and fuel it with their own awareness of how agency works.

Readers are helped to make this step into a character's perspective on the future by a process of "shifting deictic centre," as explained by psychologist Erwin Segal.

The linguistic category of deictic words is very small; it includes only those words that have an abstract and grammatical role in our discourse but actually have meaning only in context. *Here* and *there* are deictic words; so are *yesterday*, *today*, and *tomorrow*; *now* and *then*; *I* and *you*. A reader must learn to make that shift in order to make sense of the perspectives of a story. Where is *here* in this narrative? When is *now*? Who is *I*? Tenses also work in deictic ways, related to the functions of past and present and future in relation to the person who utters that tensed verb, and the shifting to a character's perspective establishes "the phenomenal present for the user of the deictic terms" (Segal, 1995: 15).

English professor Daniel Punday supplies a very useful caveat: not all forms of reading work on this basis of looking forward from inside the writing. He says, "the preconditions for thinking about narratives as future-oriented possible worlds," is a relatively recent concept (2003: 34). I find the constructs of the subjunctive mode and the deictic shift to be profoundly helpful in terms of understanding the vast majority of the reading experiences described in this project. But participants' literate relationships with the world sometimes work on a different basis. For example, some cultural materials do not operate on the basis of conventions familiar in the West. Rahina learned the Quran in Somalia by memorizing it, and almost certainly did not read it in the ways described by Bruner and Segal. She also describes learning Somali in terms of a change in bodily demeanor: "I know if my mom showed up and I spoke to her for five minutes in Somali, I'd be, like, definitely in the humble mode." She says of her hybrid life,

> Canadian is not only just the language, it's also the cultural context and the way you think about things. And, yeah, the way you carry yourself, like, people when you're walking across the street, they say, I know you're from a different country, why, the way you walk. How am I supposed to walk? Is it—um, you walk with authority, instead of just slouching.

Rahina says she reads as a Westerner, but she offers oblique hints of her access to a more deferential culture in which she would be expected to presume less on her own authority. There are interesting questions about whether such a stance reduces the individual effectiveness of stepping boldly into a different persona, but her comments do not permit a clear conclusion. She says she is not aware of much Somali writing of narrative fiction, so she is not able to provide examples of reading subjunctively within this different culture.

Similarly, Laura talks about the difficulties of reading Chinese texts in English because of their untranslatable qualities:

Margaret:	So, do you find you slide one world in, if you are reading in English and another world in if you are reading in Chinese? Does it work that way? Or do you read the Chinese as a Canadian reader?
Laura:	I think I separate them. There's a really big difference between Chinese and English literatures. In Chinese literatures, they have … these gods or—
Margaret:	Right.
Laura:	I can't describe them, like fairies, gods—
Margaret:	Sort of mythic.
Laura:	Yeah, mythical. Well, I like to read those genres, but–
Margaret:	So you would read that in English as well?
Laura:	In English, it wouldn't be like that—it's a different feeling or—they have different characters, kinda thing.
Margaret:	Right, right. So, Batman is not a Chinese god.
Laura:	(*laughs*) No. No, he's not. So, I'd say both literatures are very different and yeah, I wouldn't be able to understand it if I were to be looking at it from a Canadian point of view.

Rahina and Laura are reading in culturally different ways; there are also other ways of reading outside the frame of creating possible worlds. Roman switches reading mode when he reads for information. As a child, he was a big fan of Dorling Kindersley's *Eyewitness* books: large, heavily illustrated pages loaded with information about the world. His experiences with these books involve the creation of a reading space, but not one that is subjunctively and deictically charged.

In other words, my account of shifting *into* a story is helpful, and, I argue, necessary for most of the reading on display in this project. It is not sufficient for a full account of literacy, but it dominates the experiences presented by participants in this study. As a reader of contemporary narrative, if I occupy a character's *now* and *here* and invest in activating that character's beliefs, fears, and so forth, I have mentally moved out of my own deictic center and my own set of human possibilities. I have entered and I am inhabiting somebody else's world via somebody else's agency in that space. To that world I bring the understanding I have developed in my own space, my own schemas and scripts, my own set of visual, auditory, kinetic, psychological, and cultural references. The role of these particulars is complex, and often operates on a tacit basis so even the reader involved may have only a vague idea of how a specific, actual, known world merges into a fiction in order to bring it to life.

The move into the subjunctive mode involves lending our powers of anticipation to a fictional construct, looking forward to an unknown future, through the means of somebody else's beliefs, hopes, fears, and so forth. The deictic shift into another *here* and another *now* places our embodied knowledge at the service of the story. It allows us to set in another place our physical senses and capacities. These qualities are not just visual. Children's literature scholar Maria Nikolajeva's list of such elements includes the following:

> Sight, hearing, taste, smell and touch: however, in discussing embodied perception, we definitely need to extend the repertoire of senses to include gravity, balance,

distance, direction, speed, duration, that are all connected to our perception of space and spatiality, also known as exteroception. Moreover, we can also make use of the concept of proprioception: the sense of the relative position of neighbouring parts of the body and strength of effort being employed in movement. (2017: 69)

Punday, developing what he calls a "corporeal narratology," stresses the importance of the human body and its possible movements as essential to narrative.

In narrative ... the basis of the motion within virtual space is the human body, the object that does not allow location to be static ... [I]t is because characters are always somewhere physically in a narrative, always positioned in a way that they are able to anticipate types of possible movement and able to use different sorts of perceptual information, that narrative space can never be static. (2003: 148)

Readers, more or less willy-nilly, donate their many forms of bodily awareness to characters moving in that new *here* and *now*. Most likely, readers vary in the degree to which they are conscious of the physical movement of the characters they have thus set in motion. But Nikolajeva suggests that readers who attend to the physicality of character movement are enabled to engage with the text "cognitively and emotionally, experiencing the character's interaction with space through his concrete perception and proprioception" (2017: 72). Attending to the deictic here and now and the weight and balance of a fictional body in motion stimulates a particular kind of response: "Reading fiction becomes more like listening to music, enjoying it with multiple senses in real time, rather than stopping to search for meaning" (2017: 72).

Agency

In his abstract for an article on agency, psychologist James W. Moore offers a pithy definition: "Sense of agency refers to the feeling of control over actions and their consequences" (2016: 1). The idea that we are doing things on purpose, that we are in charge, both of the decision and of its outcomes, is an important component of a life space and can be imported in significant ways into a situation created by a narrative.

Movement is pertinent to a working concept of agency in place. Therefore, narratives must also incorporate some sense of space, the arena in which bodies and minds know how to operate. As philosopher Jeff Malpas says, "Spatiality and embodiment—and so, also, the idea of the locality in which action is embedded—are essential to the possibility of agency" (2018: 139). Narrative is in many ways the account of agency. A mind interpreting a story must incorporate at least some notional space as the field in which such agency can be exercised. A mental image of a story setting may not need to be intricately specified (readers vary in their interest in supplying background details). But even the sketchiest schema of a generic location in which fictional events can happen and fictional characters can manifest agency must incorporate some necessary complexity: "Place cannot be reduced to any one of the elements situated within its compass, but must instead be understood as a structure comprising spatiality *and* temporality, subjectivity *and* objectivity, self *and* other.

These elements are themselves established only in relation to each other, and so only -within the topographical structure of place" (Malpas 2018: 166). Reading a narrative, therefore, calls for the opening up (however metaphorically) of a mental space in the mind, in at least the minimal terms Malpas describes. Agency is impossible without at least a schematic awareness of such place.

Cave confirms the significance of agency when he talks about how we develop a skill of recognizing if a set of words "works" in creating a mental world:

> One thing that it certainly relies on is the assumption of agency. The behaviour of a living creature, whether in motion or at rest, has a peculiar kind of directedness: its movements are the expression of an intention which may be more or less overt. Perceiving the intended movement or action of another living being is exactly what makes one see that it *is* a living being in the first place. (2016: 9)

The mental space is itself immaterial, though it may be materially supported by certain kinds of brain cell activity. The ingredients with which we create it come from many sources, including our own material places in the world. Our rootedness in our own communities, however, is (im)material, involving both the real-world manifestations of our surroundings and also what we make of them.

How we invoke the virtual in developing a mental world through the act of reading will also vary. Depending on both the individual reader and the nature of the text's invitation, one reader may import a known and specific tree into an imaginary landscape and relish its particularity, whether as something to be gazed at or as something to be climbed. Another reader will be content with a vague concept of "tree-ness," or even simply "green," in the background. Similarly, the maps created for this project range from an image that is essentially abstract to a three-dimensional walk-through of a singular and individual house, rendered in highly specific detail. But even within this broad variation in how much detail is required to represent a space adequately, the composers of any virtual space must provide at least enough room for purposeful movement to enable agency.

Autotopography

Although I was not familiar with the concept when I designed this research project, I clearly asked participants to engage in autotopographical thinking (Waller, 2019; Heddon, 2002): to explore scenes from their lives with a view to illuminating their understanding of their own reading. The autotopographical method "helps to tease out further connections between the remembering reader, past reading self, and the social and spatial context in which childhood books are encountered through the life space" (Waller, 2019: 61), a description that succinctly incorporates the aims of my project. Waller says, "Reading histories are complex sites of meaning. Autotopography works to map a conceptual terrain that encompasses real and fictional geographies involved in adult memories of childhood books and their relationships with them, at the same time encouraging the reader and critic to excavate meaning over the course of the life span" (2019: 61).

The focus on maps in this project offers an explicit concentration on the "conceptual terrain that encompasses real and fictional geographies" in distinctive ways that I hope are illuminating. The maps indicate some of the overlap between the real-world places that frame and sometimes constitute our awareness of the world, the virtual space of fiction-as-read, and the crossover effect that sometimes fuses an actual and a fictional landscape. Waller refers to these three spaces as "actual geospace, fictional or textual space, and representational space" (2019: 80). We use spatial metaphors to help us understand the processes that make reading possible—and of course a spatial metaphor enables and encourages metaphors of movement and dynamism.

As I do, Waller uses the concept of the life space but she contrasts it to the "reading scene," which she defines as "a conceptual and narrative space, shaped and defined by remembering, in which individual encounters with texts take place" (2019: 23). Her version of the life space operates on the following basis: "any model of lifelong reading therefore needs to consider the reader and text as temporal entities that exist within certain sociocultural and geographical contexts" (2019: 55). The life space as she defines it is a recognizable hybrid of material and immaterial elements, like my own version of this term. Her account of the reading scene, however, is more exclusively cerebral than my messier concept of the reading space, which is deliberately (im)material, blending the tangible and the implicit in both deliberate and incidental ways.

Waller's study generally focuses on childhood fiction. She takes the concept of the paracanon from Catharine Stimpson, English professor and feminist scholar, who says, "Texts are paracanonical if some people have loved and do love them" (1990: 958). There is nothing in that one-line definition that calls for such texts to be literary, though, as with Waller, Stimpson's discussion skews fictional.

Roman was an avid reader in his childhood and continues to read as an adult, even in the context of undergraduate life with its paradoxical "anti-reading" time pressures. His map associates the ravine with a variety of fictional series, but in his discussion of his childhood reading he refers to a much broader repertoire.

> Well I did read science books, which were more informational stuff, like astronomy books, things about space and stuff, 'cause I was pretty fascinated about space. And art books as well, more visual and give you a biography or something. So yeah, those ones I would read and they wouldn't have anything to do [with the ravine experience]. I don't know if you remember the *Eyewitness* books. I was pretty big into those.

Roman particularly mentions an *Eyewitness* book about rocks, a subject you do not normally address by shifting deictic center into the perspective of the rock formations. Nevertheless, it is worth remembering Gallese's point that we draw on our own embodied knowledge of the world to comprehend "linguistic descriptions of facts, actions, and events" (2021: 379), just as much as to inhabit the world of stories. I probably don't imagine *being* a rock, but I can activate many embodied responses to reading about them. Can a boulder be climbed? How does it feel to sit on it? How readily can the feet balance on a stony terrain? What is the weight of a rock in the hand? Is it jagged or smooth? How do the hand and the eye evaluate the skipping potential of a small, flat rock? How do the wrist muscles flex at the thought of giving it the correct flip to make it skim the water? And so on.

In her discussion of paracanons, Stimpson mentions Janice Radway's work with romance readers (1984). Radway, says Stimpson, "had to relearn her critical methodology. She had to expand her focus from text to the drama between text and reader" (1990: 962). Stimpson makes a similar kind of shift: "Though noun, a paracanon summons up verbs: to read, to love what we read, to codify and judge what we read by what we love to read, to write a history of emotions and of literacy by noting what people have loved to read and how" (1990: 972).

How much of a stretch is it to award paracanonical status to the *Eyewitness* books, beloved by generations of young readers? Roman cites numerous responses to his *Eyewitness* reading: he collects rocks, he climbs on boulders, he loves to pick rocks up and throw them, especially skipping them across water. He is not as much interested in geology as in "if they look cool or not." Talking about rocks, he mentions that he has stood with one foot on each side of the equator and on each side of the Greenwich Meridian. Locally, he performs a similar ritual with the Great Divide in the Rocky Mountains. "Yeah, I like going to these really old places. That kind of storytelling is really interesting to me."

It is intriguing to me that Roman, a reader whose interests include a broad range of fiction and information, considers such geographical interfaces as a kind of storytelling. His observation suggests that "the drama between text and reader" can be expressed in many ways. While much of the emphasis on childhood reading involves the immersive appeal of fiction, many other genres of reading also entail engaging with voices and values other than one's own, encounters that contribute to how a child perceives the shape of the world. Roman has learned to see distinctions between different rocks, an enrichment of his relationship to the universe. Scholarly explorations of childhood reading frequently focus on explicitly literary materials or on fiction more broadly. Meanwhile, many child readers are—also or instead—reading informational texts and absorbing forms of virtual, rather than, or as well as, fictional awareness. The autotopographical thinking of these readers is likely to take account of such experiences. Although my own study follows the twelve readers in largely focusing on narrative fiction, I do also take account of other elements in their literate lives. The maps expand my awareness of what we can learn by starting with the readers rather than with a preselected set of materials.

Managing the Interface

How do people shift gears from being mobile agents in their own real-world environment to infusing their cognitive knowledge of movement and agency into the flat pages of their books? Bringing words to life in the mind, whether to create a fictional world or to activate a representation of the reader's own three-dimensional surroundings (the world as is), is an essential element of reading, but it is very difficult to gain access to the mental fires that make such alchemy possible. Even understanding how this process works in one's own mind is extremely challenging; creating access into how this vital operation manifests itself in the mind of another is limited even further by what that other reader can articulate of a very tacit process.

How do my key terms permit me to describe this operation? For simplicity, I stick for the moment with the example of a narrative fiction. Readers occupy a life space and when they encounter a text, they open a reading space in their minds. Both kinds of space are (im)material, activated by many contributing factors. A reading space opens to permit readers to improvise a simulation, guided by the text. A simulation of a narrative invokes issues of agency, manifested in a space that is, at a minimum, dynamic enough to permit movement, even though the detailed scope of this space may vary from reader to reader. A reader contributes an embodied sense of movement, agency, and space to the enactment of the text, and steps into the perspective of the narrative agents, transferring into the deictic center of these agents and adopting a forward-looking and subjunctive mode of hoping, believing, wishing, fearing, and more from the perspective of the characters. Such activities may be explored retrospectively through the exercise of autotopography, as readers examine connections between their life spaces and their reading spaces.

Many disciplinary perspectives merge in this brief description of reading. The fact that a coherent (if dense) account can find support from so many distinct specialist stances simply reinforces the idea that there are useful ways for us to talk to each other about this complex topic.

Gallese offers a summary description that ties together many of the elements of this chapter and of the larger project, and relates our cognitive capacities to the core elements of agency and movement—what he calls goal-directed motor acts:

> Cognitive abilities, like the mapping of space and its perception, the perception of objects occupying our visual landscape, the hierarchical representation of action course towards a distal outcome, the detection of motor goals and action anticipation, are all possible because of the peculiar functional architecture of the motor system, organized in terms of goal-directed motor acts. The proper development of this functional architecture scaffolds more cognitively sophisticated social cognitive abilities, like the production/reception of cultural artifacts and fictional worlds … The multimodal integration of what we perceive is triggered by the potentiality for action that we express corporeally. (2021: 377)

In short, we generate an improvised simulation of a textual event out of our own capacity for planning and achieving action. Such a facility is hard to monitor from outside and most attempts to understand reader activity must work obliquely. This book investigates one kind of portal into the reading of another person, exploring (only) some of the elements that make their literacy possible. Each participant in the project, reflecting on the individual experiences of a literate youth, chooses one or two representative landscapes to consider. The digital layering of their maps and the temporal affordances of the interviews offer some potential to explore the territory delineated in the maps in terms of both the incidental and the goal-directed movement that is always implicit in the marked sites.

Readers do not explicitly perceive their lives as a kind of pre-reading data sweep, in which they collect miscellaneous impressions that may, possibly, later, someday, provide useful kindling for sparking stories into mental life. Yet much childhood experience does flourish again as an ingredient in a second, fictional life or as a repertoire for the interpretation of informational text. This project asks participants to reflect on the boundaries between living and reading. The maps take us into many forms of reading hinterland, but not simply through providing access to random memories of childhood. In order to develop these maps, the participants have to do a considerable amount of thinking about how these territories shaped youthful reading experiences, even before we begin the first interview.

In their inherent and necessary plurality, the participants' maps offer different and personal views of the border country between life spaces and reading spaces. The scenarios presented here, in all their variety and complexity, certainly fulfill the conditions of "messy," and the thinking that is elucidated through the making of the maps and the subsequent discussions supplies a weight of necessary complexity to how we conceptualize the act of reading.

Geographic Spaces

The First Place

4

Home and Away: Stability, Disruption, and Agency

David Malouf says children learn about the world from what he calls their "first place." In the print version of the Herbert Blaicklock Memorial Lecture that he delivered in September of 1984, he expands on this idea:

> My purpose tonight is to look at the only place in Australia that I know well, the only place I know from inside, from my body outwards, and to offer my understanding of it as an example of how we might begin to speak accurately of where and what we are. What I will be after is not facts—or not only facts, but a description of how the elements of a place and our inner lives cross and illuminate one another, how we interpret space, and in so doing make our first maps of reality, how we mythologize spaces and through that mythology (a good deal of it inherited) find our way into a culture … For me that was Brisbane. It has always seemed to me to be a fortunate choice—except that I didn't make it. But then the place you get is always, in the real sense of the word, fortunate, in that it constitutes your fortune, your fate, and is your only entry into the world. (1985: 3)

These words were significant to my study of my own early literacy (Mackey, 2016). My personal first place, emotionally and intellectually, is undoubtedly the city of St. John's, Newfoundland. But it is not my first actual home; I was born in Halifax, Nova Scotia, and lived there until I was about twenty months old. I have no memory of Halifax except from subsequent visits to see family; and I am certain that the hills and water of St. John's are what shaped my sense of the world in the way that Malouf describes.

The concept of the first place is a powerful one in terms of understanding early literacy, and was formative in the design of the mapping project I report here. I made no specific request for participants to map the first significant life scenes they remember, but a few of them came very close to fulfilling this specification, and most of them talked about their early recollections in the interviews. In this chapter, I explore the role and shaping power of home, as manifested in singular or plural form through the maps and interviews of several participants.

Malouf's first place is largely a material site, affecting his ways of seeing the world and moving through it. In our heavily mediated world, even young children soon join Joshua Meyrowitz in combining awareness of their current physical setting with "thousands of flickering, barely conscious images of similar settings from news reports, novels, movies, television programmes, and online surfing. It is the mix of live and mediated experiences in all these settings that evoke [sic] moment-to-moment feelings of adventure, boredom, escape, romance, comfort, danger, artistic enrichment, intellectual stimulation, and so on" (2015: 98).

For most children, these immaterial flickers of *elsewhere* take place in a home setting that they are figuring out by the day, using their bodies, their senses, their imaginations, and their developing powers of thinking to make sense of the world they live in.

There is a kind of absolute quality to the notion of a first place, but the "start again" element that attends any form of migration (perhaps especially immigration from one culture to another during childhood when patterns are still being laid in place) raises the question of whether it is possible to have a second "first place," or even multiples. It is noteworthy that it is relatively easy to discern the first place of all these participants, even those who spoke of movement and fluidity as an essential part of their life story; but the "restart" component also comes through quite clearly in a number of accounts. Halia explicitly chose her first Canadian house as the basis of her map. Notably, it includes no visual reference to her initial location; which, of course, may simply be an indicator of what artifacts were available to her, though nothing prevented her from turning to Google Maps or Google Earth as others did. Rahina, as we have seen, did not provide much visual citation at all in her abstract map (though it is very clear that she understands Malouf's concept of "knowing from inside" and transfers this awareness to her reading of characters). The remaining ten participants all showed some kind of graphic reference to their initial home, at least obliquely, as in Matt's photo of his school playing field, and Suleman's family pictures.

This chapter explores some implications of mobility and stasis for a child learning about the world and about reading. But even those concepts can benefit from interrogation. "Home" is a noun, but these participants recall their different homes in terms of verbs. Amy's three-dimensional walk-through of her grandmother's house enables virtual motion on the part of the viewer, and many of the other representations imply motion through a sequence of links. Terence Cave suggests that implications of movement are "deeply embedded in our response to the perceived world. Movement is clearly of the essence" (2016: 8).

It may be a stretch to suggest that these memories of embodied movement in and around home are part of what permits the reading of the noun of home as the activation of a living organism—but I think there is enough fruitful possibility in this notion to be worth considering in the following accounts of home and reading. Cave perceives directed movement as an essential element in and for expression of agency. Our homes shape our potential agency and also provide affordances for our imaginative engagement with the world.

In this chapter, I take the idea of home as a complex form of "site of living," including both the nouns of familiar places and objects and the verbs of familiar actions and ways of being as enablers of agency. I believe such a composite definition of a core concept of childhood may permit new ways of thinking about how readers import this idea into their response to texts.

It is important to remember that, as well as these readers, their texts are also in motion. The story most extensively cited by almost all of the participants, Harry Potter, was initially published in the UK, a nation not otherwise represented in this project. Medina and Wohlwend remind us of the characteristics of the world inhabited by all these young women and men:

> Current perspectives on transnationalism, media engagement, and the politics of childhood and global markets help us understand how children engage and interpret their relationships in converging global worlds and how they accommodate and/or resist these social dynamics in their local contexts. Under these social conditions, children live multiliterate lives as they move as consumers and producers of knowledge across real and imagined spaces, across worlds and communities, and in textual diasporas grounded in traveling texts that flow through media, digital spaces, and the consumption structures of global markets. (2014: 5)

There is not a map in this collection that does not include aspects of this complex social and textual fluidity, and the ideas of agency incorporated in these accounts are correspondingly complex and sophisticated. The stories incorporate varying degrees of actual movement and cultural adjustment, and the age at which major changes occur is also germane.

John Kinsella offers the notion of *polysituatedness*. He says, "We are always polysituated. If we are talking of where we primarily live (though we might go away, travel, or relocate and return every now and again), we are talking about so many different notions of connection and alienation that 'home' simply doesn't answer the condition" (2017: 18). Not everybody in this project had active experience of displacement but all expressed plural connections. Only three (Matt, Roman, and Amy) indicate that they have lived in the same house throughout their lives, but even they talk about travel and return (to the Rockies, to New Zealand, to France) and about relocating (to Grammie's house and Grammie's rules). Furthermore, even these three who express the longest unbroken connection to a single place recognizably operate within a culture of mutability.

At the same time, all the participants have learned, at one point or another in their lives, how to *be* in a place. They all speak of specific connections to one or more significant sites. (Of course, it is important to acknowledge that this sense of connection may represent a bias in the recruitment process.) Kinsella says, "Place, for me, has become a paradoxical condition of presence" (2017: 5), and all these participants are clearly at ease with being present in one or more worlds.

But how those connections are set up in childhood plays out differently when children stay put and when they relocate. Even a few extra years of stability may make a difference. To begin this consideration, we may contrast the stories of Amy and Riya, as representatives of staying in one place through the initial years of their lives, with those of Liang and Laura, for whom a childhood move was a defining component of their experience. Lily's story subsequently serves as a reminder that no aspect of life necessarily follows the lines of what might be reasonably predicted.

Amy describes a childhood of considerable consistency and stability up to the age of twelve, and so does Riya. Liang describes an early childhood rooted in a single place, but from middle childhood onward she has moved frequently, including a shift of country and continent; Laura stopped briefly in Toronto on her way to a new life in Vancouver, but she too describes a singular childhood before the age of nine. Lily also moved at the age of nine or ten, and again a year later, but her story contrasts with those of all the others in terms of what makes a change life altering.

Security, Fear, and Fantasy: Amy

Amy is a student of environmental sciences, working on the human dimensions of environmental management. She grew up on an acreage outside Edmonton and, because both her parents worked, she was frequently looked after by her grandmother, who had a house in the city. Amy turns twenty between the first and the second interview. She mentions family connections with both Ireland and Germany. Her map is a three-dimensional walk-through of her grandmother's house (Figure 4.1), drawing on Homestyler's options to recreate it in faithful detail, though her grandmother died when she was about twelve and she has not seen the interior of the house for eight years.

Amy makes many comments about how she aimed for extreme fidelity in her rendition of her grandmother's house, but it turns out that her memories of childhood activities are largely confined to the half of the house away from the street:

Figure 4.1 Amy's grandmother's kitchen.

Maybe I'll start—the door I always walked in was here [indicating back door], this door here. And basically the center of all activities was the kitchen, this room here. I avoided this side of the house [front room] like it was the plague, because I was terrified people could look through the window and see me. Because I grew up in the country, and I did not like the city, and I was scared that people were going to walk on the sidewalk and see me. So I like hid from that room altogether and stayed in the kitchen, this room, the whole time I was there.

To this day, says Amy, the setting of all her dreams is this house. Creating the three-dimensional replica was an emotional experience, though a positive one. Specific activities happened in particular locations and her grandmother marked the passage of time by devoting one multi-slot picture frame to each grandchild and inserting the new year's school photo alongside the previous ones.

Deborah Brandt talks about the sponsors of literacy: "Any agents, local or distant, concrete or abstract, who enable, support, teach, model, as well as recruit, regulate, suppress, or withhold literacy—and gain advantage by it in some way" (1998: 166). Amy's grandmother was clearly a literacy sponsor in a number of homey, mainstream ways, familiar to many North American families. She involved Amy in much of the domestic literacy activity in her household; the list is extensive. Amy sat in the sink and read recipe cards, written by her grandmother or her great-grandmother. She helped Grammie file her domestic papers (though she was not allowed to look at the bills) and was encouraged to read the advertising flyers that came with the mail. When her grandmother acquired a new phone, Amy read the instructions and helped her get the hang of it. She used magnetic letters to place messages on the refrigerator door. They shared sections of the newspaper; Grammie read the news and Amy read the comics, did the Sudoku puzzle, and cut out pictures of the Edmonton Oilers to glue onto sheets of paper. Amy looked at the household list of phone contacts and read the Christmas cards that came to the house, grilling her grandma about the family connections represented by these links. Grammie bought magazine subscriptions from the school fundraising leaflets and read them while encouraging Amy to read her books. She also rewarded all her grandchildren for good report cards—straight As earned each of them twenty dollars, which, for an event that occurred three times a year, represented a considerable outlay. She also encouraged Amy to keep a daily journal about her time in Grammie's house; it was stored in a drawer in the china cabinet, under the tablecloths, because it was a secret even from Amy's mother. As a literacy sponsor, this grandmother took a lively interest in the achievements of her grandchildren and made many efforts to encourage and help them. She inculcated Amy into many low-level forms of literate engagement with the world around her, in ways explored and expanded on in David Barton and Mary Hamilton's study of local literacies (1998) and Susan Jones's more recent investigation of literacy in the community (2018). Absorbing their grandmother's assumptions and acknowledging her active efforts, Amy and her cousins learned to regard literacy as a foundational element in community connection.

The grandmother had rules but she also indulged Amy in some ways: Amy, for example, was permitted to select what her grandma would wear that day and Grammie always at least tried on her choices, even if she occasionally rejected them. In other ways, Amy had to fit in with her grandmother's routines. When Amy slept over, for example, she shared a bed with her grandma, who refused to switch sides just so Amy could sleep away from the window.

Her mother's former bedroom was known as the toy room during Amy's childhood, and the history of the room contributed to the kinds of activities Amy engaged in. Her mother's old dresser, for example, was filled with toys and also with tap shoes of various sizes from the childhoods of her mother and aunt. There was always a pair of tap shoes that fit, and Amy would clatter into the kitchen because the toy room was carpeted. Amy's account of her childhood in this house was animated by many such idiosyncratic details. She and her cousins played school, as many children do, making use of a bucket of "weird scarf pieces of square cloth fabric" to stand in for many elements of their play: seats, pieces of paper, and more. One of their favorite activities in the game of school involved the creation and dispensation of report cards; they clearly internalized both the significance of literacy and the locus of real school power with this operation.

Despite her phobia about windows and strangers, Amy did experience some aspects of an urban childhood at her grandmother's house. There was no sidewalk on the acreage but, in the city, she could chalk pictures and hopscotch squares on the pavement out the back. She also loved the little milk cupboard, a small shelf with a door to the outside world and a door to the interior of the house. Back in the days of household delivery, a milkman stashed a container of milk in this cupboard from the outside and the householder retrieved it from the inside without having to brace against the unforgiving depths of winter; the shelter of the little cupboard also reduced the chances of the milk freezing in the bitter Alberta cold. Unfortunately, Grammie's little door was inaccessible. Amy observed,

> I thought it was the coolest thing ever because really, it's a small door that leads to outside. But it was nailed shut and painted over so that I couldn't open it, which was always infuriating to me … I had all of these daydreams about things I could do if I could open that door. It would be awesome. It's a small little, it's its own world, it's great … But I could never open it so it was kind of disappointing. Yeah, I'm not over it, obviously.

The potential of that sealed door haunted Amy and it was clear that, despite her reservations about windows, she saw this little door as an opening rather than a threat. Perhaps its small scale gave it an allure of fantasy. Wherever her paranoia about urban dangers arose, she said it did not come from her reading, chiefly because she rejected any reading that might reflect urban reality, even at the anodyne level of *The Baby-Sitters Club* series. Her choice, over and over again, was fantasy: books about fairies and gnomes, the Harry Potter stories, science fiction.

Amy: It's better when it can't actually happen. That's my preference.
Margaret: That's a protection too, isn't it?
Amy: Yeah, it definitely is.

Margaret:	So if it's off in a world where it can't happen, then it can be more lurid and dangerous.
Amy:	Yeah. But then if I look out the window and there's a dude there, that could happen. That's happening. It's creepy.
Margaret:	Yeah. So put it behind the magic wall.
Amy:	Exactly. With the little milk door.

Although her pictorial memory for the details of her grandmother's house is acute, Amy is a very nonvisual reader. She does not care what a character looks like, and she dismisses the entire possibility of movie scenery disrupting some possible mental image with a brisk phrase: "The scenes, who cares?" The little milk door clearly resonated with her on a symbolic level, but she did not import visual details into her reading. She was categorical about not needing to do so in her discussion of Grammie's basement, which was fully finished to provide extra bedrooms for the large number of children in her mother's generation, but neglected in Amy's day:

Amy:	It was almost since they had left, she had never done anything with it, because it's all 1970s furniture and just looked weird. Just looked completely different, because upstairs was pretty modern, nice walls and furniture, but the downstairs was weird. It was old stuff, and dusty and smelt weird, musty or something. So, I would rarely go downstairs and if I did, it was because the cousins were over and we were playing hide and seek and there was the best hiding spots downstairs. But I kind of also always imagined it as the place in the house where the monsters would like. If they lived somewhere, they would be down there. Because there was all this antique fancy wood carved stuff and it was the closest thing to mystical as it got in that house. And it was also in the basement so it was dark and weird and no one ever went down there. So it was a kind of a creepy—
Margaret:	So in your non-visualizing way, when you read, would you import atmosphere from that basement?
Amy:	No, no, I didn't, but I would imagine when I was in the house, I would imagine that there were fictional characters in that house.
Margaret:	So books to basement but not basement to books.
Amy:	Correct, yes.

Given the choice of text-to-text, life-to-text, or text-to-life, Amy chose the last. If you do not need visual information in order to read, you can be free-floating in a different kind of way.

The house still exists, of course, and Amy had recently driven past it. She knew the house was sold after her grandmother's death,

> but I had never seen the people in it. I always just assumed it was someone like my grandma, because, you know, they probably have the same taste in house. This

time I saw a person. And it just set me off. It was bad ... I was like, Who's that man? What's he doing in her house? Yeah, it was very emotional.

This motif of loss recurs in the other stories considered in this chapter. The house stays put as a noun, but *somebody else* gets to activate the verbs of its life.

Stability and Specificity: Riya

Riya, age twenty-one, is a psychology major. She moved to Edmonton from India at the age of eighteen as an international student. Her map (Figure 4.2), very remote from Amy's in terms of technological sophistication, in other ways is very similar. It is a sketched floor plan on lined paper, outlining in some detail the rooms of the family bungalow in Assam, where she lived until she was about twelve. At that point, her parents divorced and she moved with her mother and brother into an apartment in the same town, continuing to visit the house at weekends to stay with their dad. Subsequent moves within India took her further afield and seem to have curtailed her trips back to this house, though at the time of our conversation, she had seen it very recently on a visit to India.

Riya's home was located in a "huge compound" with grazing animals and chickens and a fishing pond, as well as large flower and vegetable gardens. A 4.6 meter wall, topped with broken light bulbs and supplemented by a security moat separated their domain from the street. The family also kept a German shepherd, as a combination of security and pet. Riya spent almost all her playtime inside this compound because it was so big and offered so many attractions. Neighborhood children came over every day to play.

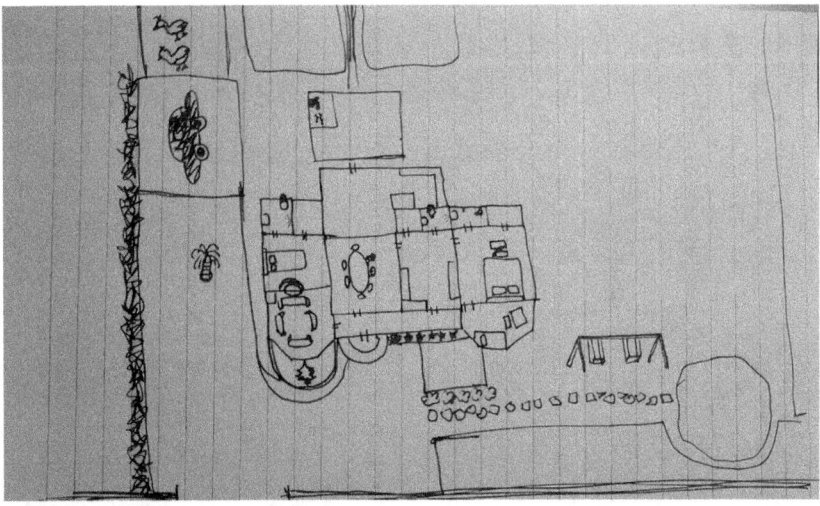

Figure 4.2 Riya's floor plan.

Like Amy, Riya describes particular locations for specific textual activities. A screened-in verandah was home for video gaming. Other locations served for watching television or playing card games such as Pokémon. There were two rooms where she did a lot of reading: the main bedroom and the guest bedroom, which she had pretty much taken over for herself. Riya was a big reader as a child, and most of her reading involved settings other than India; the only local material she read consistently was a comic called *Tinkle* (Figure 4.3). She also read *Archie Comics* and she read Enid Blyton's books about *The Famous Five* and *The Secret Seven*. She read Nancy Drew stories and other mysteries, as well as Harry Potter.

The Anglo-American mix continued in her school reading; she mentioned *Animal Farm* and *Tom Sawyer*. She also read stories in Hindi, though her first languages are English and Assamese, the language of her state. Technically, in school, Assamese was regarded as her third language, so, "it's not as intensive and we didn't do a lot of reading. But we did do some reading, like poems and short stories, but I don't really remember much of that." Now, she mostly speaks English, but she relishes her multilingual capacity: "I like being able to think in a different type of way when I think in a different language."

For Riya as a child, reading almost invariably involved invoking a world of *somewhere else*. She is a visual reader but her default visualization was "just this Western world, place." This generic setting first arose from her experience of Western television and other media, and also Western reading. She hears voices when she reads and they sound Western even if the character is Indian. "For example, if I was reading a book with an Indian character in it, I would imagine, an Indian person, but the accent is still like a regular Western accent." For the most part, Riya defaulted to white characters, picking up on textual cues such as nomenclature: "A lot of the names are Christian names in books."

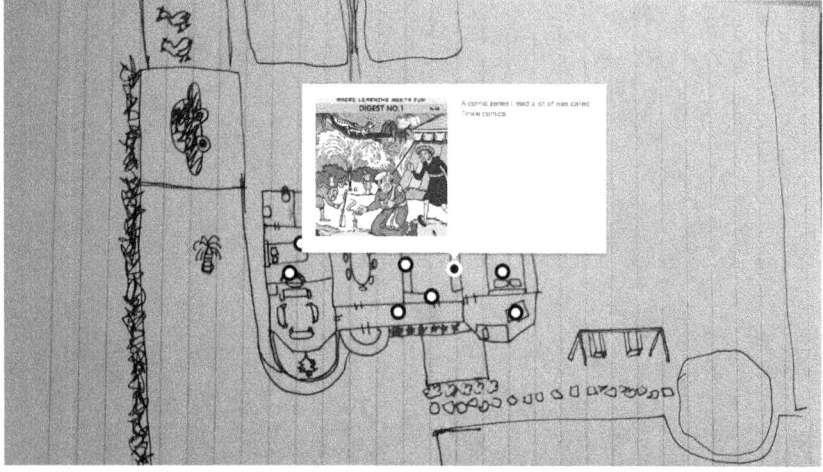

Figure 4.3 Riya's image for reading *Tinkle*, precisely located in her home floor plan.

Riya and I both read the Enid Blyton books as outsiders to British culture and we had an extended conversation on the significance of that outsider status to our reading experience (see Mackey, 2021a for details). I found the Blyton world very alien, much as I loved the stories. Riya seems to have brought a more useful repertoire to bear:

> It just felt right. I guess because I grew up reading so much of it, and watching so much Western media, that I was comfortable. I knew what a shilling was, I was familiar with British terminology and things like that, and I dunno, I always imagined the world like this. And I think that's one of the reasons, or I think that's the biggest reason why, when I came to Canada, I had close to zero culture shock. It just felt like, yeah, this is exactly what I expected, this is very normal.

In her second interview, Riya expands on that idea of "normal" in relation to Blyton. The subject of boarding school in the Blyton books arises early in our conversation, and leads me to ask what the child Riya had thought about the apparently unlimited capacity of the Famous Five to go off on adventures unattended.

Riya: Yeah, that was like a fantasy world. Yeah. That was not something that was realistic, but I think I just sort of assumed that that was white people world, and then where I live that doesn't really happen, there's more restrictions.

Margaret: Okay, so it was white people world rather than book world?

Riya: Yeah. It was the Western world, where there was not as many restrictions on things.

Margaret: So if you and I had me, time travelling in our childhood as Enid Blyton readers, and I had said to you, no way in the world would I be allowed to go camping on an island without an adult, would you have been surprised? I mean, I just assumed it was book world. And maybe the British did crazy things like that.

Riya: Yeah, maybe the British did things like that. I dunno, but I think if that were to happen, I'd be surprised, but I'd be like, wow, okay, I didn't know that. I'd just assumed this, but okay, fine, that makes sense. I guess this isn't like real life. It'd be a little bit disappointing.

Margaret: Oh, so you thought there really were hordes of children off arresting bad guys, on islands by themselves in Britain. It would be nice, wouldn't it?

Riya: Yeah, it was like a fantasy world; I wished I could have something like that.

Margaret: Yeah, yeah, so did I, so did I. I loved it.

Riya and I read Enid Blyton fifty years and half a world apart from each other, and yet we clearly responded in similar ways. One element I find striking about this conversation is how readily we each suspended "home rules" for the world that Blyton evoked, whether we ascribed the free-floating autonomy of the Famous Five to book rules, white people rules, British eccentricity, or any other readily available cord-cutting assumption. Yet what truly fueled our understanding of Blyton's world was a deep awareness of agency that we both learned at home—I in the six acres of school playing fields on which my house was located (Mackey, 2016) and Riya inside the walls of her large compound. The Famous Five simply amplified this potential.

Riya speaks of transferring information from one textual setting to another—for example, of gleaning an understanding of high school corridors full of student lockers from a succession of television programs. But such extrapolation can be two-edged. When she moved from India to Canada, she had to take account of the constructed nature of some of her previous learning. "Now I think it's a lot of unlearning, because a lot of things that happen in movies and TV shows don't actually happen in real life. I just assumed they always did. So, living here has been, like, okay, yeah, they don't actually do that."

Riya, like Amy, describes loss. After her parents separated, she and her brother would return to this house to visit their father, but it was never the same. She says, "I think that all my childhood memories, honestly, are from this place. And it feels like after I moved to the other places that I lived in, when I think of myself in those places, it doesn't feel like, I don't think of myself as a child in those places." The visits back to the house to see her dad accentuated that shift: "It's a big house, so it was really empty. A lot of the things that were there before were gone, a lot of the trees and stuff were cut down. There were trees everywhere; we had a lot of fruit trees. All of those were gone. No animals. It was really different." Riya and her brother had lost contact with their neighborhood friends, so the old games that required a crowd, "tag or whatever," became impossible.

Riya has been back to India once since she arrived in Edmonton, in the December just before we spoke. She was there for only two weeks and was obliged to visit family members in three different cities, so she found the visit rushed and unsettling. Her account of driving past her old home holds a strong tone of lament. I ask her what kinds of emotions the process of creating the map had evoked, and she replies:

> It's a mix because this was a great time of my life. It was so much fun, most things were positive memories. But it's sad, because my last few memories of this place, it was really empty. And even when I went back this time, we would drive by the place sometimes, and someone else lives there now, and they painted the walls different … And also all the trees and everything are gone. When you would drive by here, for example, you couldn't really see the house except through the holes in the gate because there were trees all along. Tall trees, but all of those are gone now, so you can literally see everything in the house. So that's unfortunate.

Amy and Riya were both twelve when they lost the home they chose to map, so they both were leaving childhood behind in any case. The significance of this sense of loss they describe is perhaps enhanced by awareness of closing the door on an early and primary stage of their own lives; in any case, they are both eloquent on the subject. Liang and Laura were both nine when they left their first home, still children. They both describe this move in terms of the mobility of the change rather than couching their conversation within the terms of the preceding stability.

Change and Growth: Liang

Liang is twenty-two at the time of our interviews. She is studying for the degree of Bachelor of Fine Arts with a specialty in painting. Like Amy, she spent a great deal of her childhood in her grandparents' house in a small town in China, but only until she was in Grade 4, aged around nine. At that point, she and her parents moved to the capital city of their Chinese province, near Shanghai, and left the grandparents behind. When she was fourteen, they moved to Canada and shifted from one community to another quite regularly; she mentions Winnipeg, Toronto, Calgary, Camrose, and currently Edmonton. Liang's map (Figure 4.4) features the small town where she spent her earliest years; it shows her grandparents' house, her own home, her parents' motorcycle store, her elementary school, and the route to school, which she drove every day with her grandfather on his electric bike.

Amy and Liang both produce maps in which grandparents feature significantly and which draw on very early memories. On the surface, the big difference between them is that Amy's is an interior map and Liang's features the outdoors. But according to the interview data, a much bigger discrepancy lies in each participant's attitude to change. Amy regularly points out elements of her three-dimensional home that were constant: the square clock on the kitchen wall, for example, old in her grandmother's time and now owned by her mother. Liang's approach is very different; her map represents the "long-ago" and the impact of the life experience it portrays is heavily diluted by subsequent experience. She has returned to China only once since she left, in 2010, so she would have been fifteen; she was there for two weeks and was sick for one of those weeks. In other words, the map is created out of memories rather than from any more recent exposure. Her automatic reactions are now in many ways Canadian. Responding to her discussion of this distant world, I say tentatively, "This young childhood is almost like it's behind a wall in some ways," and she answers, "Yes, definitely."

Like many mapmakers, Liang speaks affectionately about particular places and experiences:

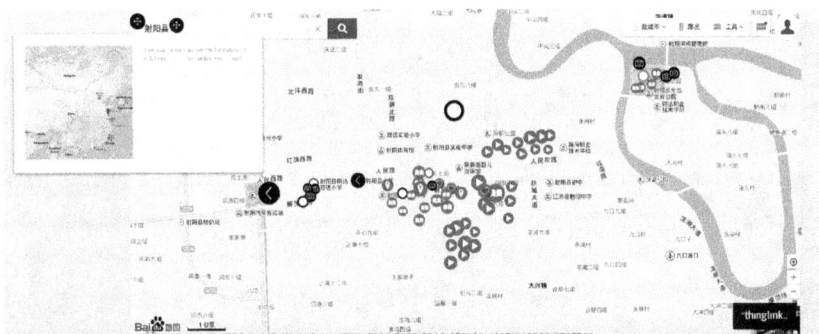

Figure 4.4 Liang's map of her early home.

There's a huge, what's it called, it's like a ground, a parking spot. It's in front of my parents' store. We used to just play badminton there and do lots of—I learned biking there. There were huge boxes from the motorcycles. [Laughs] We would play in those boxes and all the places around here. We all know each other, all the neighbours. Stores that sell stationery, sell ice creams, we all know each other. We just kind of hang out around here in this area, this whole area.

Liang speaks of this world as not only long ago but now lost. She describes playing hide and seek in the cardboard boxes and adds, "I felt like when I grew up more, I became more and more lonely. Well—not lonely but I—I just spent more time with myself." And of course the move away made irrevocable changes: "Yeah, it seems like a lot of friends in that town, they either stayed there or they just moved to other places around there. I moved all the way here." Compounding this distance is the issue of how much China has changed since she left. Liang would visit today if she got the chance, but "it's not like a really strong feeling."

As a child, Liang rendered the pictures from her books in material terms: "I really enjoyed making clothes for dolls. I loved fashion and I loved decorating. When I was reading fairytale picture books, I have always paid attention to the dresses and gowns of the princesses on the illustrations." The illustration she selects to represent this activity is relatively indeterminate in national terms but definitely "princessy" in its hyperfeminine outlines and flowing skirts and veil (Figure 4.5).

Figure 4.5 Image of Liang's model princess.

Liang is a visualizing reader, seeing "not pictures but more like a movie; there would definitely be visuals." Sometimes she sees from a distance, sometimes from inside a character's head, depending on the writing. The specific observation of the dresses in illustrations seems to be a more particular and focused activity. For the most part, her default visuals are now Western. Her fine art work also veers Western in approach, but she observes,

> I think it's more Western actually, but I would say it's a choice what I want to make this work about, I would carefully choose my way of doing it. However, I think I'm more Western—because I had most of my higher-level education here, I don't have the access to the Chinese or the Eastern culture. I don't think I know that too much, I think the Western education affected me more than Chinese education so I think I'm more of using the Western way.

Liang thinks of herself as fairly noncommittal: "I think, for me I think it's neutral because I'm really not much about nationalist, even I found nowadays a lot of Caucasian people who are very interested in Eastern culture, maybe more than I do. I think it's a lot about the personal interest. Personally I think it's very neutral for me." When I ask her outright, she says flatly that there is no place she thinks of as home, and describes her cast of mind as postmodern. We discuss the impact of her life history on her current state:

Margaret: And are you content not to have a home? Or would you like to be more settled in one place and not moving around?

Liang: [Pauses] I, I don't know actually, I think I'm kind of used to this state I have now and I think it's kind of my instinct of not trying to seek the stable; if I do it's gonna be really hard for me because I can't get it. Even now in my age I can't control a lot of things so I shouldn't be thinking about that too much ... I just try to adapt, and try to do what I can, so yeah, I don't seek for like a home place.

Margaret: Right, right. Do you think it matters that when you were small you did have a home, do you think that is part of your ability to roll with the punches now, to move wherever?

Liang: [Pauses]

Margaret: Or is that just—

Liang: I think it's very important. If I could have that state, I think I would be living more happily, but I don't think I would grow that much, so I think it's both, it has both good side and bad side—

Margaret: Right, not that—I agree with you.

Liang: So it has both, and I think I just—I think after I moved to Canada it's just been harder and harder for me; maybe it's just myself, what I feel and think, of course, that me and that age were happier, but I think it's essential for me to have this difficult period to actually have something— to actually do something in the future.

It is perhaps not too much of a stretch to describe Liang here and elsewhere in our conversation talking about change as an investment in a kind of future agency. But change comes at a price.

Although her Chinese childhood feels very much in the past for Liang, and despite her disavowal of national identity, she remains very interested in selected aspects of Chinese culture. She is currently making a study of ancient Chinese fortune-telling. She describes her painting as "more contemporary and hybrid … I like doing experimental things." There is certainly a Chinese element to her work but, she says that, having been away from China for so long, living in Canada, "I started to have a different perspective. Again, that's text-to-text, because I don't even have life experience about that culture. I kept reading and I kept doing research about that, it would be text-to-text." She would like to live in China someday "if it's still a good place."

Liang describes herself as a curious reader, "I like to read about things I don't know." She also says she is a compassionate and emotional reader. Curiosity is a driving force, and she includes it as a component of the energy that propelled her to Canada. Liking new ideas is "a part of who I am" and part of "why we came all the way, so far away, and other people stayed there; it's because we have the—we dare to take the challenge."

A Double Identity: Laura

Laura is eighteen when we meet and is a student of food and nutrition. Her sense of a double identity is reflected in the fact that her email address incorporates her Chinese name but she signs her notes with her Canadian name and says she uses it in her Canadian life with everyone but her parents; in Hong Kong, her Chinese name prevails. Uniquely among the participants, she says, "The base map is just the world map," and much of her discussion revolves around holiday trips to theme parks and amusement complexes in different parts of the world. She left her Hong Kong home at the age of nine or ten, and initially moved to Vancouver; she came to Edmonton to study and is still adjusting to life on her own at the time that we meet.

Like Liang, Laura moved away from her first home in mid-childhood. Like Riya, her early life seems to have been fairly affluent. She describes Hong Kong itself in standard terms: crowded, busy, polluted, with a lot of construction going on, and sometimes requiring its citizens to don masks for their own protection because the air is so bad. But Laura spent her early years in an apartment beside a mountain on the edge of the city (Figure 4.6). She describes apartment life briefly, mentioning scenes where she and her sister would commandeer blankets to be princesses and queens in their capes or to roll around as caterpillars, all wrapped up. She also enjoyed the view from her middle floor apartment, feeling "on top of everyone … looking through the window … from my tower." For the most part, however, her account focuses on life outside the apartment. She hiked in the mountain, but her main social life centered on the local clubhouse and its playground and swimming pool and parking lot.

Laura's school was in the city so she sampled urban life as well. Additionally, she traveled extensively, at first around Asia, on an assortment of vacations "because it was cheap!" When I ask her, for example, if her local mountain was what she

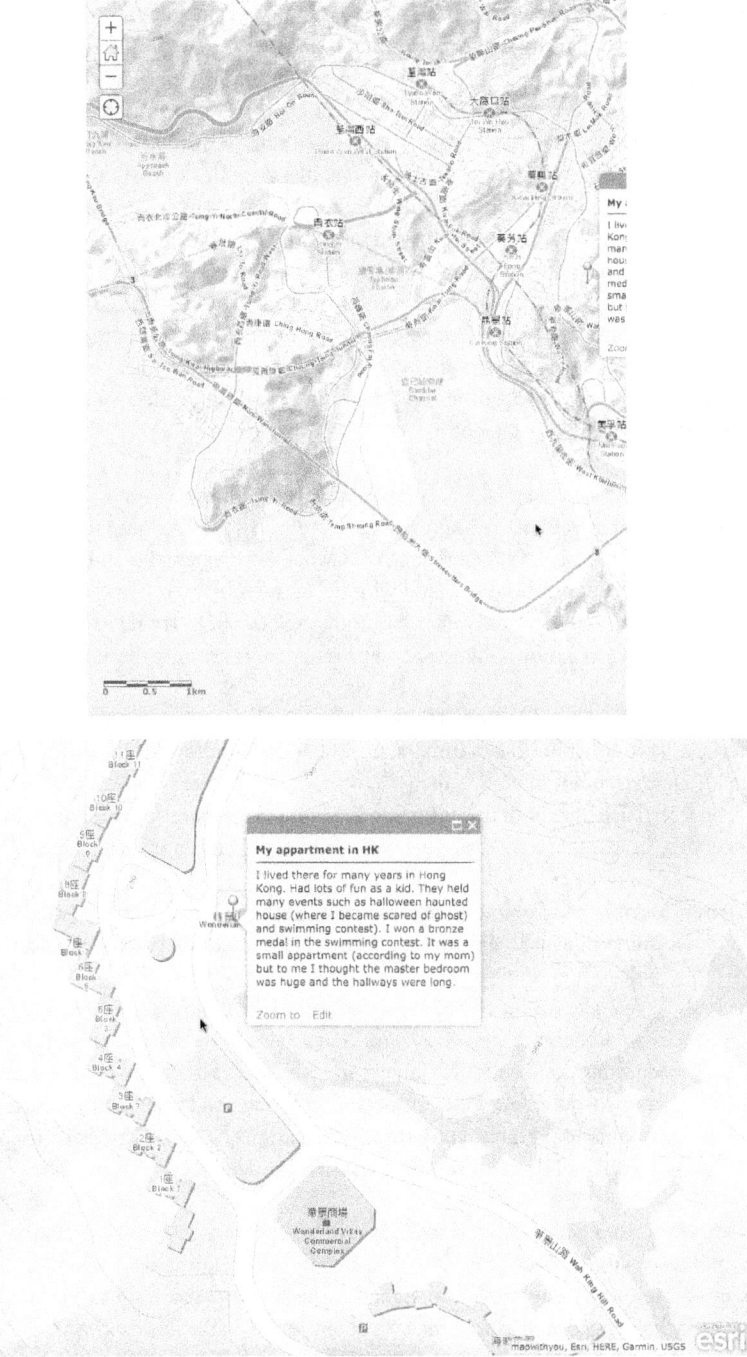

Figure 4.6 Laura's broad geographic framework, paired with the close-up perspective on her neighborhood in Hong Kong.

pictured if she read about a mountain, she says, no, her default was more likely to be a mountain in Thailand—the first mountain she ever hiked, while on holiday there. She visited Taipei and Singapore as well. One memorable experience on one of these holiday outings was a stay in a house, a novel experience for an apartment dweller. "We rented out with another family friend, and then, we just got to the house, and it was really cool. I remember it being huuuge, like a castle, almost. There's a kitchen, an open kitchen—well it's kind of common here. It has its own floor, and, like, rooms on its own floor. WOW! It was just magnificent." Laura describes the shift from Hong Kong to Vancouver (via a brief stop in Toronto for her family to explore the possibilities there) as "like a two-different-world experience." She considers that her behavior and demeanor are affected by her location; "back in Hong Kong maybe, I don't know, I have shyer personality." Depending on who you are talking to, she suggests, you "morph into a different person in a way." On reflection, she thinks she also reads differently as well.

Margaret: Do you read largely in English, largely in Chinese? A bit of both?
Laura: A bit of both, I'd say. Actually, it's more recent that I've been more exposed to Chinese. Like, before that, well, when I came here, I mainly just looked into English books … and with, what, my nine, ten years of Chinese, it wasn't enough to cover … but right now I've been trying to get back at it and learn more Chinese and just retain all my, you know, knowledge.

Laura finds her Canadian repertoire mismatched for the demands of Chinese materials: "I wouldn't be able to understand [Chinese literature] if I were to be looking from a Canadian point of view."

A bit later, I ask her about this bifurcated reading experience from a slightly different perspective. In this tentative dialogue, you can almost hear Laura's thinking.

Margaret: Is it a pleasure to step back and forth between those worlds? Is it something you enjoy doing? Or is it just something you have to do, to be able to function?
Laura: I feel like—a bit of both … It is kind of—a pleasure, I guess it is. Like, I—I sometimes can, you know, change and be, be friends or—you know, communicate with my Chinese friends [makes large and open gestures], and I would be a different person in a way. And then to my Caucasian friends or other, you know, speaking English, Canadian friends, I would—I don't know, somewhat change again.

Laura describes her childhood reading as favoring "magical and mythological stuff." Her mother read *The Secrets of Droon* to her in English, but otherwise her reading was in Chinese until she moved to Canada. She developed a taste for suspense and superhero thrillers, as well as romance. She mentioned Harry Potter, *The Maze Runner*, and Percy Jackson. If there is a film version, she prefers to watch it first, moving on to the book only if she is particularly interested. "I don't know, I'm not that into books," she says, though it later develops that she is a big fan of manga.

For Laura, an important stage in beginning to think of herself as belonging in her new home came when she started high school, "when I finally got rid of ESL lab program. I felt reborn [gestures to self]. I'm like, Yay! I'm finally learning English. Like, regular English and I—I was just thinking, yay, now I can just read the same books as everyone, and I felt—I guess, more Canadian in a way."

For a long time, Laura's focus was on learning English, on "blending in," and her reading was correspondingly Canadian. The television program *Malcolm in the Middle* scaffolded some of her adjustment to North America, as, later, did books by Judy Blume. Her textual choices today are for the heartwarming and cheerful. She read *Frankenstein* for her compulsory English course and was rueful about the experience:

> I really got connected with the creature. I just thought, aww, man! I—sometimes I feel the same and I feel sympathy for it, and I was just, wow, Victor Frankenstein is the mastermind or the evil person, you know. And, I dunno, I just felt, reading it, I understood it, but I wasn't that into it 'cause it was sad!

To Laura, growing up, Asian materials seemed to her to be what her parents would choose, and she was trying to differentiate herself from them. But as she matures, she is more invested in watching Chinese television programs and reading some Chinese books. She comments on the predictability of the plots of her Chinese texts, and says, "I think in a way that has shaped how I would read, and, even reading more English books, I would be surprised sometimes, I'd be, like, oh, I've never seen that kind of plot before." She expresses particular affection for Sophie Kinsella's *Can You Keep a Secret?* for its capacity to surprise her. Laura describes these changing tastes as a kind of doubleness, rather than as the more free-floating postmodern perspective that Liang has developed out of a life story with many common elements.

A Seamless Transition: Lily

Lily, age twenty-three and a student of civil engineering, also spent her early childhood in China. She initially supplies two parallel maps, one of her urban neighborhood in China and one of her urban neighborhood in Ontario, where she initially moved to Scarborough; before the second interview, she adds a floor plan of her Chinese apartment (Figure 4.7). Her early discussion draws attention to ways in which her life did not drastically alter when she moved to Canada. What disrupted her life far more substantially, she says, was a subsequent move to a suburban community in Edmonton, where, for the first time in her life, she could not walk to meet her friends, where she took the bus to school, where her every move was car dependent. It seems clear that many elements of life in her first place transferred successfully to her second place, and it was the third place that failed to offer the ingredients of child life and agency that she deemed essential.

Lily describes herself as completely taking in stride a move from urban life in China to urban life in Canada. In both settings, she lived in an apartment complex (symmetrically, each time on the third floor). She walked to school and the high

Figure 4.7 Lily's trio of maps.

density of the housing arrangements meant it was easy to find somebody to play with, just by going out the apartment door. In both cases, there was some green space where the children could play, and a ready source for purchasing after-school snacks (street vendors in China, the No Frills supermarket in Ontario). In an adult-oriented green space in Zheng Zhou, Lily watched her grandpa play croquet. Beside an adults-only golf course in Scarborough, Lily and the other children scavenged golf balls when the creek was low. I press her on how much she took this big move in stride by asking her if she didn't notice the change in candy and cakes; most children do. It seems her parents went often enough to the Asian markets in nearby Toronto to sustain a supply of familiar sweets, so her repertoire was simply augmented by Canadian treats. She says very consistently that the different language was the only change that impinged on her at all, and she seems to have coped with that adjustment fairly readily. She had been learning English in school before she migrated and was reading Western stories; she mentions Sherlock Holmes and Harry Potter in particular and says that when she continued to read these stories after her arrival in Canada, she found they kept the Chinese setting she had originally established for them in her mind.

Lily lists some of her favorite reading as a child in China. Two Chinese titles are a novel called *Girl's Diary* by Yang Hongying, who has been called China's J. K. Rowling, and *You Mo San Guo* by Rui Zhou (Figure 4.8), a parody of Chinese classic novels.

While still in China, Lily read R. L. Stine's *Goosebumps* series in translation. She also read an Austrian children's series, *A Mystery for You and the Tiger Team* by Thomas Brezina, that was enormously popular in China. She said,

> Each book in the series features a mystery that you can solve along with the kids in the book and there were special cards that came with the book which will reveal hidden answers at the end of each chapter. I remember playing games with other kids pretending to be the book's main characters as a child, but that stopped when I moved to Canada because nobody has heard of the series here.

In Scarborough, Lily became acquainted with *Harriet the Spy* and she and her friends pretended to be Harriet, "spying" on the people walking in the neighborhood. It is not hard to see connections with her Tiger Team play in China. Lily particularly

Figure 4.8 Image of *You Mo San Guo* book cover, https://www.amazon.ca/You-San-Guo-Lian-Ying/dp/9570838183 (Zhou, 2011).

liked the fact that Harriet did so much walking in the city. As she and her friends crossed a bridge over the creek that bordered the golf course, she imagined herself inhabiting Katherine Paterson's *Bridge to Terabithia*, but this seems to have been a more private fantasy.

Many aspects of Lily's daily routines meshed smoothly as she transitioned from China to Canada. What upended her life was the second move, from downtown Scarborough to the suburbs of Edmonton. Suddenly her autonomy was much reduced, as she relied on transport for every activity. She was also, of course, growing up, and she says she feels her final memories of childhood are all based in Scarborough. There are echoes of Amy's and Riya's stories in this observation; a move or a similar change (such as the death of Amy's grandmother) marks a door closing on childhood experiences and sensations.

Lily describes an acute loss of agency following the move to Edmonton. It is interesting to trace the issue of agency through the other stories, though the risk of gross oversimplification is very great and I will not pursue this line of thought in any detail. Amy and Riya may both have lost a sense of personal agency when they lost the arena of a place where they felt securely at home. Liang describes a process of gaining authority over her own life, but it came at a price of increasing solitariness. Although she doesn't use the word, Laura is describing aspects of personal agency when she talks about being a different person in Hong Kong than she is in Canada; she establishes herself in terms of the society in which she finds herself at any point.

Malpas says, "Embodiment—one's extended and differentiated location in space— and the grasp of such embodiment would thus seem essential to the possibility of agency, and therefore of experience and thought" (2018: 137). Each of these women is describing an embodied place in the world and exploring the possibilities of agency within the specific conditions of that world.

Purposes of Reading

None of these participants reads as much now as she did when younger; Riya probably comes closest. Currently, Amy and Liang both read for information. Amy is intrigued by sustainability books "like *How to Make Your House Green*, *How to Use Grey Water*, and *How to Make a Vegetable Garden and Composter*, love those books." These topics relate directly to her major in the human dimension of environmental management. Amy volunteers at different nature conservation lands, which also ties in with her academic interests—but she also does competitive archery and is interested in graphic design.

Liang expresses an interest in vintage clothing and reads about Chinese fortune-telling, connecting with like-minded individuals online and consulting with masters who have studied it for many years. There are many complications with the associated reading materials. The books are very old; she says,

> Even if we know Chinese we might not understand the ancient Chinese who wrote that clearly. And based on the master's experience and studies, they would teach kind of translating … The books … are just online texts. And I found it difficult to read. Because I like physical things. When I print them out, it's still, it doesn't feel like you're actually reading a book. And I've found it difficult for me to read Chinese now. I could understand, but it's, I don't know, it's difficult, it's not that easy. Because I haven't read a Chinese book for so long.

Much of Liang's knowledge of this topic comes from social media: "We had the group chat and even we had the class through online too."

Laura reads manga today and she is starting to read Chinese materials after a long hiatus during which her main focus was on reading in English. Riya can read Hindi, but she finds it laborious and she defaults to English. Her tastes run to fantasy worlds (she mentioned *Game of Thrones*) and Paulo Coelho's philosophical writings, as well as books on topics that interest her such as criminology and autobiographies. Unlike any other reader in the project, Lily's discussion of her adult reading mostly consisted of her picking my brain for books that would satisfy her desire to read about nontraumatic immigration (she mentioned *The Kite Runner* simply because it does contain the immigrant experience in a very different context) and about urban street life (she mentioned *City of Bones*). The topic sent her back to her childhood experiences and she mentioned enjoying the television series of *Corduroy* and Ludwig Bemelmans's books about Madeline explicitly because of their urban settings in New York and Paris, respectively. She regrets that she has not kept up her Chinese reading and would like to regain that skill.

Like Liang, Amy prefers a physical book, and would rather read a paperback than a hardback. Although she reads about her environmental concerns with interest, one of her great pleasures in reading remains the ability to lock out her real world fears.

> Honestly, I hate windows still, I really do. All windows of a house. I hate sleeping by windows. All of it. I lock everything. I'm still like that really, and I still have a tendency to read not realistic books. Because it's more fascinating to me than, I don't know, most of my friends read books about how to be more successful or how to improve your life in this way and it's literally so boring, I can't. I need to read something that's not real because I do so much real stuff all the time anyway, that it's more of an escape than anything.

Matching up sets of readers in a study like this one is an odd experience. I can frequently find points of comparison. In this case, grandparents play an important role in the lives of Liang and Amy and Lily, though they each lost significant contact with those grandparents in different ways. Liang and Amy both enjoy reading for information, and they both describe the appeal of physical books. And yet in other ways, their reading behaviors are completely divergent. Lily sees "very very vivid" mental images. Liang takes for granted that she will see some kind of visual, a "movie" in her head. Amy rejects that kind of reading so strenuously that she regards a movie adaptation of a book as a serious and long-lasting interference with her reading pleasure. Today Liang defaults automatically to a Canadian background for her reading unless something in the text particularly calls up a childhood that she now regards as long ago and far away. Lily imports a setting from the culture in which she first encountered a story, so a Chinese setting lingers even when she reads subsequent titles while living in Canada. Amy defaults differently, simply rejecting the importance of a background at all, and placing all her interpretive energy into the exercise of living inside a character's head. Liang is familiar with this stance also; she alternates it with watching a "movie" run-through of the story, according to how the writing positions her. Laura, on the other hand, uses the movie version as a guide to how she reads, rerunning film scenes in her head as prompted by the print descriptions. Riya maintains a generic, even schematic Western background unless the details of the text invite a more specific reaction.

None of these readers provides a detailed description of the experience of reading a particular text with a couple of partial exceptions: Amy's account of how watching one Harry Potter film interfered with her internal sense of the story when she finally read Book 7, and Riya's more generic reflections on reading Blyton. They do, however, describe using reading as part of their own sense of personal agency. Liang reads about ancient fortune-telling, in part as a way of connecting with her childhood culture that she seems to feel is otherwise fading. Laura also turns to reading in Chinese as a way of revisiting her past. Riya, on the other hand, continues to choose Western books. Amy reads fantasy to block out aspects of the real world that perturb her. Lily is on the hunt for urban stories, not caring what city is involved but particularly valuing characters who walk through their lives and adventures. In all these cases, we see reading as something they *do* to help shape the adults they have become—and are still becoming.

Reading Spaces

Liang is bicultural, though she now feels more Canadian than Chinese, and has no place that feels like home. Laura is also bicultural and reads differently according to the cultural context. Lily describes a freer flow between her Chinese and her Canadian life. Both Amy and Riya express a strong sense of a home now lost but definitive in its importance to her childhood.

Riya drew on a generic Western repertoire to help her understand the books she read as a child. Of *Tinkle*, the comic that provided the only "Indian-ish" material she encountered, she says, "The stories were based in India so a lot of the things in there made more sense. A lot of references to Indian culture that you wouldn't get unless you lived there." In the context of *Tinkle*, she defaulted to assuming an Indian background and Indian characters, even when the evidence of the text was that some characters were white (she cited an educational series, "with this professor and these kids that he would teach science lessons to"; as a child, she assumed they were all Indian, but she has subsequently noticed that they were not). It is interesting to observe that Riya's override button is two directional; she describes defaulting to Western and defaulting to Indian in different contexts. But the *Tinkle* experience has not motivated her to seek out more Indian reading material, even now with the breadth of choice made possible by her access to a large university library.

Liang's early reading was almost entirely in Chinese but she read many translations. She encountered Grimm's fairy tales and Hans Christian Andersen in a variety of versions: "I had picture books, storybooks just in text with some illustrations, some with just some picture books with just illustrations, some DVDs, sometimes they're shown on TV, sometimes they're actually in textbooks, I think." Her mental vivification of these stories included white people speaking in Chinese but she thought of the settings as "very original," somewhere else, a world enlivened by Western television and computer images; she specifically cited the little documentaries in *Teletubbies* and a broader range of information television on the Discovery Channel as resources for creating her background visuals. Her mental world was at least 90 percent created out of other texts, she said, rather than her own life. Such a stance is inherently portable and, after she moved, Liang drew on viewing experiences such as *High School Musical* and *Hannah Montana* to help her understand Canadian school customs. Lily read broadly, both in China and in Canada, and, while describing Sherlock Holmes as important to her developing an understanding of Western culture, she mentally placed him in a Chinese setting and kept him there even after she moved away.

It is tempting to speculate that the deracinated features of a text-to-text form of repertoire development may contribute to a postmodern sensibility. We might expect a more rooted kind of reading experience to be cultivated out of Amy's significant attachment to her grandmother's house. Two factors weigh against such a pattern. One is Amy's great fear of those windows and her willingness to cut off certain kinds of life experiences and to be very selective indeed in her reading choices (fantasy only). The second element at work is Amy's very nonvisual style of reading. She is indifferent to background scenery, as she made clear in her discussion of Harry Potter, and she wants to be inside the heads of the characters looking out.

So many factors are at work here that discerning patterns is just about impossible. As autonomous readers making their own choices, these children took insights and options from their environments and then converted them through the lenses of their personal tastes and predilections. These accounts of their experiences have been filtered further through their decisions about what to include in or omit from their maps, through the focus of our conversations and any ensuing digressions, and through the selective way I have chosen some quotes and passed over others. The reading spaces of even just these five women are infinitely more complex than what I am able to present in these pages.

The sense of home as an arena for certain kinds of childhood agency come through clearly; Malouf would certainly recognize this deep connection between home and agency. He concludes his essay on the first place by addressing what "we might trace back to the topography of the place and the physical conditions it imposes on the body, to ways of seeing it imposes on the eye, and at some less conscious level, to embodiments of mind and psyche that belong to the first experience and first mapping of a home" (1985: 10).

In some essential ways, it might be possible to say that each of these women also speaks of home in terms of a "first loss." Amy dreams of her grandmother's house. Riya considers that all her memories of herself as a child involve the bungalow and its surrounding compound. Liang thinks she was happier in her childhood home than at any time since. Laura looks back on the apartment on the mountainside that seemed like its own mansion to her as a child, and also to the many "cheap" holiday outings to theme parks across Asia as sources of happiness and adventure. Lily laments the loss of autonomy that occurred when she relocated to a car-oriented suburb, and connects this move to the end of her childhood. It is perhaps not too fanciful at this point to mention Amy's beloved little door to the milk cupboard: the little door in their psyches that might lead back to their childish lives does not open or provide any true access to the past. But they did once have the chance to live on the other side of that door, and their memories retain specificity and texture. Malouf says, "A landscape and its houses, also a way of life; but more deeply, a way of experiencing and mapping the world" (1985: 8).

Social Spaces

5

Family Matters: Relationships and the Development of Reading Spaces

Maps specify places and the links on the maps in this project frequently highlight experiences; and, of course, most places and experiences include other people. All the participants in this project speak of family and friends. Have some of these people played a role in the developing literacy of the twelve mapmakers, and is it possible to discern their impact?

Madeleine Grumet suggests that our connections to other human beings prime our capacity to take note of the world: "Knowledge comes to form in human relationships. *The world we notice is the one that someone we cared about once pointed to*" (1992: 6, emphasis added). What Grumet describes here relates to the notion of joint attention. We learn by attending to what other people, important to us, encourage us to notice and help us to understand. The social context of that learning is part of the experience.

Marah Gubar talks about our kinship connections to other people and how they affect the discourses that we learn:

> We are akin to one another in that from the moment we are born (and even before then) we are immersed in multiple discourses not of our own making that influence who we are, how we think, what we do and say—and we never grow out of this compromised state. We are always channeling the voices of other people, ventriloquizing but also deviating from and improvising on the many different and sometimes conflicting discourses that inform our lives and shape our identities. (2013: 454)

The participants in this project do not discuss their reading in such abstract terms, but in the interviews, they all "people" their maps to greater or lesser degrees, and it is possible to observe the impact of some of these people on how they developed their ideas of what reading constitutes. In this chapter, I discuss both explicit and implicit accounts of the role of other people on readerly growth and change, focusing particularly on the accounts of Suleman, Amani, and Halia.

Strategies of Access Management: Suleman

Suleman registers very high on any kind of notional scale of the importance of relationships to his life; and both his map and interviews highlight ways in which such relationships have affected his reading capacities and interests, in both positive and negative ways. Because he is so explicit about the significance of other people to his own reading, I investigate his story in some detail.

At the age of nineteen, Suleman is an international student from Pakistan, who has been in Edmonton for only a few months at the time of our meeting. He has just completed his first year of engineering, and he says more than once that he is also very interested in business. He lived in the same town in Pakistan until his high school years, when he and his mother moved to a larger town for the benefit of his education (his father could not obtain a job transfer and stayed behind, visiting regularly).

Suleman is a man to whom relationships are clearly very important; he speaks with much more enthusiasm about his connections with his parents and his extended family than he ever does about any connection with a book. He is an aficionado of television cartoons and he conveys this passion in terms of how he negotiated access with his uncle and his grandfather (he could not watch at home because his parents decided it would be good for his education if they did not own a television set). Suleman's favorite television cartoon, *Dragon Ball Super*, a Japanese anime series, was on at nine in the evening, conflicting with the news program that was supremely important to his relatives. His constant viewing of cartoons at other times of the day when he was visiting was a matter of some negotiation between him and his uncle and grandfather (he implies that his aunt and grandmother were a bit more accommodating). "Yeah, my childhood is described on this picture right now," he said, opening the screen to a montage of cartoon images (Figure 5.1).

It may be fanciful but, as Suleman talks, it is almost as if I can see the faces of significant people peeping out from behind this image: his mother, who thought cartoons were bad for his education; his uncle and grandfather, who were concerned at how avidly he consumed them while at their homes; and his cousins and friends, who shared some of his interests in particular shows. Suleman had many literacy sponsors who were local and known to him, and his conversations about literacy invokes their presence over and over again. Additionally, more distanced institutional sponsors also had an impact on his developing literacy in different ways.

Suleman describes himself at the outset of our conversations as someone who is not interested in reading. As our discussions continue, however, he begins to remember episodes of reading particular kinds of text at one or other point in his life. It is fascinating to watch his self-assessment change over the course of two relatively lengthy conversations. Initially he thinks of reading in terms that would fit in with the definitions approved by his school, or his mother. As his sense of his textual life becomes more expansive, he begins to speak of reading comics and a monthly magazine, of exploring a CD-ROM encyclopedia, of developing a vast knowledge of the world of television cartoons.

Figure 5.1 Suleman's map of cartoons important to his literate life.

Being an only child is a significant element in Suleman's identity. Throughout his youth, he and his parents did everything together, courtesy of a motorbike that accommodates three riders. His mother is a school principal, and his father is an accountant; they both place a very high value on school achievement. Suleman recounts an incident when he came first in his class with a test mark of 85 percent; the second-place student scored in the seventies, so Suleman thought he had done very well. But his parents scolded him for a mark below the 90 percent cut off that they considered to be the lowest permissible outcome.

Studying, therefore, dominated Suleman's home life throughout his childhood. His mother gave him academic work to do even during the holidays. The ethos was competitive, with Suleman's achievements being compared to cousins as well as classmates. Suleman acknowledges that this ongoing pressure gave him the grades that provided international options for his further education. Despite the fact that he received a number of acceptances and scholarship offers in other countries, his friends and his school counselor all assumed (correctly) that his parents would insist on him attending the University of Alberta because there are cousins in Edmonton who could take him in and provide guidance to the new culture. The long flight from Pakistan to Alberta was his first flight ever, and his first real foray into the world on his own.

Suleman offers an anecdote about the day he left home, and explains how this incident sums up his relationship with his parents:

> On the day of my flight, I ordered some shoes from the shop. I said, "Okay I'm just going to pick it up," it was five minutes ride with a bike, and my mom was like, "No you can't go alone," I was like, "Oh my god! [Laughs] I have a flight, I'm flying right across the globe in an hour and now you're stopping me from going ten minutes across the neighbourhood." So yeah, wherever we went, we were a family of three, and a general bike there—three people can sit on it so wherever we go shopping or going for something big: just getting a pack of biscuits or visiting someone, we would all go together. It was a close-knit family; it wasn't like my dad was somewhere and my mom's not going, or I'm going somewhere; we would mostly stick together and go everywhere.

Suleman's youthful experience of literature was mostly governed by very utilitarian considerations. He says,

> The way they taught us, I still am angry about that. It was like the novel we read, we didn't read it for the literature or the story of it, we actually read it for the words. The way they taught us English was they would pick out the hard words from that story and write the words and their meanings, and we would keep memorizing them for the exam, because we have to write it exactly the same way.

He and his classmates read "mostly just for vocabulary or passing the comprehension test, the question. I read *Oliver Twist*, so what did Oliver's mother say when she was dying?" His mother reinforced this kind of drill work at home, setting math problems, and dictating pages of books for her son to write out.

One teacher in junior high set up a readers' club, and Suleman appreciated the care she took to introduce books to readers. Friends of his persuaded him to tackle some novels, but the experiment was short-lived. He read about four books before exam time intervened and he had to stop reading in order to study. *Black Beauty* was one book on that brief list; another was *A Walk to Remember* by Nicholas Sparks. He refers to this short list of four more than once and laments that exam prep had cut short his budding sense of establishing a new hobby.

Suleman initially says he did not read by choice at home at all, though he later modifies this account as he reflects more deeply on the literacies of his childhood. His parents wanted him to read, but, he says, "You can't impose a book on someone. You have to make that person like it."

The publication he read most frequently was a monthly children's magazine (Figure 5.2), written in Urdu and very popular in Pakistan. *Naunehal*, produced by Hamdard (a company that also makes gripe water for babies and is clearly a significant institutional sponsor of Urdu literacy in Pakistan), offers material for and by children (see Jaffri [2017] for a very brief video offering a glimpse of its pages, literally a flick through). The production values appear to be modest, but its reliable appearance every month undoubtedly delights many children.

Figure 5.2 Suleman's most-read monthly magazine, *Naunehal* by Hamdard (https://archive.org/details/HamdardNaunehalMarch2016HDPdfbooksfree.pk_201604/mode/2up?view=theater).

Suleman describes this publication in the following relatively formal terms in a link he creates for his map:

Naunehal by Hamdard is my most read book. They issued a book every month. This book was the complete package of everything a child would like to read.

I still remember in the start of each edition there was a note from the author for children and after that there would be many stories. One of them was an untitled story and whoever would make the best title suggestion would receive a cash award. There was a section of pictures of children which were sent by the parents of the children to be published in the book. There was also a section where they published the drawings made by the kids. My favourite section was about the jokes. I would directly open that section to read that first.

In his interview commentary about this title, he lays much greater emphasis on the jokes. His mother was very keen for him to read more broadly in this little publication, but it took a cousin to make him see it could be enjoyable.

What Suleman liked more than anything else were those cartoons. His connection with these animated television programs was interwoven with his family relationships, as this description underlines:

> I would purposely go to my grandmother's house. Whenever [my mother] said, "hey can you do this" for my grandmother, I would just, I would often wait there, watch a show, and then come back and make an excuse—hey I met someone on the way, or someone stopped me there. I would make these kind of excuses and watch shows.

He negotiated with his mother to be allowed to go to his grandmother's house:

> There were specific times of dramas there, I would go there. It was like a great joyful moment when my mother would allow me to do that. She would be like you have to write three pages of this, solve this many math problems, do this, and I would spend my whole day doing that just so that she would allow me to go in the evening to my grandmother's house and I'd watch an hour drama.

Suleman's aunt and uncle looked after him when his parents were both working and he watched cartoons at their house as constantly as he could manage. "My uncle there was mostly fed up of me because all I did was watch cartoons ... I would switch on the television and keep watching it, keep watching it, and my uncle would say, you just watched this episode three times in a row." Suleman says there were forty cartoons he watched regularly ("in high school, we actually made a list of them") and the titles he mentions include *Scooby-Doo*, *Swat Kats*, *Bob the Builder*, *Baby Loonie Toons*, *Beyblade*, *Digimon*, and *Pokémon*. He speaks very passionately about the significance of these cartoons to his childhood (and is quite sure that today's cartoons are not as good, though I would not be surprised to learn that many of those available to today's children are the identical shows).

Suleman read some comic books associated with these titles but says his favorite fictional character appeared in a comic that premiered in his youth. The hero was Umro Ayar, "this man who had a bag which could fit in everything irrespective of its size." Shahzeb Ahmed, in the Express Tribune (2013), describes how this character features in the first Urdu comic book, launched in 2013 after two years of testing the waters on social media; a complete history of this comic would undoubtedly produce a complex study of literacy sponsorship. The comic was also published in English to appeal to the international market. Suleman says, "There were many stories about his adventures. I would order these stories and would spend hours reading."

Everything Suleman saw or read through the first part of his childhood was translated into Urdu. He assumed for a long time that all his media materials were local, or, at most, brought in from India; it took him a long time to realize that many of his cartoons, for example, were Japanese or American. But when Suleman's father installed Encarta on his computer before they had ready access to the internet, the boy read it in English. Encarta liberated him to the extent that he could follow his own line of interests and absorb some English language understanding without having to memorize vocabulary. He was around eleven or twelve at this point and was very taken with the multimodal elements of the text:

> It was appealing to me. I would say it was more interesting to me because of its features, its graphics and sounds. There would be a program, which animal sound is this? I would actually say something. The technology was not so common there, so you would be, okay, what sound is this? Even though I've never seen that animal, never heard of it, never heard any such voice before, I would still check something and then it would tell me okay and now I know. Then I'd do something else, then it's about countries, which country is this picture from and there's a few things like that, and then the right word. I don't exactly remember—there are a few things I can recall; that animal sounds was one of them, and especially the interface of it. I guess that was the first graphically advanced program I ever saw, so it was very appealing to me.

When Suleman gained access to the internet a few years ago, he joined Facebook to play *Farmville*, a highly social text. He owned some Pokémon cards and a couple of Beyblades tops (he also crafted a homemade Beyblade out of washers and said its weight made it a very successful competitor against his peers). He was familiar with *Pokémon Go* but said it was not easy to participate in Pakistan because you risked having your phone stolen if you played in a public place.

What is striking in Suleman's account of this reasonably varied textual life is how it all interweaves with personal relationships. It was a cousin (at his mother's behest) who persuaded him to read beyond the jokes in *Naunehal* and then loaned him a stack of back copies of the little magazine. His cartoon watching was under constant social negotiation. A couple of friends persuaded him to give author Nicholas Sparks a try. At some point, he read *The Fault in Our Stars* because everybody was reading it and he did not want to be left out. When he got enough bandwidth to make it possible, he watched movies, in miniature, on his phone, constantly being interrupted by his mother who thought there were better things for him to be doing. He selected his movies through an online list of 100 movies everyone should watch. Suleman's map is highly populated, and almost every textual reference in his interviews is introduced by means of a connection to a human being in his world.

It seems clear that a major obstacle to the child Suleman becoming as keen a reader as he was a consumer of other media lay in how long it took him to grasp the big picture in any book he attempted to read. "I'm not a reader," he says. "But once something makes sense to me, when I'm halfway through the book and I'm like, I understood all of it, I am compelled to read more." He is prepared to take an incremental approach, gleaning a greater sense of overview through multiple exposures to different versions of a story. He tried to read *Thirteen Reasons Why* on the recommendation of a friend, but it made little sense to him; he says his English was not up to the challenge. Then he watched the television series and grasped the main concept: "Then all of it made much more sense to me, what actually happened. There was some girl who made these recordings for people and made people look at how they were responsible for her death. But I didn't actually understand most of that part of it [while reading]. So I watched the series." His literary education did not help him assess and understand the larger narrative thrust of a text. In emphasizing vocabulary memorization and comprehension through questions about fragments of the text, his schooling did him no favors, as he recognizes.

Suleman watched his cartoons more on a basis of accretion. At the time of our interviews, he has just discovered a large batch of *Dragon Ball Super* cartoons on YouTube. Although he starts with the intention of watching only the ones he has never seen before, he winds up viewing the whole set, to the detriment of his plans for studying for an exam. His recurring consumption of so many short-form fictions (the cartoons, the *Naunehal* jokes and stories, the Umro Ayar comics) probably also contributed to his fragmentary reading of long-form texts. His capacity to bootstrap comprehension from multiple sources is a strategy that works more holistically; he is talented at forging scaffolding out of any available source.

A Relational World of Reading: Amani

Not every reader is as socially oriented as Suleman. Certainly, the interviews with other participants do not so consistently establish the particular social provenance of different materials through identifying the person who introduced them to the reader. But, to some extent, Suleman simply makes explicit the kinds of literacy sponsorship that every reader relies on to a greater or lesser extent. As Brandt observes, "It is useful to think about who or what underwrites occasions of literacy learning and use" (1998: 166).

Amani is age twenty-one when we meet, and a student in Elementary Education. She has a sister three and half years younger and a brother five and a half years younger. She has always lived in Edmonton, but moved frequently, sometimes changing schools. Her map features city parks (Figure 5.3), and much of her discussion refers to outings to these parks with family and friends. These relationships feature significantly in her discussion of her reading life.

Amani's connections to the world around her are affected by her relationships to other people and also filtered through texts. It might be accurate to refer to her friends as cosponsors of some of her literate activities. She was frightened to go into the trees behind one park, but in outings to this site, she was in charge of the decisions so she simply avoided them. She was also ambivalent about rivers, in part because of a near-drowning experience in her youth. Perhaps not surprisingly, she was frightened of a particularly shaky bridge that crosses the North Saskatchewan River from Rundle Park, but, in this case, her parents stepped in. Her comment was heartfelt as she pointed it out on the screen: "And then this, oh God this bridge, I hated it, but my parents would make us go over it to get over our fear, I guess, of the bridge. It works, but I still think it's pretty terrifying!"

Amani immediately knows what I am talking about when I ask her if she ever draws on this experience of the bridge to illuminate her reading:

Figure 5.3 Amani's generic park and the fountain at the entrance to her favorite park.

Margaret: But would you use the terrifying bridge for other things, if characters are terrified of something, would you draw on your experience with that bridge just to make some sense of what it feels like to be terrified?

Amani: I think so, like I would relate the feeling to, oh yeah, I felt that way at the bridge, yeah. Or, perhaps they went to a bridge and it was a scary bridge I would say, I know what that's like.

It is worth asking (though I think there is no way of answering) how much Amani's associations between the bridge and feelings of terror also draw on her relationship with her parents—not in any particularly good or bad way, but simply in the form of their connection with her experience of the bridge. Such deep drilling into the makeup of our reading as it involves emotional connections with an event, or even simply with a phrase, is beyond exploring by anyone except the reader herself and is indeed often beyond the reader's own capacities to disinter. But implicitly or explicitly, these connotative trails frequently include a relational charge.

Amani also provides an example of a complex set of connections between the books she read, her friends, and her daily routines. Sometimes, during her junior high years, in the lunch break when they were permitted to leave school, she and her friends would strike out together to inspect a neighborhood park not previously known to them. She says,

> Actually, what I used to do was I'd go through the White Pages [of the city telephone book, a paper artifact that is no longer produced]. You know, those books. And

they'd have the maps in the beginning. So then I'd look for like different parks, and I'd say guys, let's go hang out there, and my friends would actually do it. It seems kind of strange when I think about it … We'd name these little places, these parks, things like, let's call this Narnia.

Not every association was encapsulated in a name of a fictional territory, but Amani made connections nevertheless:

Amani: I think there was one, it was very far. I remember walking to it in winter. And I think, I don't know if that one had a name. No.
Margaret: Just the journey.
Amani: Yeah, just the journey was very, yeah, I just remember it was a big disappointment. We can call it that, I suppose, the disappointing park. Or just 'the disappointment'. Yeah, it kind of ties into this, *The Little Prince* I read. And I guess I could see myself having the little adventures and visiting the new lands like he does, when he goes to the different planets throughout the book.

Amani kept these adventures private: "My family didn't really know. I remember I would find the places when everyone was sleeping or after they went to work. So they wouldn't know I'm journeying off into these foreign lands [laughs]."

These outings drew on fictions already incorporated into Amani's way of thinking, as we can see particularly from the comment about *The Little Prince*. But it also seems clear that she feeds this sense of questing back into her reading experience, including the relationships with the friends who accompanied her and the attendant awareness (undoubtedly appealing to a girl in early adolescence) that her family did not actually know where she was as she moved into territory previously unknown to her. The "journeys" provided an experience of liminality that sometimes turned into the main feature of the expedition. That she had some concept of this threshold state is clear from her observation about the fountain at the entrance to Rundle Park; she was always pleased to see it as it marked the entrance to a pleasing world.

Amani: This is the fountain, I didn't spend too much time here but it's important to me because I remember when we'd drive in, I would always just see it, and I was, it was nice [indistinct].
Margaret: It means you were there.
Amani: Yeah, exactly, and we'd be so excited we be like, ah, there it is!

Amani's park encounters include experiences of liminality (the fountains marking the entrance), of fear (the bridge, the trees), of the unknown (the expeditions), and of the very familiar (her local parks). This repertoire is not just literary in nature, but it fosters literary understanding. And in her description of these encounters, Amani includes the people who were with her at the time.

The Social Face of a Reading Life: Halia

The social surrounds of reading are varied and individual. Halia is another reader who discusses many aspects of her reading history through the lens of social connections.

Halia is nineteen when we meet, and an Education student, majoring in biology and minoring in English. She immigrated to Canada from Iraq at the age of six. At that time, she was an only child, though she now has a younger brother and two younger sisters. After they arrived in Edmonton, her parents were nervous about her going outside; consequently, she read a lot. Her map focuses on the interior of her first house in Canada. A friend lived on a farm and read many horse stories; Halia preferred unicorns. At the school book fair, she said, there would be horse posters and cat posters and a child had to choose to be a horse person or a cat person. Following her friend, she chose horses, and her preference for magical horses led to a moment of cultural attunement:

> And then after that I found so many interesting stories about horses that are magical and things like that. And coincidentally, my dad told me about this mythological— it was an Arabic, Islamic, something like that, mythical creature, and it was more of like a Pegasus. I was, like, wow! You know, I was, like, oh my God! So—and there's actually an Arabic storybook, probably the only Arabic storybook that I read, and it was more like an audiobook that I listened to. It was really interesting because it mentions how the Prophet actually encountered this creature. And back then, I was, like, wow, that's amazing, that confirms that unicorns are kind of—

The emotional power of this moment when her different cultural worlds coalesced was so overwhelming that, even retrospectively, Halia is unable to finish the sentence.

Like Amy, Halia furnished the rooms in her virtual house. She used RoomSketcher (https://www.roomsketcher.com), and comments on the kinds of reading she did in different spaces: "So this was the living room and if I read Arabic I probably read here (Figure 5.4), cause my parents wanted me to, they really wanted me to, [pauses] not for great reasons." Whatever pleasure she got from her Arabic reading (and she says she read Arabic as effortlessly as she read English), there also seems to have been an element of performance taking place in this scenario.

Halia describes her reading experience as culturally "mixed," a label she defines in relational terms:

> It's my own cultural and family experience, and I think that influenced a lot of what I took from the Canadian experience. There was a lot of things I didn't understand but I liked, and there was a lot of things I couldn't accept. I remember—what was it? I read this strange story about this boy and it was really strange to me how he was treated—how he treated his family and the way he treated his friends and stuff. I guess my family was a lot more conservative … For example, the concept of leaving home at the age of eighteen or something was quite strange for us. You're family forever! You do your own thing, but you stay together.

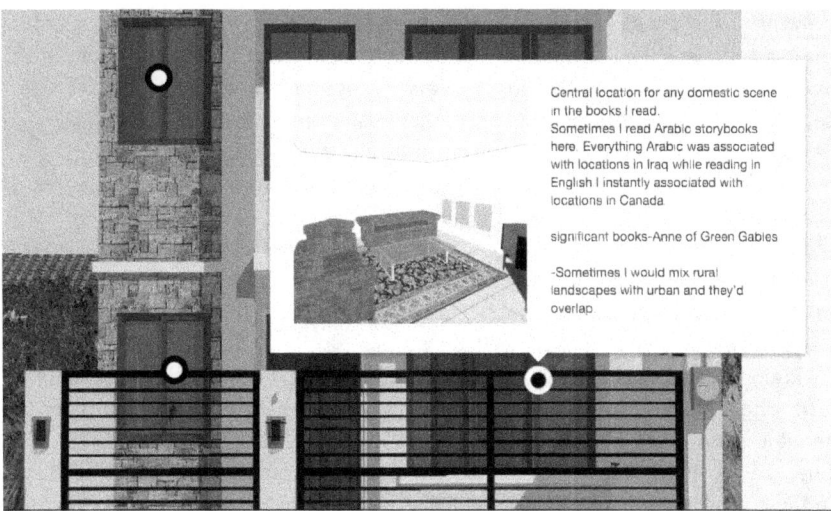

Figure 5.4 Halia's living room, where she did her Arabic reading.

What she describes as "a very cross-cultural experience" became more of a clash of ideas in junior high. "At a younger age, I felt very attached to everything I learned previously: religion, culture, ethics and stuff like that. Those were very ingrained into me. But the point where that changed was in junior high where I met a lot of new people. I went to a different school and it was a completely new perspective." Her new friends were very positive about LGBTQ culture, and at least one friend was a lesbian. "And because my friends were so interested in it, I would also read books about those kinds of things … That's definitely not something I could explore at home. So that's something that I found big, a big change growing up: considering gender identity, orientation, and things like that." Her friends also introduced her to graphic novels and manga. "I was very influenced by my friends because they were the gateway to everything." At this time, her mother was unwell, and she relied on her friends very heavily. "Their interests were my interests. I was interested in knowing what they knew and that's why I guess I took all those strange things in."

Halia has visited Iraq three times since she moved to Canada. She loves these visits; her large family is very kind and very welcoming. "It's like two completely different worlds, and I felt like I loved both of them." Interestingly, she dislikes stories about migrants moving between cultures. "I don't know why. I never liked them at all. I felt like they kind of undermined who I was, it's not that this is who I am, this isn't the point of the story. I just feel like it's so much more enriching to have this experience, but it's not something I would like to focus on." Her preference is for coming-of-age stories; she cites *Great Expectations* as an example of an "existential search for truth." Again she turns to a relational explanation. "I find myself thinking about these things a lot. I try to balance between. I feel like I really, really love my family, but I feel like there are a lot of demanding things to that side, there's a lot of expectations and things like that. But growing up in Canada, it's so much more open." It is a challenge to find ways of striking that balance with family members whose core experience is of a different culture, and she appreciates "any storyline with a sense of going from a certain place to just something bigger, just coming of age." Halia's hijab displays one form of relationship to "something bigger," and her manifest curiosity about the world is very broad.

Halia's reading history connects very strongly with her social experiences. In elementary school, although her teachers were kind, the other children were not. "I didn't have any friends, and it was a rough time. There was a lot of bullying. It was not a good place to be, so that kind of made me reclusive." With her parents also struggling to come to terms with a new country, Halia retreated to reading. "I felt like the lonelier I was, the more I read."

Junior high offered a major change of scene, in many ways. Halia went to an all-girls school and made a number of friends. She spent her junior high years reading about worlds new to her, being introduced to young adult fiction, particularly LGBTQ titles, and investing heavily in the fictions of graphic novels. She immersed herself in these worlds, regularly drawing and writing alternate storylines. For example, she and her friends delved into the world of *Naruto*. "I read it and watched that animated version of it and then I spent hours every single day re-drawing the characters." She and her friends spent their recess times role-playing scenes from their current series, and sometimes, she said, she continued to inhabit the story even during class time. She also reworked storylines. "I didn't want Naruto to die, so I kind of took him out and I recreated a mini-comic where he's alive, and he's just having a normal life." She lived inside the fictions to an extent that she now considers not entirely mentally healthy, and in Grade 12 she began to make the effort to back out of such total immersion in her story worlds. Recently, she began reading *1984* but did not finish it because she did not like it. She contrasts her current more detached and critical reading stance with her earlier deep immersion in illuminating terms:

> For example, if I had picked up *1984* four years ago, I would have fully immersed myself in it and I would have, I kind of would assume that this is almost righteous, everything I read was kind of true. But now it's more like, I'm actually more opinionated. I do like certain styles of writing, so that's probably why I couldn't continue.

Halia's assessment of how she would have read *1984* more emotionally in her youth is intriguing. She would have identified with Winston, since she always attached herself to "the characters that changed, that had problems, that were emotionally distressed." Like her imaginative life more generally, her reading seems to have involved relating to characters. Connecting with people is important to her, in real life and in imagination.

Reading and Relationships

Other people may impinge on literate behaviors through virtual online relationships. Riya lurks online to check out what other people have to say about an issue in a book that troubles her. Rahina communicates her deepest thoughts and ideas to her Tumblr friends. Halia posts fan art. Matt gathers real-life friends together to interact with the virtual elements of Pottermore.com.

Playing with friends within a fictional framework also arises in the interviews. Amani and her allies in exploration visited a nearby park and called it Narnia; Lily and her friends crossed the bridge over a local creek and she conjured up Terabithia. Roman's cohort played *Pirates of the Caribbean* in the sand beneath the swings in the park; Matt and his buddies galloped through Quidditch games with their imaginary broomsticks between their legs. Halia and her classmates acted out their favorite graphic novels. This kind of post-reading performance of a fiction is redolent of childhood, but it is fair to say that some of the same kind of imaginative work has transferred onto the internet. Rahina, for example, extends her reading life into certain kinds of online writing performance, and the presence of friends remains important, even though she chooses a rigorous anonymity in her exchanges with them. Just as the playground games represent an extension of a fictional encounter, so Rahina's fan writing helps her stay inside the world of the story. Similarly, Halia speaks of the role of fan art, and talks about drawing her favorite characters in an alternate universe, posting the images and getting feedback.

These extensions need not be social; Birkerts speaks of the shadow life of reading, saying, "If we have been deeply engaged by the book, we carry its resonance as a kind of echo, thinking again and again of a character, an episode, or, less concretely, about some thematic preoccupation of the author's" (1994: 103). In such a case, the relationship is shared simply between the reader and the text, rather than involving others. It can be simply a case of continuing to dwell in the story inside the mind, or it can involve more active solitary play. Halia, for example, operating alone, searched her basement "like, five times" for the hidden door that features in *The Secrets of Droon* ("I was very hopeful!"). How such a relationship is established remains obscure. Vivian Gornick, in her consideration of rereading, says "the deepest of all human mysteries" is the question of "emotional readiness," which is "responsible for every successful connection ever made between a book and a reader—no less than between people" (2020: 117). Rita Felski talks about such connections as a form of attunement, and says it "cannot occur without a nascent state of readiness; aesthetics cannot forgo or dispense with the first-person response" (2020: 52).

Some of the readers who inhabit two cultures speak of a different kind of relationship to particular books or television shows. Certain stories serve as a kind of cultural translator. Rahina talks about Junie B. Jones and Alice McKinley as her early keys to understanding the Western lifestyles her school friends took for granted. Liang describes making use of *High School Musical* and *Hannah Montana* for similar purposes. Halia gives no titles, but says the LGBTQ fiction she read in junior high helped her to understand her friends better. Laura picks up cues from watching *Malcolm in the Middle*. From a slightly different perspective, she talks about Geronimo Stilton and his detective work as providing a parallel to her own cultural work in adjusting to Canadian life; Geronimo, a mouse detective, is himself a character in translation as he originated in Italy. Later in Laura's life, an author she thinks was Judy Blume introduced her to a more complex sense of emotions.

The relational openings provided by these stories offer young readers from cultures different from that of their current host society a safe form of connection in which they can explore confusions and try out reactions. It is almost as if particular stories, through some kind of relational power, offer a double Janus face to their readers: one, opening to the reader herself, drawing on some kind of emotional connection to the characters to establish a working link; and the other, facing onto that reader's new society and demonstrating persuasive ways of interacting with it. The potential for safe rehearsal within the space of this relationship is very powerful.

The bicultural readers in this participant pool also had a "home" culture inviting a continuing or renewed relationship. Of this particular group, Riya probably expressed the most sustained indifference to any kind of text set in her homeland of India. Rahina describes herself as torn; Liang maintains a postmodern stance of no home at all. Lily incorporates the background of where she happened to be living when she first encountered a story.

Laura, on the other hand, finds the cultural frameworks of Hong Kong and Canada so distinctive that she cannot incorporate much crossover into her reading and maintains two different mental stances. She shares this approach with Halia, who automatically associates a Canadian background with reading in English and an Iraqi setting for reading in Arabic, and also with Riya who enjoys how a different language invites different thinking. Laura prefers to read about Hong Kong in Chinese rather than English: "With English, it's kinda, I don't know, not as authentic." Reading in English relates to her Canadian culture. Yet much of her early childhood in Hong Kong is now forgotten. "I was just focusing on English and, you know, blending into the Canadian culture that I kinda just forgot what was back then. So, I think a lot of memories have gone, just disappeared in my mind, and if you ask me, like, what my childhood friends were, I'm like, mmm, I don't remember." Getting out of ESL so she could be with the "normal" kids was a high priority for her, and this relational ambition overtook past memories.

Laura's account of her first elementary school, which she attended for just four months, highlights some of the ways in which relationships govern repertoire. She loved this first school. She made many friends "and the playground was amazing, and I got to learn how to do monkey bars for the first time." They moved soon after arriving in Vancouver, and Laura then attended a school that she liked much less, one where the children were substantially less friendly to her. Even today, if she reads about an elementary school, it is her first temporary school that floats into her mind.

Relationships can become all-consuming. Halia, interacting with her junior high friends, became so immersed in her fantasy life, drawing and, for a while, writing alternative stories for her favorite characters, living her life as somebody else, that she made a deliberate decision to withdraw. For the past three years, she says, she has been attempting to back away, to give herself a reality check. It was "a process" to change her wholehearted commitment to her fictions.

> I would read and I kind of learned how to enjoy things without assuming I was *in* this kind of—that was also a process. It kind of took away from the joy of it. I was trying to disassociate … I felt like it was kind of an unhealthy extent before.

I was learning how to read differently ... Like I said, it took away a lot of the joy of reading, and at first I regretted it and every now and then I would go back and I would get into a book so much and I would just spend a week drawing, thinking about it, things like that. But eventually it stopped.

Halia says she does not regret making this change, but she misses her former sense of immersion. Her account of what might be called an extreme relational form of reading is poignant:

Everything I took emotionally. I never took anything that was very abstract. It was a very emotional association; this character was doing this, I felt it, and it was that kind of association I had with the character. Also, sometimes I read strictly for characters. I was very attached to character building. I didn't care if the plot was weak if it had interesting characters.

Interestingly, Halia sets this intense relationship with fictional characters firmly in the context of her friends and their tastes and recommendations. "I was very with the flow of my friends."

In this participant pool, Suleman is the newest to Canada, and probably the person who expresses the most diffidence about reading in English. He is studying engineering along with a frequently expressed enthusiasm for business. After we turn off the recording instruments at the end of his second interview, he fishes in his pocket with an air of triumph, announces that he is now choosing to read voluntarily, and produces a book about being an entrepreneur, featuring Elon Musk. Gornick's concept of emotional readiness need not apply only to literary materials.

Life Spaces and Reading Spaces

It is obvious to the point of banality that the life spaces of these participants contain an assortment of other people: family, friends, teachers, and many others. In these layered accounts of their reading histories, I believe we may see the impact of other people inside the reading spaces as well. Adam Lively, in his article on the connection between joint attention and literary reading, describes a persuasive "bridge" between these two notional spaces: "Narrative 'competence' cannot be abstracted from its 'performance' in a particular situation" (2016: 529). As people perform reading inside their reading spaces, they often invoke an implied audience for that performance: the friends who have recommended the story and who are waiting for a reaction are only the most obvious set. As Rahina performs a reading of Junie B. Jones in her bedroom with the door shut, she is inhabiting ways of being mainstream Western that place her in the implied company of girls like the ones she knows at school. As Halia reads the graphic novel series *Naruto*, it is with a view to acting it out with her friends at recess time. In a different kind of social framing, her reading of LGBTQ novels gives her a space in which to rehearse a greater understanding of her friends and of a society run by rules and conventions different from those she internalized in childhood.

Even when these readers describe childhood activities, the time when a response to reading is most likely to be externalized in play, they are nevertheless describing these spaces in (im)material terms. The long journey to the disappointing park is a real-life event for Amani and her friends, even as the disappointment itself is ineffable. The real sand by the swings lends verisimilitude to a fantasy of piratical adventures. The running is real even when the Quidditch broomstick is imaginary.

What also comes across here is how reading spaces and life spaces open to each other. The fiction adds shape and a kind of glamour to the actions of children's bodies in an ordinary space, so a basement may contain monsters or a secret door. Some of the bodily knowledge they gain—the weariness of a long journey, the sensation of sand under feet, the imperative to hang onto your broomstick at all costs—possibly transfers back into the reading space, either in terms of the text explicitly mentioned or, more generically, stored up for next time. They develop relationships with their friends that include connections to texts held in common. They pick up particular titles to read, already knowing that their friends have invested in the worlds being presented. The reading space is deeply private and the life space is very often public, and the crossover is complex.

Domestic Spaces

6

The Home Range: Rehearsals and Repertoires

Children interact with their local landscapes in many ways. Their power to change and shape the world they inhabit is limited by physical restrictions, and also by different forms of timidity: Roman was afraid to climb into the tree house in the ravine; Amani quaked on the bridge and was too scared to investigate the trees by the park; Amy shrank from half the windows in her grandmother's house. As well, family cultures may restrict a child's relationship to the world; Halia and Rahina mostly played indoors.

But if the children, with their physical and psychological limitations, do not directly shape their landscape, they manifestly possess another skill: they transform it with their developing imaginations and their participation in childhood society. Halia, for example, roamed her basement looking for the magic she found in her books. "Because we have the capacity to configure what lies around us, we bring patterns and structures into existence in the landscape," says Maxine Greene (1995: 73). Children learn to impose particular patterns on the setting in which they happen to find themselves. We will investigate one such setting by considering the scope and limitations of a child's "home range," the area in which relatively independent decision-making is possible. We will explore the home range in both geographic and textual terms, and investigate the crucial impact of independence on child development.

Life on the Geographical Home Range

"Home range," say Little and Derr, "refers to the range or distance from home in which children can travel autonomously" (2020: 161). It also describes the microcosm within which children can learn about and practice agency.

Not every participant in this study was offered much of a home range during their childhood, but it is clear from their commentary that they all recognize the concept, though without using the label, and they are readily able to describe their childhood in terms either of its presence or its absence. It is not always possible to discern how old they were at the time of the particular home range they mention, so the scope of freedom on offer to one is difficult to compare with that available to another. There are gradations of independence as well: when Roman was younger his mother took him and his brother to the ravine, but later, the two boys went together or with friends; Amani's parents took the kids to Rundell Park but then sent them off to cross the terrifying bridge on their own; Ying Yu's mother walked in the river valley with her, but it is clear that Ying Yu feels some psychological ownership of this territory. One explicit example of a home range in this sample lies in Lily's story: there is no question that she felt her home range was comparable in China and then in Scarborough, but her capacity for autonomous activity was drastically curtailed when they moved to the Edmonton suburbs. Riya's home range was protected by walls and a gate. Amy had two such territories, one at her grandmother's and one on the acreage, but she chose to describe only one. Laura's territory included the parking lot for the local social club; Liang was at home among the motorcycle cartons in front of her parents' shop (Figure 6.1). Matt had the run of the school playing fields and the trees behind them (Figure 6.1). Rahina and Halia had less access to autonomous outdoor life as children, though they both greatly admired the trees through the window. Suleman did most of his traveling on the three-person bike with his parents, but he seems to have been able to move independently between the homes of his different relatives.

For convenient reference, I assembled a table of the home range of each participant as indicated on the maps and in the descriptions. Many of them obviously had other home ranges. Amy, for example, had some kind of home range on the acreage where she lives, but it was not specified in any way on this map, nor illuminated by her discussion. Halia had an early life in Iraq, which she did not describe in any detail. Only two maps did not graphically represent at least some of the participant's home range: those of Rahina and Suleman, though the family photos I have not shown in this book do allude to a background space where the latter felt at home. Halia, whose range (as described in this project) was probably most restricted of all, presented an image of her home and her links were mainly to indoor spaces, though she did refer to a small area immediately outside her door and to those important trees out the back.

Questions of gender, class, and culture clearly affect home range for most of these young people. Many of them had to establish home range more than once, in more than one location. Oliver Picton and Sarah Urquhart, writing about Third Culture Kids and their experiences of places, point out that current studies exploring the impact of a secure relationship with a particular place on the identity and resilience of a young person are heavily biased in favor of a stable, even intergenerational relationship with a single place (2020: 1578). They observe, correctly, that an ever-increasing mobility means that many children grow up in multiple sites, and draw on Doreen Massey's more plural definition of space to call for a more open-ended version of place-based education (2020: 1594). The accounts presented here confirm the significance of such plurality and, although it was never a direct focus of discussion, it is possible to pick out hints that children learn to reestablish a new home range after a move (unless, like Lily in the suburbs, they are utterly frustrated by the cancellation of their autonomy).

So, what kinds of activities took place within these home ranges? How did the children use their autonomy, however limited, for social and intellectual growth?

Figure 6.1 Liang's urban home range outside the motorcycle shop, which is behind the trees; Matt's suburban soccer pitch with the trees behind.

Table 6.1 Home Range Discernible in Participants' Accounts of Their Childhood

Name	Home Range
Amani	Parks, lunchtime walks to unknown parks, four-year period of a fenced-in back yard
Amy	Inside Grammie's house with brief reference to sidewalks outside
Halia	Indoors mainly; visual references to trees
Laura	In the vicinity of the social center and swimming pool of apartment complex, and in the parking lot
Liang	In the large area in front of the motorcycle shop, including in and around the motorcycle boxes
Lily	Neighborhood area around apartment complex in both China and Ontario
Matt	School playground, trees behind
Rahina	Indoors mainly; visual references to park and active mention of library
Riya	Inside the walls of large gated compound
Roman	In the ravine; in local playgrounds
Suleman	Between parents' and grandparents' homes
Ying Yu	Local neighborhoods in Edmonton

Without any question, one challenge they explored involved experimenting with developing forms of agency.

Rehearsing a Repertoire with the Body

Children need to learn about "everything out there in the world" (Pullman, 2015: 215), and, of course, they start with the version of "everything" that surrounds them. But they do not simply accumulate a compendium of things out there. Their awareness of the world is shaped by how they experience it. Only very young babies gesticulate randomly at the world, as they experiment to bring their limbs under some kind of control. From mid-infancy onward, children engage in purposeful motion as part of their exploration of the world. The motivations of these actions vary: some are task oriented, aimed at achieving a particular end, and children learn to refine their own motions toward a successful outcome. Other actions are governed by the relatively more arbitrary rules of games, and children become more skillful at managing their own bodies to accomplish goals that serve as their own satisfaction.

Proffitt and Baer provide an accessible account of the importance of agency to a child's development: "The cradle of knowledge is exercise and play. Children learn to interpret their experience by actively creating it via crawling, walking, falling, and so forth. Moreover, what we learn in childhood forms the foundation for all the new experiences and discoveries that are to come" (2020: 12). And the knowledge develops as the experiences change. Karen Adolph provides intriguing evidence about the situated nature of infants' world knowledge. As they gain experience in sitting, for example, they become more skillful at estimating how far they can reach for a toy without toppling. But when they start crawling, they must learn a whole new set of estimating skills, as the balance between their bodies and the ground is altered, thus changing their capacity to lean toward the desired object:

> Learning may be posture-specific because each postural milestone represents a different perception-action system with different relevant control variables. Sitting, crawling, and walking postures, for example, involve different regions of permissible sway for different key pivots around which the body rotates (e.g. the hips for sitting, the wrists for crawling, and the ankles for walking). In addition, each postural milestone involves different muscle groups for executing movements and for generating compensatory sway, different vantage points for viewing the ground, different patterns of optic flow as the body sways back and forth, different correlations between visual, kinaesthetic, and vestibular information, and so on. (Adolph, 2000: 291)

Infants need to sit, crawl and walk for themselves in order to gain insight into how to manage their "perception-action system" in each new posture. The work these babies accomplish is salutary reminder of the physical conditions that govern our relationship with the world, and the requirement for us to learn them autonomously. An adult may tempt a sitting or a crawling baby to reach for a toy by dangling it nearby, but it is the infant who must actually learn to make the necessary calculations about the consequences of reaching too far and who literally "takes the fall" for an overly ambitious assessment. The situation is perhaps not quite so stark for older children who have mastered the basics of stability and mobility alike, but they remain very busy with learning—with adult scaffolding or with peer scaffolding or through relying on their own actions and feedback.

Children's games are often active feedback mechanisms. I well remember watching a pair of two-year-olds play a joyful game of hide-and-seek in a bedroom. One closed her eyes and counted to five; the other, without fail, hid in the closet. The seeker went straight to the closet; there was a triumphant scene of discovery with many shrieks of laughter, and then they exchanged roles and repeated the process. At the other end of the hide-and-seek spectrum, most of us have probably had the deflating experience of creating such a successful hiding place that all attempts to find us fail and the seeker gradually loses interest, while the hider becomes frustrated and bored. There is a balance of reciprocity in a successful game of hide-and-seek that falls somewhere between these two extremes. The game also develops according to the affordances of the environment—a cluttered basement and a collection of large motorcycle boxes outside the shop both make their appearance in this study, and each permits certain kinds of hiding and not others. The child's body also places limits on the game; there comes a point where what was once an excellent hiding spot is outgrown and new crannies must be established. Some hiding successes will work only once; I remember myself, at the age of about eight, successfully standing stock-still behind a plank leaning against a cluttered shed wall. Nobody thought to look at the wall, so nobody noticed that most of me remained visible, and eventually I had to reveal myself. But, of course, I could never do it again; after my success, seekers routinely cast their eye along that wall as they ran past.

I do not want to belabour the list of (im)material life lessons gleaned through playing hide-and-seek, but it is extensive. Children learn about the limits of how much they can compress their own bodies into a given space, and then must relearn it as they grow. They learn (eventually) that it is not enough to persuade themselves that they are invisible; they must take account of what somebody else sees, a highly focused and temporary transfer of deictic center. They learn about social cooperation and rules and turn-taking. More tacitly, they learn about the suspense of hiding and the strategic demands of seeking. Crucially, perhaps, they learn about the potential and limits of agency. They decide to set up or join a game, but then they must bend their own agency to the requirements of that game. As agents, they decide it is to their advantage to follow the rules.

Participants in this study specifically mention walking, hiking, hill climbing and tree climbing, biking, sledding, and swimming. They played on swings and slides and merry-go-rounds, and learned to master the monkey bars. They also cite particular playground games: hide-and-seek, tag, hopscotch, Red Rover, grounders (a variant of tag, in which the player labeled as "it" operates with closed eyes, listening for footfalls). They played competitive sports such as basketball, badminton, cricket, and (field) hockey (and were explicit that these games were pickup affairs, organized by the kids themselves, not by any grown-ups). A couple of them mention more organized sports (Matt played soccer from an early age; Suleman played cricket for a number of years). Participants also discuss imaginary games: these may be as simple as Amani's quests to previously unseen neighborhood parks; as generic as a game of pirates or shark attack, also mentioned by Amani as good park activities; or as elaborate as Quidditch or a reenactment of some essential activities from *Harriet the Spy*.

We can see an escalating complexity in these pursuits. The first list includes the development of physical skills that allow the participant to relate to the surrounding world in particular ways. The "rules" of swimming or biking or climbing a tree operate in the form of physical constraints and physical consequences. The playground games offer a form of relatively primitive decentering; the players operate on a contingent basis, performing the disposition of their bodies *as if* a particular set of rules holds meaningful significance. The organized games have external rules and scores (though some of the rules remain local; Suleman mentions playing pickup cricket in a small street area and talks about the importance of recruiting children from as many of the neighboring houses as possible, to facilitate retrieval of the ball when it disappeared inside the open door of a house). The organized sports introduce a more formal concept of teamwork.

With the imaginary pursuits, children recast their own bodies into the role of somebody else, thus shifting the point of their sense of agency to a fictional end and practicing some short-term deictic shifts and, in the more elaborated cases, some invocation of a subjunctive mindset. Marie-Laure Ryan describes exactly such a process in her description of what happens in reading:

> In the case of mimetic texts, an essential aspect of reading comprehension consists of distinguishing a domain of autonomous facts—what I call the textual actual world—from the domains created by the mental activity of characters: dreaming,

Figure 6.2 The toy room in Grammie's house where the fabric squares lived and the games of house and school took place.

hoping, believing, planning, and so on. Mimetic texts project not a single world but an entire modal system, or universe, centered around its own actual world. (2015: 72)

A schematic account of the glimpses of childhood games provided in these maps would outline the bare bones of a sequence: an initial life space leads to the organization of spaces bounded by rules and/or animated by pretending, which in turn leads to the capacity to open up a reading space where the primary partner for the participant is a text. Without a doubt, this linear progression is highly oversimplified, but it does offer some potential for understanding one possible relationship between life spaces and reading spaces.

All the activities in the foregoing section involve children learning to manage their bodies in particular ways. At some point, they also learn to use and adapt objects as part of the game. The clearest example in this set of transcripts lies in Amy's account of the protean qualities of the pile of fabric squares in her grandma's house (Figure 6.2); her description offers the most fine-grained account of a transfer of agency. She outlines a quintessential element of early childhood that most children and their parents would recognize: a versatile capacity to pretend and then re-pretend, applying a variety of different use values to some very humble raw ingredients:

> We also had this bucket of weird scarf pieces of square cloth fabric that we would fill these drawers with, because there was nothing else to go in there, other than toys. But we would always use the scarves for everything. When we would play different imaginary games like house, where you would pretend you had your own house and you were the mom, and my cousins would be the kids or whatever,

or when we would play school where I would pretend to be the teacher and my cousins would be students or whatever, we would always use those little square scarves as, oh, this is your seat. This is your piece of paper or whatever. So, they kind of acted as the objects for everything. We used the heck out of those scarves for everything. It was very weird because we had real paper we could have used but no, we had to use a scarf instead.

Even in these very generic make-believe games of house and school, Amy and her cousins clearly took pleasure in prescribing the functions of the fabric squares in a fictional setup that also required them to name the roles of the human participants: mom, kids, teacher, and students. A piece of paper simply being a piece of paper in a game of school is manifestly not as dynamic as a square of cloth *performing* the role of a piece of paper. The scarves provide a kind of blank canvas to the pretending children; whether they are to be turned into a seat or a sheet of paper is within the power of the pretender to determine.

The very generic nature of this familiar story of make-believe suggests that most children learn early on that they can project imaginary qualities onto neutral objects, bringing them to mental life in a variety of ways that can be explicitly agreed among participating players. This homely account of children negotiating the terms of their collective pretense also provides a glimpse of these same children acquiring a formidable toolkit for the projection of imagined life into the attributes presented on a page of print. It seems likely that the toy room presented a more autonomous space for such pretending as opposed to the kitchen, which was clearly Grammie's domain; even interior domestic sites may offer more or less of a home range, may be more or less supervised and regulated.

Amani, who moved frequently, lived for four years in a house with a closed-off backyard. She speaks acutely on the significance of having some control over your territory. I ask if there were games played only in that backyard and she replies, "With my siblings, we used to play pretend. So that's where we would play it, because it would be our space, because it's our home." If they played house, the pattern of the game was "pretty similar" every time. "But otherwise, if we were just playing something like pirates, or were just playing around with our toys, then it would change from time to time." The yard contained a swing set, and, as well as enjoying their private capacity to use it for its designed purposes, Amani and her younger brother and sister incorporated it into their game of house. "It used to be, like, rooms, I guess? So it would be, like, the slide is your room, the teeter totter is someone else's room, and the swings are my room." Like Amy with the fabric squares, the children's capacity to repurpose a known space is highly functional in the cause of make-believe.

Amani also speaks briefly about imaginative games in the public space of a park. A bench would provide a little refuge in a game of pirates, but it couldn't be the primary ship. The main ship would need to be "probably somewhere bigger. Like the merry go round." In a larger park, with more elaborate playground apparatus, what she called an "attached" structure "would make a great ship. They're fun, you have lots of slides for playing and all that good stuff."

Every reader brings individual life and reading experience to bear on a text. Amy's report of her make-believe games involving her cousins and that stack of fabric squares comes very close to being a classic account of such games, as does Amani's description of the rooms of the pretend house distributed across the elements of the swing set. What can we learn if we look at their words in terms of learning to step *into* the world of a text? How does Amy's playacting help her start the process of enlivening the words on the page? What processes do Amani's many imaginary games set in motion in her head?

The child Amy, becoming a mom or a teacher, is shifting her deictic center to a new perspective, one that offers her a new relationship with her cousins, who transform into the kids or the students. They all operate in terms of the *as-if* of play. Cecire et al. point out a crucial ingredient of play, one that also entails a deictic shift to a new temporal framing, a new *now*: "Essential to playing is the suspension of possible outcomes: allowing, in a moment, for your play to take any number of directions. Such uncertainty requires a kind of *not knowing* and openness to action within this state of indeterminacy" (2015: 11). This kind of *not knowing* can also apply in reading. When we move into a character's subjunctive world, we shift deictic center to a *now* that does not include awareness of the ultimate outcome. We can make this shift even when rereading; Richard Gerrig describes the experience of "anomalous suspense" (1993: 79), in which, "once we undertake a performance of the narrative world" (1993: 80), we are confined to the perspectives and information available "inside" that world.

Amy's relatively plain description does not illuminate her internal life as she makes the transition to the role she decides to play, but Philip Pullman describes what we bring to bear on this exercise: "the stuff in our minds, the ideas, memories, emotions, conjectures, fantasies, dreams" (2015: 215). He is invoking the subjunctive mode: I feel that, I wish that, I dream that, I imagine that. We experience these states for ourselves in this account of the pre-reading workings of the mind. Our capacity to shift these open-ended stances from our own perspective to those of characters in a story is prefigured by the kind of deictic shift that very young children practice over and over again in their imaginary games. Marie-Laure Ryan calls this process of recentering an essential element in the experience of reading, particularly reading fiction: "Insofar as fictional worlds are, objectively speaking, nonactual possible worlds, it takes recentering to experience them as actual—an experience that forms the basic condition for immersive reading" (2015: 73).

Amani comes close to expressing this kind of transfer in explicit terms. Talking about her "journey" to the disappointing park, she calls up *The Little Prince* and says, "I guess I could see myself having the little adventures and visiting the new lands like he does, when he goes to the different planets throughout the book." The uncertainty of the outcome is what turns a walk into a little adventure.

At a very young age indeed, children learn to move in and out of the world of make-believe ("Daisy can't really talk; she's a stuffie," a three-year-old recently told me). They experiment with the transfer of agency and with a variety of modalities both as participants and as spectators. Through these brief references on the maps, we can see many of the participants in this project describing such intellectual rehearsal "played out" in physical form in different countries and continents.

The provisional nature of these commitments to the affordances of particular landscapes and local structures is underlined by Ingold in a discussion of an ingredient rarely mentioned in accounts of landscape: the weather. My mapmakers do not talk about weather either, apart from the rare mention of snow, but I find Ingold's invocation of this inevitable ingredient of the scene a useful reminder of the improvisational nature of so much of what occurs as children make sense of their universe. He says, "In reality, of course, the landscape has *not* already congealed from the medium. It is undergoing continuous formation, above all thanks to the immersion of its manifold surfaces in those fluxes of the medium that we call weather—in sunshine, rain, wind, and so on" (2011: 130). One or two participants mention change in the landscape of their maps, but it is mainly in terms of urban development in that their Google Earth image, for example, does not truly represent the world they remember. Nobody addresses the ephemeral changes from day to day, caused by different weather conditions for their play. Yet, once reminded, we are all aware that, as Ingold says,

> Rather than thinking of ourselves only as observers, picking our way around the objects lying about on the ground of a ready-formed world, we must imagine ourselves in the first place as participants, each immersed with the whole of our being in the currents of a world-in-formation: in the sunlight we see in, the rain we hear in and the wind we feel in. Participation is not opposed to observation but is a condition for it, just as light is a condition for seeing things, sound for hearing them, and feeling for touching them. (2011: 129)

Ingold's invocation of a three-dimensional self, one that affects, however modestly, a landscape always in transition, in the ever-changing conditions of daily weather, is a useful reminder of the active nature of these children's different forms of engagement with the world. Their play in the lively zones of their make-believe gave them all kinds of cues for how to establish and furnish a reading space. But to create this space, this borderland, most of them also drew on more virtual experiences as well. They describe what I am calling a textual home range, unsupervised contact with particular forms of mediation.

Building a Repertoire from a Textual Home Range

There is an organic quality to the development of children's ability to play games that permits them to imprint at least a modest form of agency onto their behavior. But the trajectories that Massey describes as filling the space we move through comprise more than organic movement, more than the innocent assumption of more powerful roles. Charlton et al. draw on Massey's conception of space as a theoretical framework for their study of children's awareness of their own place in the world, and also make use of Louise Rosenblatt's idea of reading as a transaction in which readers "construct meanings as they read over time in particular contexts of spaces" (Charlton et al., 2014: 156). They say,

> Readers draw on their prior knowledge to construct meaning from texts; texts change readers' prior knowledge; new meanings are thus formed. The process

is dynamic, not static. The reader's trajectory meets the text's trajectory to form a constantly shifting process of space-time which, following Massey, becomes a simultaneity of stories-so-far. (2014: 156–7)

In the previous section, I explore how the participants describe making use of the spaces that surrounded them in the home range of their childhood (cardboard boxes, basement clutter, monkey bars) and exploiting the humble raw materials at their disposal (squares of fabric) in order to create worlds that operated on rules imposed by the children. In this section, I turn to issues of textuality and fictionality that are investigated in the context of what we might call a *textual* home range. In this part of the chapter, I begin the segue to the section on textual spaces that follows.

The idea of the home range may productively be applied to children's domestic access to texts. What texts are children effectively left alone with, to manage on their own terms? The answers will vary according to the age of the child and also on the priorities of the parents. It is not difficult to imagine a house where an infant's encounters with books are scaffolded by adults but where the same small child is allowed to play more autonomously with the advertising flyers that come free in the mailbox, since it does not matter if they are crumpled. Some kinds of television and movie viewing are actively curated by parents; in many homes, children do not watch the news or adult drama, for example. Similarly, many parents may sit in on television viewing that they perceive as educational in order to augment the value of the child's viewing experience, but be rather more inclined to "park" the children in front of the TV screen on their own when the material on offer is a set of repetitive animations or the umpteenth showing of *Frozen*. The home range of texts, the material to which children have self-governed access, may, in some homes, include mother tongue materials. Alternatively, they may develop new language skills from watching television; Laura says, "I think I learned most of my English conversational things all from *SpongeBob Squarepants*. And his hilarious jokes of course, yes." For many children, the format to which they have the earliest and broadest independent access is the animated cartoon. What may they learn from this commonly available genre?

I am surprised at the paucity of general research on children watching television cartoons. No matter how I refine my search terms, I find sustained evidence of academic attention to only two topics: responses to cartoon violence and the impact of cartoon viewing on both brand recognition and eating habits. Very few studies explore the experience of the viewing itself. One such study, conducted by Rachel Barr et al., looks at children's different experiences with programming directed at adults and at children. Adult programming may distract a child from playing, particularly with audio signals, but the child whose attention is attracted cannot make sense of what is being highlighted, so the experience largely remains one of simply being diverted from something else. Programming designed for infants and young children can follow up on that audio signal with salient visuals. Barr et al. observe, "With age and experience, children learn that perceptually salient formal features, such as sound effects, can guide their attention to interesting, informative content, thereby moving them from a strictly reflexive to a purposeful attentional strategy when they hear a sound effect in a television program" (2010: 40).

Cartoons are not necessarily produced for the very young (though some are specifically addressed to toddlers). Nevertheless, their colorful, noisy, lively antics may retain the attention of young viewers even as their understanding is only partial. With an adult co-viewer, a child may pursue a higher form of understanding by asking questions about the baffling elements of an animation. Watching on their own or with other children may give them practice in the habit of satisficing, of making do, of achieving a good enough understanding to keep watching without reaching a point of actual coherent meaning-making (a topic to which I return in rather more detail in Chapter 9). Ying Yu, in the different context of watching Hong Kong detective dramas in Chinese, sums up the essence of this kind of viewing: "I'd understand it. But then I'm not sure if I could say it back so other people would understand." Young viewers of the random and silly narratives of some cartoons might similarly enjoy them on a moment-by-moment basis but be bewildered by the overall arc of the story. Left to their own devices in this home range zone, they learn to persevere through early bafflement, an important interpretive skill set they are frequently never taught in any explicit way. Of course, they sometimes simply remain confused or they lower their expectations that a text ever should make any coherent sense; there is no virtue in romanticizing a child's uncomprehending exposure to the kaleidoscopic cacophony of some cartoons. Nevertheless, it is worth looking harder at what is going on when children watch cartoons on their own.

One of the virtues of a home range is that you can set the parameters of your own awareness without answering to anyone else. You can make do with satisficing for as long as you need, gradually and independently moving to a position of greater understanding and then to a focused alertness and awareness in relation to a particular program. Lori Schafer describes watching *Scooby-Doo* and learning to resist the eponymous hero's invariable gullibility about ghosts. "As viewers, we know better, because we know how it always ends" (2015). Knowing how a formulaic cartoon "always ends" is a local and undervalued skill, but it may represent a triumphant achievement for a child watching alone, who moves from an initial state of perplexity to the powerful capacity to make successful predictions.

A second issue arises out of the implausibility of the cartoon world. Maria Nikolajeva discusses the importance to children of coming to terms with the whole concept of fictionality. She says, "Recognition of narrative conventions and therefore the ability to detect deviations from them are acquired cognitive skills, and exposure to standard as well as metafictive narratives enhances these skills" (2014: 45–7). The hypothetical child featuring in her pages is learning these valuable lessons from a succession of print books, but, of course, large numbers of children pick up many of these concepts from television, and particularly from whatever diet of cartoons is available to them. This large set of thoroughly unrealistic texts made a major contribution to the "simultaneity of stories-so-far" of some participants.

By the age of five, children can separate fictional worlds from reality and register that characters in different fictional worlds are not likely to know each other (Skolnick and Bloom, 2006). Abraham, von Cramon, and Schubotz (2008) established that different parts of the brain are involved in recollecting information about real and fictional people. Ryan cogently summarizes these findings:

It turned out that different regions of the brain were activated for real and fictional characters: for Cinderella, a region that corresponds to established facts; for George Bush, a region more open to revision ... Since fictional characters are created by texts, they are the product of a limited corpus of information. With real-life characters, on the other hand, the corpus is open-ended, since it is always possible that new information will turn up, and that it will lead to a revision of our image. (2010: 472)

One of the powers of play, of course, is its capacity to bridge these gulfs, to develop a hybrid world where characters from different ontologies mix and mingle. The capacity to perform an override of the limits of fictional universes provides a potent sense of agency—and reinforces the concept that these worlds are, indeed, made-up and malleable. Young children are early proponents of fan culture when they invest in hybrid pretending.

Hodge and Tripp, in their seminal discussion of modality and children's television, follow Nikolajeva in exploring the need to develop an understanding of the concept of fictionality, but they use the idea of degrees of modality to discuss this topic. "Modality," in this case, "concerns the reality attributed to a message" (1986: 104). A text with weak modality is highly artificial, more distanced from reality; and clearly, animated cartoons are very artificial indeed. Their conversations with groups of nine-year-olds show that these children had no difficulty in specifying what contributes to the weak modality of cartoons. The images are drawn, and "coloured in. Not like real people" (1986: 110). The dimensions and characteristics of the characters are not believable. The sound effects are fake. The events are unrealistic, and overall free from actual consequences.

A full-length animated feature film, speaking very generally, probably pays somewhat more attention to a reasonably plausible development of cause and effect, simply because it needs to sustain a plot over a longer period of time. It may operate within a relatively realistic setting, compared to the sparse and/or repetitive scenery of many cartoon shorts. Nevertheless, as one of Hodge and Tripp's nine-year-olds astutely observes, even comparatively well-developed cartoon characters belong to their own world, not ours: "And you can't go out and see a cartoon character walking across the road or something. It's just ... [others laugh] piece of paper" (1986: 110).

Short cartoons are clearly fictional, and many of them are anarchic in nature. Some of their slapstick may also be slapdash; not every cartoon is highly crafted. Repetition is a significant feature in many series. Many are also commercially saturated, either from the outset or after the event, by the development of associated commodities and collectibles. Some are heavily stereotyped; others are subversive. Many include violence (often very stylized). It is not a particularly attractive list when laid out so baldly. Their comical inversion of the possibilities of the body may have particular appeal to the young, who are still busy sorting out the potential of that body and its place within the forces of the world. The animator, says Mary Slowik, both observes and defies the laws of gravity. "In this way, animated films can reinforce and then shatter their most insistent divisions and keep us situated literally and figuratively in an uncomfortable, non-gravitational, gravitational space, which activates our visceral fears, in this case of falling, while teasing our exhilarated response to floating and flight" (2016: 151).

Having caught the attention of young viewers with this primal appeal to very early fears and fantasies, animations may also introduce some sophisticated forms of reflection on the process of storytelling itself. Slowik says, "Animated films at their best also unabashedly reveal their own artifice, adding a distinctive layer of narrative self-consciousness to the animal fable" (2016: 151). Audiences are often treated as knowing, and, as children occupy this stance, they do gradually begin to understand what the animation is assuming of its viewers.

Douglas Bruce makes a thought-provoking observation: "Animations are the rhetorical heirs of the nursery rhyme" (2001: 230). It would certainly be a fascinating challenge to compare and contrast the contributions of nursery rhymes and animations to the development of literate awareness. Like cartoons, nursery rhymes are often lurid, anarchic, violent and/or erotic, and fossilized at a particular point in history so that they may make little contemporary sense. Like nursery rhymes, as Bruce observes, "Cartoons can do forbidden and disruptive things because unlike 'adult' media they are not taken seriously" (2001: 231)

The role of nursery rhymes in the development of early literacy has been well established. In 1989, Bryant et al. could confidently assert in the opening line of their abstract, "Nursery rhymes are an almost universal part of young English-speaking children's lives" (1989: 407). They built on studies showing mothers in England reciting nursery rhymes to babies as young as three months old, and established that knowledge of nursery rhymes at the age of three could be connected to reading achievement three years later, most likely through increasing sensitivity to rhyme, alliteration, and a subsequent development of phonemic awareness.

Nursery rhymes, as a rule, are scaffolded by adults; it is when they segue into playground rhymes (which often manifest similar qualities) that they become a part of children's textual home range and a feature of their autonomous lives. And in the school playground, we may see the footprint of the textual home range expanded into autonomous play. As Jackie Marsh and Julia Bishop note, playground rhymes themselves mutate, often in response to television viewing experience (2014: 68).

Children must obviously have some adult assistance in gaining access to animated shorts and full-length films, but they are often left on their own to make what interpretive sense they can of the multimodal array of information that a cartoon has to offer. Their playground rites offer one kind of insight into a child community of interpreters; in many cases, the route from television viewing to playground reenactment is unscaffolded by any form of adult attention.

Cartoon Watching

Nine of the participants mention watching cartoons in their childhood. They watched what their siblings or cousins watched, or they quarreled over controlling the remote, or they turned to other strategies. Amy watched *Bugs Bunny* because her brother liked it, but when he switched his preference to *Power Rangers*, she gave up and turned to reading. Some viewers were highly selective; Lily, for example, chose to watch *Corduroy* and *Madeline* because of the urban setting that she also prized in other materials. Suleman, on the other hand, wanted to see everything going. Adults who wanted to watch sports or the news simply took over the remote, so all the children's choices had to fit round these constraints. In effect, their vernacular textual pleasures flourished in the shadow of ultimate adult control of the screen.

Cartoons were translated or dubbed from English and Japanese into Chinese or Urdu or Arabic. Probably the most international example comes from Halia who, while still in Iraq, viewed a very loosely adapted Japanese series of *Anne of Green Gables*, dubbed into Arabic. Later, after she moved to Canada and studied the novel and the Sullivan miniseries in elementary school, she continued to think of Montgomery's story as Arabic at its roots. She failed to register either the Canadian or the Japanese connection because of the lingering power of that first animated impression.

For some young viewers, immigrants to a new country, cartoons and other kinds of television provide ongoing access both to their new and to their "home" language. The exaggerated actions and caricatured characters of a cartoon offer a comforting and familiar scaffold as viewers aim to improve comprehension in a new tongue, or maintain fluency in a known language, perhaps now used less often.

The focus of this project is on reading, so most mention of cartoons is incidental. Two participants make a much more significant case for the importance of cartoons in their lives.

Rahina articulates a very solid testimonial to the teaching potential of television as a gateway to reading:

> I'd say TV is definitely the first medium into the world of literature because by having images and motivations, and just character baselines, then I could take those and when I'm reading books, stitch things together … Junie B. Jones and Dr. Seuss, I did not understand the motivations behind characters' hysterical actions until I connected them to TV shows I watched.

The kind of television Rahina was watching at this time, according to the list she readily recalls, included *SpongeBob SquarePants, Fairly Odd Parents, The Simpsons, The Berenstain Bears, Teletubbies, Arthur,* and *Barney*. Her television viewing is "family-oriented" to this day because of her numerous younger siblings. She says of children's television,

> You pick up a lot of themes, character portrayals, and the fact that they use animals and they can get away with it, most TV shows. That helps you … Sometimes they actually put ethnicity in the background, you know that? Like, for example, a cat is Japanese. So there's way more I can learn. As a story creator you have more of a repertoire, not repertoire, you have more of a cast that you can pull from, like a pool.

The most committed aficionado and expert, of course, is Suleman, who negotiated so hard to squeeze as much cartoon viewing as possible into his daily life. What may he have learned from these shows? At one level, they certainly look like a hodgepodge of cultural artifacts. It is not difficult to picture him working out at an early age that one of these cartoon heroes was unlikely to belong in the world of another. He did not absorb much in the way of background information about the cultures that produced them, since his assumption was that they were all produced in Pakistan, or, in the most remote option, India. He heard them all in Urdu.

Suleman makes it clear that his parents were hostile to these cartoons and the very act of watching them in the homes of his other relatives may have been a way of carving out a textual home range away from his mother's watchful eye; but this comment is speculation on my part. There is no question that his viewing life gave him something he still values.

These cartoons also gave Suleman and his friends a rich repertoire for imaginary play. They made up pretend games about many of the characters. Suleman dabbled in collecting Beyblades as far as he could persuade his parents to part with the purchase price, and once even crafted one for himself. He read related comics when he could lay his hands on them. And he still values his expertise in relation to these cartoons; it is a lively form of (relatively uncritical) cultural capital for him.

Suleman's enthusiasm for these texts and the variegated inner life they offered him is not a negligible asset. It is an interesting but unanswerable question whether greater access to full-length animated movies might have offered him a viable transition into more extended textual interpretation and practice with sustaining attention over a longer narrative arc. It didn't happen, so there is no way of knowing. But his delight in what these short animations did give him is unmistakable.

The Textual Home Range as Glocal

The playground games described by this little group of international participants seem to transcend borders: hide-and-seek in China, tag in India. It might be possible to evince universal elements at work in these games. The textual home range, however, embodies a different kind of paradox: rather than being universal, it is global. Children negotiating access to a screenful of cartoons are participating in a complex international operation, described by Medina and Wohlwend in the following striking terms: "Children's social imaginations in contemporary times are embedded in fluid but also disjointed and fragmented cultural practices with multimodal textual resources that are not static or tethered to one particular place yet carry attached histories and ideologies that become traces of multiple localities" (2014: 5).

Medina and Wohlwend ask a question that certainly dogs this project in many vital ways: "How do we study the material consequences of global corporate markers, media, and transnationalism without leaving out multiple overlapping experiences and knowledges that are too difficult to simultaneously map?" (2014: 18). There is no short answer to this question, of course, but it seems important to acknowledge that many children organize their first tentative steps into a relatively autonomous relationship with media by engaging with the products of huge international media conglomerates—a paradigmatic example of what is now called glocal experience, both global and local at once. Whatever the commercial and ideological motivations of these media companies, what the children do with their products is profoundly domestic. However they express their commitment to their favorite programs, they see themselves as agents in this relationship. And in the process, they join a highly dispersed form of affinity group, sharing interpretive experiences and affective priorities with other small children around the globe.

For some years, I lived near an international graduate student family housing complex. The children from these homes often arrived in our neighborhood elementary school with very little English. I regularly walked through the school playground to catch the bus, and it intrigued me to observe that in one respect a very polyglot group of children formed a focused community of interpreters. No matter what the country of origin or the mother tongue, nearly all the children were familiar with Disney animations. Disney-speak offered a lingua franca in the recess-time exchanges and games of these very diverse children.

Suleman and his friends were a less international group, but they played pretend games arising from their cartoons. They improvised; he mentioned using long balloons for swords in a game of *Samurai Jack*. They held Beyblade competitions with purchased and homemade tokens. And they played with Pokémon cards:

Margaret: So if you had a stack of cards of, say, Pokémon characters, would you pretend with those cards? Or were they just for trading and talking about the shows with? Would you say, would you take—
Suleman: We would argue, this one's more powerful, no this one's more powerful. We wouldn't pretend or anything—
Margaret: You wouldn't have mock battles with them or anything?
Suleman: No, not the mock battles. It was more of an intellectual thing.

This child in Pakistan, maneuvering to watch as many of his beloved cartoons as he could possibly manage in the face of adult disapproval or scorn, participated in global culture even as he naively (but possibly productively) believed all these animations were local productions. We can see very precisely here an example of Medina and Wohlwend's observation that "the local moment of engagement within play, dramatic experiences, and literacies is not a given but is always produced by the multiple localities children navigate and the histories and possibilities they bring to the creative moment" (2014: 11–12).

Apart from Suleman and his Beyblades and Pokémon cards, participants in this project spoke very little about television-related playthings. Depending on the intimacy—and the affluence—of the home range group, it is very possible that some children may regularly manage their play through cobbling up some stand-in for the official franchise toy or accoutrement. In other play regimes, owning the official object may be a major focus. Marsh and Bishop draw our attention to the way that text-related play may be distributed across a variety of sources and resources, but there are not many mentions of this kind of approach in my transcripts. These particular young people are more likely to refer to themselves as simply imagining what they needed for a game, sometimes drawing on the local affordances of a playground or a stand of trees or a bridge or, for that matter, a pile of fabric squares.

Their power to imagine collectively from the starting point of a simple structure provides a form of social glue.

The textual home range is a complex and contested territory; while its reception is intensely local, it inculcates young children around the globe into some elements of a common culture. If I had brought my dozen participants together, I suspect the swiftest way to open a broad conversation among them all would have been to say, "Let's talk about animated cartoons you watched in your childhood." Both the shorts and the feature films appear in the interviews over and over again.

In Bartlett's terms, this international and corporate framework is one of the filters through which these participants mark their place in the world. The newly arrived children at my local elementary school possess at least one element of exchangeable social currency with their Disney knowledge, and I suspect it is a lifesaver for some to find any point of common interest and knowledge with their new classmates. The degree of autonomy permitted by their daily and textual home ranges ironically serves to "school" many children in understanding what independent interpretation entails. Just as Amani and her friends filtered an ordinary walk to a nearby park into an expression of adventure and significance, the home range activities, live and textual, offer practice in ways of being in the world.

Textual Spaces

Border Country

7

Fundamental Scenes of the Reading Space: The Forest

Philip Pullman talks about fundamental particles of narrative as essential building blocks of story. "I'm going to say straight out that I think stories are made of events, and that the fundamental particles of story are the smallest events we can find. So small, in fact, that they are more or less abstract" (2017: 194). The example he uses in his Richard Hillary Lecture at Oxford, is the particle-level event of pouring something out of a container, and he provides many fascinating examples of the impact of such a particle in many very different stories.

In this chapter, I do not descend quite so far down the scale to the level of particles. Pullman comments briefly on the place of being human: "The scale on which we live, with our bodies and our normal everyday consciousness, is round about the middle scale of size between the cosmic level and the quantum level, and one of the characteristics of this middle scale is *individual difference*, every person, every face, every story being recognisably itself and different from everything else" (2017: 194). I wish to borrow Pullman's analytical approach but to remain at this middle point in the scale where human activity is visible. Let us call it a fundamental scene: an ingredient of many people's accounts of their reading that exists more or less on the same point of the scale as people themselves, but shading off into something more abstract, less individual. The fundamental scene I explore in this chapter is a set of experiences of the forest, both real-life and imaginary.

Many participants mention the setting of a forest. This trope obviously plays a big part in the Harry Potter books but, of course, its significance is broader. Only three readers fail to mention some concept of the forest: Suleman, Liang, and Amy (for what it is worth, they were children in three different countries, so they do not represent a single topography in which trees are not important). Laura's only mention of trees comes in her description of her arrival in Canada, but she makes no connection to her reading: "I was just amazed how I just travelled maybe ten, twelve hours in airplane flight and then I got to this place. I'm like, wow, there's snow, which you don't see in Hong Kong, and there's big, big gigantic malls, huge, and land is huge too. I've never seen that much trees, wow."

Eight readers raise the topic of the forest independently and ascribe literary significance to it. Their individual landscapes are undoubtedly distinctive, but their analysis of the role of the forest in a reading life is surprisingly connected, in relatively abstract ways.

Amani makes a connection between a scene in a book and a real tree. When the heroine of her story "climbs the tree, I do think of, like, a specific tree that me and my siblings used to climb." But more of her references to forests are atmospheric. One of the four parks she mapped had a concrete area used as a skate park, and behind that area was a small wood. "I remember those woods very clearly because there was a lot of stories around them," Amani says. She never went into the woods because she was far too frightened, but she called on the atmosphere when it was helpful. "I think there was one book I did read, I believe it was *Goosebumps*, where they did go into the woods in the scenario, and I did definitely think of those woods, because I had heard horror stories around it, and I was yes, this is what it would look like." I ask, "So it's not just wood-ness in your head, it's scary wood-ness?" and she replies, laughing, "It's like the classic slasher wood-ness, I guess." Her best guess as expressed in the first interview is that the woods are nowhere near as sinister as she projected in her youth: "I think it was just child talk. I mean, thinking back now, if I probably went there, I'm not even sure they were really woods; it might just have been a bunch of trees. I haven't been back there in a few years, so I think it was definitely heightened, as a kid." In her second interview, Amani returns to this topic.

> I remember last time I was talking about the scary forest. Behind Kirkness. Well, I did some research—well, I looked at Google Earth—and it turns out it's just a few trees behind the park. [Laughing] I found that kind of funny, though; I imagined it as a huge forest, but, in hindsight it was just a few trees.

This imagined forest also underlay her reading of a *Choose Your Own Adventure* book, and animated Harry Potter's Forbidden Forest.

Halia does not mention Harry Potter but she makes similar reference to a few trees behind her house (also unvisited, in this case because her parents, newly arrived in Canada from Iraq, were uneasy about her going outside on her own). This small stand of trees that she depicts in her map (Figure 7.1) substituted for any number of forests in her reading: "For sure, the forest would be twenty more trees than the ones outside my house, and, like, pine trees and things like that. We didn't have that in Iraq; we had palm trees, so pine trees were very interesting at the time for me." She would look out her window at the view of the courtyard and the trees. "And that's where I would like, that's where all my imaginings were, all the unicorns were, and all that."

As a child in a new environment, Halia eked out her scant local knowledge to make do with imagery that was adequate to keep her going in the story. A more detailed accounting of the process will appear in Chapter 9. Both she and Amani expanded on the minimal input of a few local trees, and inserted their makeshift forest as needed into a range of reading experiences.

Ying Yu, another urban reader, talks about the psychological impact of trees in her environment: "Because the neighbourhood is pretty old, the trees are pretty high up. So then, when we were small, it feels like, oh, there's so many trees towering over us,

112 Space, Place, and Children's Reading Development

Figure 7.1 The few trees behind Halia's house that fueled her mental schema of a forest.

so it feels like an adventure just walking there." These "high up" trees did not provide detailed visual information so much as atmosphere, but Ying Yu went on a field trip that enhanced her schema of a forest with some up close and detailed investigation that fed back into her reading. It is interesting that she commits herself only to the idea that "it feels like a forest," raising the possibility that she too is extrapolating from a small stand of trees to something larger.

> So, for the fairies, or the travelling, adventuring, hiking kind of stories, usually there's lots of green, there's tree trunks, and then sometimes there would be the fallen tree trunk. And for the more mysterious type, I think I read—I think it was *The Iron Daughter, The Iron King*. She just discovered, oh she's half fairy, so then, just that moment of travelling there, everything seems kind of fuzzy, everything's kind of blurry, so I'd imagine, oh yeah, okay, there's mist, there's fuzz going on, or it's dark, not a lot of sunlight. And then, for field trips, back in elementary, we actually went to, I think we went to the forest, or near the forest. It feels like a forest to me when I went there. We got to see the trees, we got to see the fungus. And then there was fallen trees, and then we got to see the rings inside the tree trunks too. So that would kind of be incorporated in the images in my mind.

Ying Yu includes three images of a forest in her map (Figure 7.2), and adds a comment:

> I am very aware of nature. As a child, I have climbed trees, gone on many road trips to see more nature, as well as lived around big trees and lots of trees ... When I read books about fairies and nymphs, when the plot is in the forest, I usually

Figure 7.2 Ying Yu's atmospheric forest images.

> incorporate memories of how a forest would look into the images in my mind. There would be fallen logs, lots of tall trees, bushes, small trees. The image is usually an up-close image of how it looks. Detailed and less vague, because it gives off a stronger nature feel.

When she is walking among trees, says Ying Yu, she feels as if she is on a journey. This kind of heightened sensibility is mentioned or implied by a number of participants.

Rahina explicitly speaks of the importance of the forest to her imagination, even though, like some of the others, she mostly observed from indoors:

> I've been very lucky with living in cities my entire life, so I've got to see not only the buildings but also the natural forests behind them. So, in Toronto, there was a huge forest behind my house. Even though I lived smack in the middle of the city, there were still mini forests, they were sort of national parks? But somewhat smaller. I was really grateful for how these helped me think beyond just the TV, and going to school, and back and forth.

I ask if she was ever allowed to go out into the forest. She replies, "Sadly no, because I was five or six; my mom had to take care of two other children so she couldn't always go out for walks."

But the forest made a great impact on Rahina, nevertheless. On her map, she links the forest and the library. Of the former, she writes:

> The most monumental and visceral landscape of all is that of natural scenery. Nature provides me with wonder, humility, possibilities to imagine worlds outside this one, and an escape from reality. In Toronto, we lived in a twenty-five floor

building that overlooked a mini forest. It wasn't a national park, but there were pathways for those who wanted to take a walk. From Grade 3 to this day, I have made a habit out of gazing out of the window for at least an hour quite regularly. The abundance of natural life, the swaying of trees, the cool night air, the vast open sky, the mesmerizing stars, and the buildings dotted throughout the horizon was my first glimpse of a landscape capable of riveting beauty and nostalgia inducing memories.

Her comparison to the values of a library is explicit:

The link between the forests and libraries is that they mimic each other in the quality of being limitless. The vast array of books, the possibility of eternal entertainment and occupation, and the calm that they bring were best reflected in the lush and silent greenery found in forests. Because forests aren't exactly imagined, their ubiquitous presence helps me feel at ease, free, and connected to the world of books, where a person is never far from some real needed mental stimulation. Forests and libraries are real places, they can be lost in, wandered in, and found enlightening to their observers. Even if I knew next to nothing back then about the real dangers of getting lost in a forest, I imagined that the trees were living, breathing, silently watching beings who taught me patience because here they were, standing still their whole lives, and never once complaining. I envied their silence, fortitude, and perseverance to live through winter after winter.

Rahina says that "forests or trees or woodland or anywhere like that" offer "a sense of wonder, just how much there is outside of you."

Riya's take on the forest is more schematic. Her own tea garden landscape in India included trees, but she does not speak about these real trees in any detail, except to lament that they were cut down after she moved away. Imagining the necessary elements for the children's escapades in Enid Blyton's Famous Five stories, however, she decrees trees and bushes to be necessary for a satisfactory image of Kirrin Island, where the Five have many adventures (see Mackey [2021a] for more details). Her imagined island is a generic image she tracks to her school geography book: a smooth semicircle of land rising out of the water. But it needs trees, in her mind, to be an appropriate setting for adventure. I contribute the notion that some running water would be equally essential to a satisfactory adventure, and she is happy to go along. In fact, to my considerable surprise when I reread *Five on a Treasure Island* some time later, Blyton is explicit that Kirrin Island is rocky and treeless and without fresh water of any kind. Clearly, both Riya and I had retrofitted this setting with conventional scenery to suit our own assumptions.

Lily mentions trees on both her maps. Her Chinese setting includes a "tree-lined" street near her apartment building, and she associates these trees with bustling urban life:

The trees were all French oaks. They imported a lot of them from France I believe, and my dad used to talk about them a lot because they were really huge trees. It

Fundamental Scenes of the Reading Space

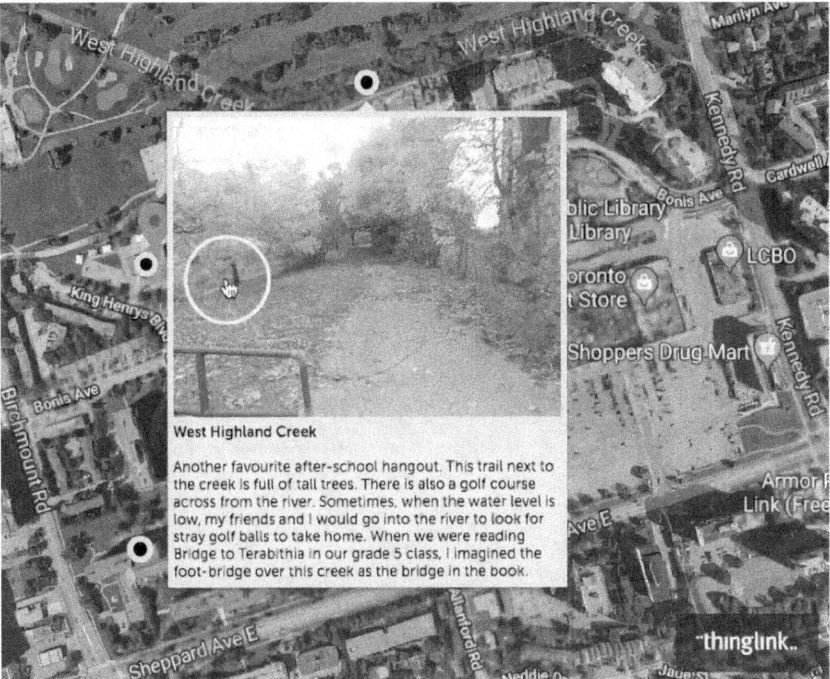

Figure 7.3 A view of the tree-lined walk toward West Highland Creek.

was shady in the summer so a lot of these streets, they had vendors on the side, so it was like kind of like Whyte Ave [an Edmonton neighborhood with shops and cafés]. So you have little shops, just little mom and pop shops where you can go shopping, along here and here [pointing], so I used to have a great time after school just walking around and then spending my pocket money. And then there's street food as well so there's lots of activities going on here, so that's why I marked them.

Her play time involved a green space alongside this street, and, in her account, the trees were simply part of the scenery, providing the atmosphere of something special and the practical advantage of shade.

In Scarborough, Lily similarly lived in an apartment block, purchased her after-school snacks in a No Frills supermarket and played on a green space, "greenery and trees all around." Many of the children's games were played in a space defined by a traffic roundabout, but they also imagined themselves into some of their favorite novels (*Harriet the Spy*, *Bridge to Terabithia*) in a nearby park space (Figure 7.3):

So, this is West Highlands Creek; you can't really see it from here. It's tree-lined, so there's a creek running down the neighbourhood. I think it goes here [pointing to

Figure 7.4 Matt's "forest" behind his school's soccer pitch.

the screen], so this is like a hiking trail and it was really pretty there. A lot of times after school, some buddies of mine would just go walk around there and they would have a bridge and you can just go on the bridge across the creek. And then there's a fence here that looked into a golf court, and you couldn't go in but you can go into the creek and find golf balls and stuff, so it was like a fun activity sometimes.

Lily does not expand on the role of trees in their imaginative games, but it is not difficult to perceive them providing helpful atmosphere and a small glimpse of something wilder than the city. There is just a glimmer of what Amani and I called "wood-ness" in Lily's account of her imaginary games. "Here, I think it was *Bridge to Terabithia* that we were reading in class; we thought that bridge kind of looked like it. I just pretended that I was there."

Matt makes detailed and literary reference to the Forbidden Forest, and he too starts with the same kind of basic schematic unit of a small stand of trees as mentioned by several of the others. In his case, it is "sort of a forest" behind his school (Figure 7.4). This "forest" fuels his immersion in the story.

I spent a lot of my time in there building forts … It was a lot easier to imagine yourself being in these stories and re-enacting these stories when you have an environment like that around you … So this, for me, is a very strong narrative where I can take things from my childhood and visions from my childhood and imprint them on the literature I was reading.

Like Amani, Matt assesses the forest in terms of atmosphere. More than any other participant, he describes the Forest in literary terms. This exchange on the Harry Potter books is worth quoting at length.

Matt: So, it grows more as you read in the books. In the first one they don't describe it a whole lot. In the second one they describe it more when they go meet with the spiders. But you know it's mysterious, it's dangerous, it's dark. It's kind of the dark area to the otherwise bright landscape. It teaches a lot of things and it kind of helps you, as a child at least, encounter brief encounters of fear. So like—

Margaret: Yeah, that you're holding in your hand. It's not all around you.

Matt: Yeah, I mean they talk about the first book, I can remember my mom was reading it and she was talking about the dark figure that was sucking blood from the unicorn. And it was definitely like, there was an element of fear. It wasn't as scary as watching a movie, but it was definitely something I thought about in my sleep. I thought that was a unique ability that books had … it's kind of that idea of testing your limits a little bit so the more you read it, the more you want to read more of that, so having a dark environment like the Forbidden Forest kind of creates a little bit of a want to see more of it, but in small steps.

Margaret: You really are testing yourself as well as the characters, aren't you?

Matt: And in the books she did it brilliantly. They take small steps in the first book. They see this happen and in the second book it gets even bigger and they see a big spider and they spent a lot more time in there. And then by the third book, you're pretty comfortable with the Forbidden Forest and a lot of the story takes place in these woods in the second half of the book. A lot of what happens near the end takes place in this area which you're more familiar with and you're not really—you don't have that element of fear as much. You still know it's dark and mysterious and there's things that—

Margaret: But it's familiar by now.

Matt: Yeah, and so it's kind of an achievement in itself by reading these books you get to kind of master this fear and have an understanding of a really interesting place … The third book, the characters gain a sense of independence and I think you as the reader kind of gain it along with them.

Margaret: You go right along with them, don't you?

Matt: Yeah. So, again, for me I could remember times running through this forest pretending that one of us was a werewolf and the rest of us were playing tag. Or just—I mean the trees are so—because a tree is a tree, as much as in a book they can give a lot of description to trees. Like the Ents and whatnot. But if they're talking about a forest, you immediately will think of the most closely surrounding forest that you interact with. So, for me, it was this one, so if they talk about logs, I'm picturing the logs from this forest, if they're talking—and this forest was kind of the

Forbidden Forest that I imagined. And a lot of it was because it had a lot of knocked over trees. And then, I mean as much as this Forbidden Forest meant a lot of knocked over trees, it had a lot of exposed roots and it had areas that they were tripping on and stuff like that. So for me, I was, oh, I've got this visual in mind now.

Matt, who raids his mental scenery from one book to furnish another, often plunders his mental image of the Forbidden Forest in this way. To him, the forest also represents a state of mind:

It's one of the things that I steal a lot of imagery from when reading about other forests. Throughout the books, you get a lot of description of this forest and kind of the mysterious, dark, eerie aspect to it. The reader has kind of an expectedness of the unpredictability of it, and I feel like there's a lot of books that have a forest sort of like that, so the description that they put into the forest and the understanding that I was able to gain of this landscape really related to a lot of other books I was reading. Because I think a lot of fantasy novels use forests and very primitive landscapes, which is why I think the forest was easy to relate to other books.

He is explicit in relating the characters' challenges in the Forest to the growth of the reader.

I feel like as a reader you kind of gain a bit of independence as well as the characters gaining a sense of independence … It calls for wittiness and cleverness of getting out of situations and it requires being able to be on your feet … I think the forest was kind of like a maze in that sense, and it relies on the characters' own qualities to get out.

Of all the participants, Roman is equipped with the most complete forest experience. In his childhood, before housing development reduced its size, the ravine was extensive enough that he could find himself relatively "deep in the woods." He takes this landscape into his reading, as this brief fragment of dialogue demonstrates:

Roman: When I read, I see images. I don't see words. So it's like a film in my head, and I guess some of the setting, or the context for the stuff that's going on, I'd see pictures of this ravine.
Margaret: Right. So let's just make up an example. You're reading *The Lord of the Rings*. They could be marching through this ravine of yours.
Roman: Yeah, or when they go into Mirkwood or something. That's the kind of forest.
Margaret: Right. So this is available for forest scenes in anything that you read?
Roman: Anything. Anything and everything.
Margaret: Yeah, it's funny how that works, isn't it? And you're not troubled by the fact that it's always the same forest?

Roman: Well, it's not always the same forest, 'cause as I grew up, the ravine wasn't the only place that we went. We went to the mountains, we traveled across Canada. So I developed a deeper bank. And I also went to New Zealand, so that helped.

New Zealand, of course, provided the site for the filming of *The Lord of the Rings*, so Roman is mentioning a specifically connected setting in this final remark, skewing the (im)materiality of his account in a slightly different direction. But the generic "woodness" of his time in the ravine clearly serves his reading well.

The Forest of the Reading Space

In Matt's reading space, the forest is very richly specified and redolent of physical and psychological challenges. But other readers make do with a much more sketchily outlined forest. With Riya, for example, the hypothetical Blyton forest is really little more than a precondition for adventure. Halia's forest is a make-do extrapolation of a few trees. Ying Yu supplies close-up details from her field trip, and she draws on larger elements of atmosphere from her walks in Edmonton's river valley. Rahina's forest provides a richness to her imaginative life, even as her childhood mostly involved looking out the window at the trees. Lily's tree-lined walk to the creek includes some imaginative essentials for her pretend games. Amani's forest is heavy on scary atmosphere but rather shorter of specified details since she was too frightened to head into the trees in her neighborhood. Roman, on the other hand, has fully saturated experiences of the forest in his ravine that he brings to his reading.

The space of the forest is a space where things happen. If the smallest fundamental narrative particle is an event, it seems as if the fundamental scene of the forest enables certain kinds of events to happen. A forest may be inspirational (Rahina), adventurous (Ying Yu), adversarial (Amani), schematic (Riya, Halia), atmospheric (Ying Yu, Lily, Amani), or a fully developed sensory experience (Roman, Matt). There is no way of assessing the implications of the obvious gender divide represented here. The boys had by far the greatest free access to playing among the trees. Rahina and Halia were discouraged by their parents from playing outside at all. Amani was afraid. Riya simply does not say. Of the women in this project, only Lily and Ying Yu mention even walking among the trees on a regular basis and only Amani and Ying Yu talk about climbing. Nevertheless, no matter how slight their experiences of actual trees, these readers invoke a forest very readily when one is needed to furnish a reading space.

The interface between the words on the page and the particular kind of space evoked is encapsulated in the standard literary term of *topos*. The Greek word literally means *place*, but the dictionaries define its use in English as meaning a traditional theme or motif or literary convention, a stock topic in rhetoric (https://www.thefreedictionary.com/topos). A forest, of course, provides an extremely conventional theme/motif/topic and at the same time it is a distinctive *place*, its own visual, sonic, olfactory, and atmospheric space.

Children's literature specialist Jane Suzanne Carroll pays very serious attention to the role of place in children's literature and talks about the need to acquire "footfall knowledge of the landscape" (2011: 9). While her book is fascinating and thought-provoking about the connections between the geography and the history of a particular place and the geographical and historical strata embedded in the landscape of a text, she does not incorporate individual readers into her complex construct. Her approach of "topoanalysis" (2011: 3) is heavily focused on the world of the text; but there is definitely scope to consider how a reader's "footfall knowledge" of a home territory aids reading about other places.

Up to this point, I have been using the word "atmosphere" in its vernacular sense. Architect Juhani Pallasmaa offers a more specialized account of place and atmosphere, though not in relation to forests; nevertheless, he provides a description that resonates in this context.

> It is evident that the experiential quality of a space or a place is not merely a visual perceptual quality, and in fact, focused vision makes us outsiders in relation to what we are seeing in focus. The sense of insideness in a space or place calls for unfocused, peripheral, enveloping, and enfolding perceptions and interactions of various sense experiences. Atmosphere is a kind of virtual, experiential, and multi-sensory place, which usually has shapeless, indefinable and ephemeral boundaries, and experiential qualities ... Atmosphere defines a specific location or place with distinct experiential qualities and emotive suggestions. (2015: 131–2)

Hans Ulrich Gumbrecht invokes the German word *Stimmung*, which he says is difficult to translate, though he offers the English words *mood*, *atmosphere*, and *climate*. He quotes a line from Toni Morrison (without providing a citation): "Being touched as if from inside." He then expands on this idea: "She was interested, I imagine, in an experience familiar to everyone: that atmospheres and moods, as the slightest of encounters between our bodies and material surroundings, also affect our psyche" (Gumbrecht 2012: 4). Concentrating on atmospheres and moods, says Gumbrecht, is a route to "vitality and aesthetic immediacy" (2012: 12); atmosphere provides a form of presence.

Imagining a forest offers a shortcut to atmospheric awareness and vivid presence in just the terms that Pallasmaa and Gumbrecht supply. The issue of "insideness" arises in different ways: a forest may touch us "as if from inside" and/or we may read ourselves to a position "inside" the forest—and/or, at a different level again, we may locate ourselves "inside" the structure of words that creates the structure of the forest. There are intriguing questions about the degree to which atmosphere establishes itself in a reader's mind in ways that feel spontaneous, immediate, and nonnegotiable. Gumbrecht suggests that the impact of atmosphere can never exist "wholly independent of the material components of works—above all, their prosody. Therefore, texts affect the 'inner feelings' of readers in the way that weather and music do" (2012: 5).

It would be easy to supply multiple literary examples of forests to illustrate the (im)material qualities being described here. Instead, I offer a single extract, partly on the basis of its splendidly apropos title. In *The Word for World is Forest*, Ursula Le Guin provides atmosphere, mood, and a setting for agency and adventure. Through the powerful cadences of this description, she invites us *inside*.

> No way was clear, no light unbroken, in the forest. Into wind, water, sunlight, starlight, there always entered leaf and branch, bole and root, the shadowy, the complex. Little paths ran under the branches, around the boles, over the roots; they did not go straight, but yielded to every obstacle, devious as nerves. The ground was not dry and solid but damp and rather springy, product of the collaboration of living things with the long, elaborate death of leaves and trees … The smell of the air was subtle, various, and sweet. The view was never long, unless looking up through the branches you caught sight of the stars. Nothing was pure, dry, arid, plain. Revelation was lacking. There was no seeing everything at once: no certainty. (1972: 35–6)

Le Guin invites her readers to enact the absence of certainty in these thick woods, frustrating any drive for either security or purposeful movement, with hampered sight, insecure footing, and a scented air redolent of the forest's permanent and never-ending capacity for growth and change. Her evocation of "footfall knowledge" is resonant.

When I look, I find many scholarly, critical, and artistic associations between forests and reading. But it is important to note that none of these are in my mind when I begin to notice the repetition of ideas of forest among the transcripts. The readers raise ideas about trees and woods unprompted. It is possible that the very process of mapping draws participants' attention to the way that any group of trees can serve as a landmark; but, whatever the cause, the overlap in their accounts of the fundamental scene of the forest is striking.

The Cultural Forest

Some years ago, I flew across Europe after crossing the Atlantic overnight from Edmonton. Having dozed fretfully on the long-haul flight, I fell heavily asleep as my second plane left Heathrow, and woke, disoriented, to find myself flying over an unknown territory. Below me, I saw a heavily forested region, dotted with small clearings containing even smaller villages.

So far, this is not a very interesting anecdote. What was noteworthy about the experience was my immediate reaction to the scenery below: a startled awareness that this landscape was utterly and profoundly familiar to me. I stared down, puzzled by the intimacy of my connection to this geography. It resembled no place where I have ever lived, yet I had a very powerful sense of knowing this land, even *owning* it in some intense way.

Eventually I made the connection: below me spread the landscape of folktales, the village, the clearing, the surrounding deep woods. In the moments just after waking, my relationship to this setting felt elemental. It was a highly (im)material experience. The geography below me was real and so was the catch in my breath when I first spotted it. But the intense sense of connection arose out of the immaterial impact of many, many stories.

The resonance of the forest in children's literature has been noticed by numerous commentators. Francis Spufford's memoir of childhood reading, for example, is eloquent on the significance of the forest to children's early literature:

> There was a forest at the beginning of fiction, too. This one spread forever … Up in its living roof birds flitted through greenness and bright air, but down between the trunks of the many trees there were shadows, there was dark. When you walked this forest your feet made rustling sounds, but the noises you made yourself were not the only noises, oh no … This was a populated wood. All wild creatures lived here, dangerous or benign according to their natures. And all the other travellers you had heard of were in the wood too, at this very moment: kings and knights, youngest sons and third daughters, simpletons and outlaws; a small girl whose bright hood flickered between the pine trees like a scarlet beacon, and a wolf moving on a different vector to intercept her at the cottage. (2002: 24)

This quote offers only a fraction of Spufford's evocation of the literary forest and its challenges to both characters and readers:

> You could no more avoid the encounters of the wood—all significant, all in their way tests—than you could cross it on a neat dependable path. It existed to cause changes, and it had no pattern you could take hold of in the hope of evading change. You never came out the same as when you went in. (2002: 25)

Spufford's forest confronts readers with tests and trials; Sara Maitland, exploring the connections between forests and fairytales, sees it as rather more emancipatory: "And forest became the pure place of primal innocence, where children could escape from their adults, get away from the order and discipline of straight roads and good governance, and revert to their animal origins" (2012: 5).

According to Maitland, fairytales show us how to look at forests (and vice versa, I suspect):

> I am suggesting that we walk in all the forests with a double map: a rich, carefully researched but still incomplete map of the history (economic, social and natural) of woodland that spans not just centuries but millennia; and a second map which relocates the forest in our imaginations and was drawn up when we were children from fairy stories and other tales. (2012: 49)

Umberto Eco, in his evocatively titled *Six Walks in the Fictional Woods*, relates forests to story itself, and uses this metaphor to emphasize the importance of the reader:

> Woods are a metaphor for the narrative text, not only for the text of fairy tales but for any narrative text …
>
> Even when there are no well-trodden paths in a wood, everyone can trace his or her own path, deciding to go to the left or to the right of a certain tree and making a choice at every tree encountered.
>
> In a narrative text, the reader is forced to make choices all the time. (1994: 6)

Zoë Jaques discusses a variety of possible relationships between humans and forests as represented in different texts either written for children or taken up by children. J. R. R. Tolkien, she suggests, belongs to an ancient "tradition of tree worship" (2011: 4). Philip Pullman's *His Dark Materials* places value on a complex ecosystem, particularly in *The Amber Spyglass*. Pullman, said Jaques, "goes much further than his predecessors in representing a heavily symbiotic nature, where trees are not simply for 'use', they are for nurturing" (2011: 6). But the Harry Potter series of J. K. Rowling "departs strongly from the seeming evolution of children's literary texts towards ecological awareness." Instead, "the narratives depict nature as a commodity which should be harvested for human need" (2011: 7). Competitive consumption of wands and broomsticks represents a more predatory approach to the forest.

The participants in this project who discuss the Forbidden Forest, however, did not see it as a source of consumables (which is not to deny the significance of the material economy described in the books themselves). The primal joys and fears described by Maitland and Spufford come closer to accounting for their attitudes to these and other fictional woods.

Border Country

The notion of the borderlands, like the idea of the fundamental particle, comes from another lecture by Philip Pullman. Although he does not use the expression, his account of the land along the borders seems to delineate an (im)material reading space:

> The land along the border is the space that opens up between the private mind of the reader and the book they're reading. It'll be different for every individual, because while parts of the borderland belong to the book, other parts belong only to that particular reader—to us: our own memories, the associations we have with this or that particular word or landscape, the aspects that resonate with our own individual temperament; so whereas many readers might be reading the same book no two of them will read it in exactly the same way. However, we can talk about our experiences of it, and compare our part of the borderland with other people's. (2015: 216)

How do we learn to bridge that gap from what we know about the world and about our own internal panoply of feelings and wishes *into* the world of a text? What do the participants and their maps tell us about how they learned to invest energy and agency into a set of written words? What forms of rehearsal appear to have been productive in terms of creating a reading space, furnished with many active details from a life space?

The forest seems to offer one kind of transition zone, a borderland. No doubt there are others, but this set of readers is certainly aware of the inherently liminal nature of the forest, both as an actual real-world site and as an image redolent of symbolic potential. A forest is a place where agency makes a genuine difference, so it offers all kinds of scope for plot development. It is perhaps not too much of a stretch to say that simply being among trees almost adds a bit of plot potential to the ordinary daily world. A forest is usually beautiful on its own terms; but it is alluring in many other ways. It can be mysterious: what (or whom) is it hiding? It can be treacherous: the unwary always run the risk of getting lost. Trees can be urban, as we see in many of the comments, but a group of trees almost by definition also has an edge of wildness to it. Almost any forest provides an object lesson in registering atmosphere.

In short, as these readers frequently acknowledge, trees make life more vivid, even if only for a moment. I think such vividness is at least a part of what makes a forest, real or extrapolated, such a successful transition zone into a textual world. In a world created by words, everything is significant, just by virtue of its presence in the story. A forest offers a chance to rehearse such a sense of significance. As Halia, Rahina, and Amani all demonstrate, you do not even need to enter the grove of trees to acquire a sense of its potential for proximity to many forms of narrative magic.

The setting of the forest matters in Harry Potter and in many other stories. It is striking how many participants describe extrapolating a full fictional forest out of life experience involving only a few trees. Readers create their forests out of the raw ingredients at their disposal, even when they only look at the trees and do not walk among them. The process almost seems like a mini case study of the formation of a certain kind of (im)materiality: the small stand of real trees merges with the intangible atmospheric forest scene of literary evocation and understanding.

In their different ways these readers create a conceptual forest out of two ingredients: the landscapes at their disposal and what they observe to be the demands of a text. It is clear from their assorted descriptions that they value the atmospheric charge of a forest. They also perceive a forest as a prime site for the expression of agency. Matt provides the fullest description, but the idea is implicit in other accounts. A forest offers opportunity for purposeful movement. These opportunities can be frustrated, as with Halia, Rahina, and Amani. Their existence in the imagined world can be makeshift (Halia) or largely symbolic (Riya). Yet the forest retains its potential for significance for very many of these readers.

My own startled recognition of the familiarity of the forested landscape beneath my airplane window was fueled by repeated childhood reading of European (and especially Germanic and Scandinavian) folk and fairy tales. The experts I quote in this chapter on the significance of the literary forest are all British or European, and the resonance of forested land, both historical and contemporary, is certainly powerful in North America as well. I am not knowledgeable enough to speak with authority about other places and cultures. It is impossible to make much of the international range of my little group of contributors since the numbers are so small; but it seems important to mention that not all the readers who specifically bring up the significance of the forest are rooted in European traditions (though much of their childhood reading was in English). Halia's first reading was in Arabic; other readers drew to varying degree on the traditions of Chinese literature. A different study might pursue the role of the forest in childhood reading as a colonial import for some of these readers, but this study cannot offer more than the question.

It is worth noting the goodness of fit between what these readers describe and Malpas's account of space being a necessary component of agency. In different ways, these readers create a mental space as an arena for mental movement. They draw on their own backgrounds to flesh out the setting but in evocative rather than static and specific ways. What they import is, to a very significant degree, a *feeling* of a space. That space in a reader's mind is both alive in the simple sense and lively in the active sense; *being in* that space entails *moving through* that space. And the space is populated by fictional beings, often frequently in movement. Halia's forest contains ravens drinking at a stream—and also unicorns. Matt, in his own memorable wording, makes room for "Ents and whatnot." Ying Yu provides fairies and also adventurous travelers. Riya sets the stage for the Famous Five. Lily calls up the spying Harriet and the two friends Jessie and Lesley. Rahina conjures a forest that is itself alive.

And maybe in that final sentence lies one clue to the appeal of the forest. Unlike many other scenes, the forest itself is alive and active; it has its own forms of agency, and shelters protagonists and antagonists alike. "The sense of secrets, silences, surprises, good and bad, is fundamental to forests and informs their literature," says Maitland (2012: 129). Later, she observes, "Even the most benign magic is not safe, cannot be safe, because it is unfamiliar, spooky, weird and eerie. The woods are chaotic and wild; life goes on unseen within them" (2012: 206). Something in that chaotic wildness clearly speaks to the urban readers of this study, inviting them, at some deep level, to acknowledge the potential for story on the edge of their daily lives. Whether they advance into the woods or shrink away or simply watch from a distance, they acknowledge that challenge (material or imagined), so close to their own doorsteps.

At the beginning of this chapter, I place the idea of the forest at the midpoint of Pullman's scale that measures "between the cosmic level and the quantum level" (2017: 194). This midpoint where "we live, with our bodies and our normal everyday consciousness" (2017: 194) is the human point where individual difference matters. Trees share this midpoint with humans; trees flourish in our everyday city world and carry with them some of the import of the wilderness. They offer a border country where human scale segues into something more cosmic and where daily life becomes an adventure. The participants in this project clearly recognize both the quotidian and the literary value of trees. One reader after another describes a process whereby a very modest life space is expanded by means of a few mental tricks into a highly resonant and powerful reading space. The text calls that space into being, and the readers respond with the raw materials at their disposal. The (im)materiality of the mix of actual trees and what these readers make of them is a very potent brew.

A Shared Fictional World

8

The Many Reading Spaces of Harry Potter

With its focus on reader-selected priorities, this book aims to provide at least a glimpse of what I call "reading in the wild." But despite my commitment to making a priority of individuality and diversity, there is one major point of convergence among nearly all the transcripts. The twelve participants were born during a brief span of years between March 1993 and July 1999. In other words, their collective youth took place throughout the time period in which the Harry Potter books were published (1997–2007) and the Harry Potter movies were released (2001–11). They were too young to have been the very first readers of Harry Potter; but they grew up during the era when the "Potter phenomenon" was at its height.

This timing is reflected in the transcripts. Only two participants (Halia and Liang) do not mention Harry Potter at all, which does not mean that they were unaware of the books or that they did not read them; they simply do not refer to them, and I do not ask. The other ten readers present a broad range of awareness of and response to J. K. Rowling's series. Knowledge of this story is clearly important to the cultural literacy of this generation, shared across the globe; participants speak of reading or watching Harry Potter in China, India, and Pakistan, as well as in the West. In Bartlett's terms, the filter of Rowling's textual universe is built into how they connect with and move around their own daily world. This allegiance to a phenomenon of their time is a generational marker, among other aspects. The international ubiquity of Harry Potter is a taken for granted feature of their childhoods in a number of countries. Harry Potter crossed borders with them when they moved and supplied a kind of currency for communicating in different surroundings.

Their generation finds ways of incorporating Harry Potter into their lives. As sociologist Antoine Hennion puts it, "Works 'make' the gaze that beholds them, and the gaze makes the works" (2005: 134). A paradigmatic account of this process is described in an article in the *Christian Science Monitor* about the impact of Rowling's series on child readers. Shayna Garlick introduces Marcus:

> Marcus credits the series for getting him interested in reading. He says his grandfather read him the first five books, but he wanted to read the sixth one himself. Since then, he loves to read medieval, fantasy, and science-fiction books,

he says. He also now likes the many books he reads for school—even though the majority aren't his favorite genres, he says. (2007)

Marcus is of same generation as the participants in this study, and, at the time of this article, is eagerly awaiting the publication of Book 7. He is planning to go straight to the final page before reading anything else, out of an acute need to discover whether Harry survives. The books have "made" a gaze very invested in the well-being of the character; the gaze of Marcus, and millions like him including participants in this study, have created a world where excitement about Harry is private and emotionally significant—and also a source of connection with other readers round the world. Harry Potter "made" Marcus a fantasy reader who says he now reads fifty books a year. In return, Marcus will "make" *Harry Potter and the Deathly Hallows* a reading experience that begins with the ending. This version of events, of course, is simplistic, but there is no question that the enormous and global community of interpreters was created by these stories at the same time as the experience of reading *within* this community created a particular kind of reading act. The allegiance becomes part of the reading and viewing, while being created through it. (After our interviews were long concluded, Rowling's published views on gender provided another opportunity to explore the impact of community, as many of her previously avid fans searched for ways of resisting transphobia *inside* the "Potterverse," because abandoning a lifetime of such allegiance was so complex and wrenching for them. Obviously, what one reader calls the "battle for the soul of Hogwarts" [Evans, 2020] between the books' author and their readers was not an issue in 2017 and 2018—but the light shed on the phenomenon of Harry Potter by this reversal is exceptionally intriguing, and worth mentioning in connection to issues of reader loyalty.)

Simone Murray helpfully locates Harry Potter in a framework that includes a "conception of the book as both text *and* object—one that is always embedded in fluid social, cultural, political and economic networks" (2021: 5). By consuming Harry Potter in the diverse ways they choose, the participants join these networks. Discussing music, Hennion says that (like books), "it is perpetually transformed by any contact with its public … It is a performance; it acts, engages, transforms, and is felt" (2005: 135). The importance of Harry Potter is definitely "felt" by the readers in this project (and differently felt by Potter fans after 2020); and it is performed diversely: through the material books, movies, websites, and more, and also via a more inchoate and immaterial sense of belonging to an important "club."

The Harry Potter saga fits well into the kind of virtual world described by Black, Alexander, and Korobkova in terms of transmedia:

> The concept of transmedia draws our focus not just to the media and technology but also to the ways in which consumers are afforded multiple points of contact and entry into a complex ecology of literate practices that often involve the translation, and even construction, of meaning across different systems of representation. These entry-points may be commercially produced … or developed by consumers … but all play a role in creating a multifaceted literate context in which the lifeworlds of consumers are intertwined with the storyworlds of producers. (2017: 4)

This "multifaceted literate context" makes it possible to observe a variety of forms of (im)materiality at work. In this study, I am looking at such (im)materiality from the point of view of the readers, but a fascinating study by Maria Sachiko Cecire (2019) places Rowling's books in their own (im)material frame. Cecire explores how much of the great British fantasy writing for children in the twentieth century (including the Harry Potter series in a second generation kind of connection) arose in relation to the University of Oxford curriculum for English studies and its strong focus on medieval writing. It is probably no coincidence that much of the filming of Hogwarts that followed the publication of the books took place at the University of Oxford. Thus, the rich immaterial world of the series is rooted in the concrete decisions and committee meetings that go to the formation of a curriculum, and then reexpressed in the material setting of Oxford's old and evocative buildings.

Cecire makes another perceptive point: "The Harry Potter universe's palimpsest-like existence just beneath the surface of everyday life lends itself to imaginary integration with the real world" (2019: 264). She suggests that this quality "opens up space for fan-driven revisions of the Wizarding World's racial and cultural norms" (2019: 264), but the participants in this study do not explicitly mention any such reworking. With the exception of Lily's default process of setting the stories in a Chinese landscape, these readers and viewers seem to have woven Harry Potter into the fabric of their own lives without resisting or reworking the elements that comprise that world. A literate connection of one form or another then feeds into their own relationship to a world in which international boundaries have many importantly mutable qualities.

That palimpsestic quality fuels the forms of reader/viewer responses to the series, collectively composing the kind of textual space that, as Catherine Butler comments in a different context, may become "a much larger and more multidimensional territory, where physical, affective, and cultural geographies are all in dynamic play" (2020: 229). The ubiquity of Harry Potter, its series format, the interaction between the publication of new book titles and the production of new films during the time these participants were young, the proliferation of fan and commercial outputs—all these ingredients and more contribute to the idea of Harry Potter as continuously in motion throughout the childhood of these consumers of the franchise. For these enthusiasts, reading one book, watching one movie achieved a kind of *after* but also served as a *before* to the next encounter. And for some participants, a kind of ongoing *during* seeped in and out of actual textual encounters to inflect daily life in a variety of ways. When I start exploring the large number of responses to various forms of Harry Potter, I think of the series as a kind of focal point, but working with the maps and interviews makes me realize that this concept is far too static for the dynamic imaginative exercises that comprise this expansive fiction.

I did not enter this project paying any particular attention to Harry Potter and its many manifestations, so, in the interviews, I do not pursue the topic when it simply arises in passing. In several cases, participants make thoughtful observations about their experience with this saga, and I do follow up on such comments. This chapter reports on both kinds of response.

Most of my previous research with readers has involved presenting participants with a common text, the role played by Harry Potter in this chapter. In this project, however, as was the case with the broader theme of the forest, all reference to the series is initiated by participants themselves and is grounded in their own individual approaches to a global phenomenon. For this reason, it seems plausible that a deeper exploration of their divergent responses to the Potter series may shed light on some aspects of the significance of such variation. In effect, Harry Potter is the prism (a prism in constant motion) and the responses outlined here represent the scattered and flickering light. The lifeworlds of these participants are indeed intertwined with the story world of Harry Potter, as Black, Alexander, and Korobkova suggested, and in very diverse ways.

The Readers

Ying Yu encountered Harry Potter through movies alone. She does not make any reference to wanting or trying to read any of the books. Suleman's encounters with the series were largely film-based, but he did once try the book experience as a child. He says,

> I actually loved the movie, but I was in the library when I saw its book. I guess it was *Chamber of Secrets*. I took it out. It was so big. And when I started reading it, so much text, and I said, "No, I can't read it." I was actually scared of text books [by which he means books containing words only].

Eventually he discovered that there was no film version of *Harry Potter and the Cursed Child*, and he felt obliged to read it to complete his knowledge of the story. He described the play script as "the thickest book I ever read." But by then, he said, his English was good enough and "I had enough context in my mind."

Material publishing conditions are reflected in three transcripts. Amy read six of the books in paperback; she bought the seventh as soon as it was released, so was forced to read a hardback, which she found a distraction. Both Suleman and Riya (each from South Asia) mention issues related to reading pirated versions. Suleman assumes that most Pakistanis cannot afford the very expensive originals and that most of what anyone reads would be pirated. Riya speaks hypothetically. We are discussing her ability to "see" characters and I ask her what she would have done if there was a contradiction in the description between one book and another. She would take such confusion very seriously, she says, and, as a child in India, she would have asked her mother. Her mother would have offered suggestions, including, "Maybe you got a fake copy or something." Such alertness to provenance is less prevalent in the West, especially in relation to books, which are generally deemed authoritative.

Most of the diverse ways that Harry Potter features in the lives of these participants are not so culturally and economically specific. Many participants (not all) make use of life experience to animate the stories and settings in their minds, but the intimacy and individuality of that connection is a common thread.

Lily, for example, initially encountered the books while she was still living in China. Her experience fed into the setting in particular, and that influence lingered. "Harry

Potter too was set in a more Chinese landscape until I moved here, and then I don't think it ever changed; Harry Potter would always be the Chinese landscape." Her mother read her some of the adventures of Sherlock Holmes before they left China, and those stories, like Rowling's books, retained their Chinese setting in Lily's mind. In contrast, for books she read after her arrival in Canada, her mental settings were Western, frequently related to her daily walks through downtown Scarborough. Sounding somewhat surprised, however, she observes that something had started to shift when she recently read *Harry Potter and the Cursed Child*. "I think I pictured my Edmonton townhouse." Maybe this alteration reflects more time in Canada, a different format, an extended time lapse between books, or the fact that *Cursed Child* deals with new characters, thus breaking the spell of continuity. Perhaps all these factors are at work.

Laura read only some of the Harry Potter books but she liked them, though, in general, "I'm not that into books." Her approach is to watch the movie first, and in many cases, she actively checks the book against the movie as she reads. "In a way I was imagining how the actor was going, how they were acting in that scene and how that relates with the book." The book often serves as a form of mnemonic for the film; "I kinda disregard the text in a way, I'm just thinking of the movie." But not all images in her reading come straight from the screen; some are imported from her daily life: "Going to the magical school, I did kind of relate that with my memories as well," tying it in to her own daily travels to school in China.

Amy, in contrast to Laura, attempts very assiduously to avoid the movie until after she has read the book. She finds importing movie visuals into her reading to be simultaneously irresistible and annoying. She tried extremely hard to avoid all the Harry Potter movies until she had read all the books, but waiting for the seventh title to be published finally defeated her. "So I actually caved. The seventh book hadn't come out yet, but I watched the first movie before the seventh book came out, which was a mistake because I didn't like knowing, particularly Hermione, I was really mad about Hermione." Amy was not troubled about being provided with a concrete and specific setting ("the scenes, who cares?") once she had seen the movie, but she was distressed to lose her internal focus on the characters.

> It was just really frustrating to not be—I don't know, in the body of that person. It was more like now I just have to watch her do everything ... And it was harder to read ... Because it was—I don't know, I wasn't as engaged. I was like, this isn't happening to me anymore, and that's what I kind of like out of reading, is that I kind of live someone else's life for a few minutes at least. But it wasn't like that after, because I could *see* her character.

Amy's reiterated point is that as a reader she is effectively on the inside of a character such as Hermione, participating in the Harry Potter story world. The film irrevocably drags her to the outside, and obliges her to watch Hermione from the perspective of an external spectator. Once she made the mistake of watching one of the films, she found that even the books she had already read were somehow changed. The seventh book, which she read for the first time after having had film visuals inserted into her mind, remains "an outcast."

Rahina shares some of Amy's reservations about movies, drawing on very similar terms to describe her preference for reading. "I like characters when they're described on paper. I don't like it when I can actually see them. When you can see a character, it's just like any other human being on the streets, like whatever, or your friend. When they're described, they're a set of characteristics that emotionally I connect to." Rahina read the Harry Potter books very young, as they were released, and calls the series "a gemstone of my childhood," but, unlike Lily, she provided no background mental landscape whatever. Because, like Amy, she enjoys connecting to characters in an internal way, she is not interested in visualizing them or their setting.

> People's faces do not map onto what they're like. Like if I say the character of Harry Potter, Daniel Radcliffe, and you gave me no description of him at all, I would not know—he'd just be like average white guy to me ... He would not be remarkable at all. But because I know this guy is an extremely resilient, courageous, and often looked-up-to character, he will forever be associated with that face. Faces are limiting.

Amani read a lot of Harry Potter and seems to have registered flashes of local recognition through particular details. Her map, drawing on city parks, cites a line from *Harry Potter and the Order of the Phoenix*: "He sunk onto the only [swing] that Dudley and his friends had not yet managed to break." In the interview, she comments, "I thought that was funny because in Abbotsfield Park, they always had broken swings. Those hood rats would always swing them off. [Laughing] Yeah, so that was close, that reminded me of the swings." Similarly, Amani animates her vision of Magnolia Road with a local image: "How Magnolia Road was full of large square houses, perfectly manicured lawns, very clean cars. I think that is what Kirkness was for me because out of the neighbourhoods I've lived in, I think that was most well maintained."

Riya also read Harry Potter intensively, valuing accuracy and consistency in her settings. She began with discrete scenes and adjusted their relationship with each other as necessary, a process she found easier before she watched the movies and had to compromise with a different vision. "I imagine, when they say Hogwarts is here and Hogsmead is here and the forest is here, I sort of imagine them as three different entities almost, and I put them together at random ... And then when I read something in the book later that contradicts that, then I'll put them somewhere else if I really, really have to." Even as she makes adjustments, Riya is clear that she is moving discrete scenes that do not themselves necessarily change very much. She makes this mental investment in getting it right because, "especially if it's a series, the same scenery is gonna happen again so I need to make sure it's right."

Riya also places a high priority on reading carefully enough to get characters and faces correct,

> but only if they describe the face and describe the person. Otherwise it's pretty generic. Reading Harry Potter, they all had faces because J. K. Rowling described their faces and described their features. So, Hermione had big front teeth, and bushy hair and brown eyes, or something like that, so that was her face. Same

Figure 8.1 Roman's image of the cycle path between the pylons—the transition zone to the ravine.

with all the other characters. I think she did a really good job of describing each character's major features. But if they don't and I'm reading a book, then it's just pretty generic.

Roman pictures faces and hears voices for his characters; he draws on life experience to add texture to his reading. His map involves black and white analogue photographs of a ravine near his house (Figure 8.1), and images from the ravine fed his reading: "When I read, I see images. I don't see words. So, it's like a film in my head, and I guess some of the setting, or the context for the stuff that's going on, I'd see pictures of this ravine." Like Riya, he sees discrete scenes: "I have a hard time with spatial areas. I'll have the book leading me through, and then I have to go back and check the map at the front, 'cause I don't know where I am. But I know what it looks like."

Although his orientation is visual, Roman seems invested in qualities of experience as well as in pictorial details of setting. He provides an image that he connects to reading Harry Potter.

It is worth supplying some detail of how Roman describes the relationship between this path to the ravine and the world of Harry Potter.

Roman: These giant power lines that run through the whole neighborhood, I relate a lot to the Harry Potter series because the ravine was so different from my neighborhood. It was like a magical place to go, where you see stuff that's not normally in your neighbourhoods. And the trail that we took all the time was this giant greenway to go all the way to the ravine. And it was that play of urban and ravine, kind of.

Margaret: And was there a moment of threshold where you stepped into the ravine or was it gradual?

Roman:	This helped the separation. You're going on a journey somewhere so I guess the way I related it when I was reflecting on all these images and stuff was with the train that goes to Hogwarts. It was like, you're going on that trail to go to the ravine.
Margaret:	So, you're in the in-between zone?
Roman:	Yeah, the in-between zone. Before your adventure into the ravine.
Margaret:	Right, so it's almost like a ceremony of walking through the pylons.
Roman:	Yeah, a little ritual you gotta do before you go and have fun and stuff. So yeah, leaving your normal life to go to the other life, the experience that ties into the books.
Margaret:	Now do you think, which came first, the ravine or the reading? Do you think you would have thought of this particular ordinary-looking walk as a threshold experience without all the reading that you did? Or would it have been—?
Roman:	Yes.
Margaret:	It would have been magical in its own right?
Roman:	Yeah, because I'm pretty passionate about nature and going into those environments and exploring and stuff. So, without reading I still had my pretty vivid imagination to, to draw from. Yeah, I think it was a magical experience regardless.
Margaret:	So, it was not so much fiction lending magic to this experience, but this experience grounding the magic in the fiction.
Roman:	Yeah.
Margaret:	Right. I don't want to put words into your mouth but I just want to be clear that I've got it.
Roman:	That's better put than I said, yeah.

Roman played fiction-based games with his friends, choosing, for example, to play *Pirates of the Caribbean* in the sand around the swings for greater verisimilitude to the beaches of that story. But throughout his youth, the ravine existed in a different category; he experienced it very fully and evoked that experience to supply feelings and atmosphere to his subsequent reading.

The most committed reader of Harry Potter is undoubtedly Matt. He is eloquent on the series' importance in his life and is able to articulate many details of his reading process.

Growing with Harry Potter: Matt

Matt is a 23-year-old student of industrial design when we meet. He grew up in a dormitory town on the edge of Edmonton with one older sister; the family background is Dutch. Of all the participants, Matt speaks least about his life and most about his reading. His map is the most oriented to a fictional landscape: the world of Hogwarts and its surroundings. It was a deliberate decision; he says, "I thought about using— because I live fairly close to the school and I could have probably drawn a map to the school and a couple iconic areas there that related to books I was reading. But for me, a lot of it is grounded in these fantasy worlds."

Matt is very interested in music, and takes pride in recommending material his friends will enjoy. He reads regularly, despite other demands on his time. He says his taste for fantasy has waned somewhat; he reads graphic novels and, at his girlfriend's behest, is giving F. Scott Fitzgerald a try. He describes the kind of trail through potential reading material that many readers will recognize:

> I recently learned that Leonard Cohen published a couple of his books before he started his career in music. And I read some of his poetry, so I'm pretty intrigued by him, and I kind of want to read some of the stories that he made because I think a lot of it is set in Canada, and a lot of it is Canadian literature, which would be something I really have never gotten into. So, I might pick those up and read them pretty soon, but—yeah, I mean, it's just making time for it. Usually in the summer I have more time to read, but, come school, it's pretty much—

He is also open to looking at poetry:

> I do have a couple books of just poetry. One of the books they made me get in university was the *Harbrace Anthology of Poetry*. And that one, I've kind of flipped back to, a couple of times, to—I don't know, sometimes I like inspiration. I play music in my spare time. I'm not a songwriter or anything like that, but I do appreciate the construction of songs and the construction of poems and the metaphors and the figures of speech that they can use in them. I really appreciate that. So I think poetry's really interesting because of that.

Talking about the book he is currently reading, Fitzgerald's *Tender Is the Night*, Matt comments on the contrast between fiction based in the known world and fantasy.

> A lot of what places he's describing are real places, so he doesn't put a lot of description into it. So, it relies a lot of just understanding the landscape and, if you've never really been there, then you're kind of excluded from it in a certain sense. If you don't really know the Champs-Élysées in Paris, you've got no frame of reference. And so, that's why it's kind of refreshing to go back and read some more fantasy novels and have a bit more appreciation of just the overall importance they put onto those landscapes, and ensuring that the readers understand what they are because there is no frame of reference for it.

I ask if he would ever put down the book and go look at, say, the Champs-Élysées on Google Earth. "Probably not," says Matt, "but I've been to Paris and I've been to southern France, so I have those frames of reference to think of it." In any case, he adds, looking up the setting is "kind of cheating." Picturing the setting "is not really the point, the point of reading a book is to have that response to it." It is fair game, however, to go back to the story map, if it exists, in order to establish where one setting lies in relation to another.

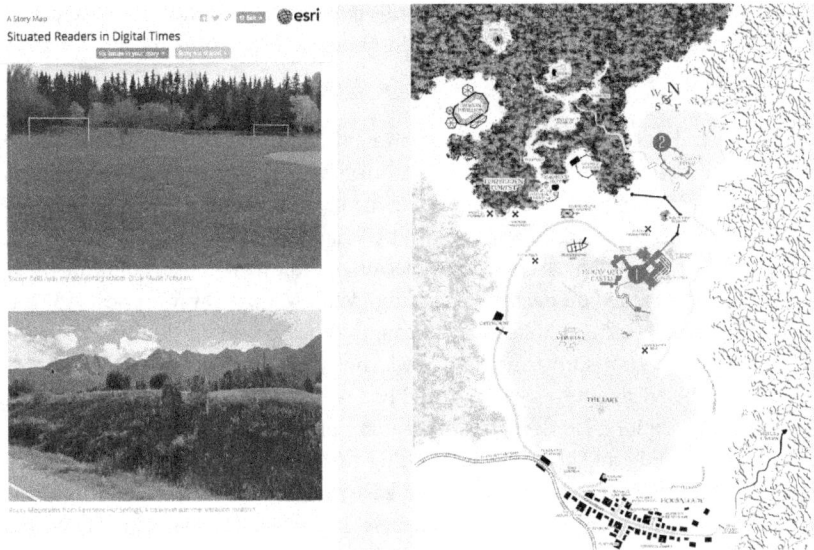

Figure 8.2 Matt's map including images of the school soccer pitch and the Rocky Mountains, both of which he incorporated into his mental setting. Hogwarts © J. K. Rowling (original map Mize and Elder n.d.).

To develop his Harry Potter site for this project, Matt researched potential online maps to suit his purpose; he was determined that the mapmakers' perspective on this world should be accurate according to his own reading of the books. Once he settled on a map (Figure 8.2), he highlighted segments indicating movement through the environment, and augmented this movement with photographs and links relating to his own life.

Perhaps not surprisingly, Matt's account of reading Harry Potter is also, by far, the fullest. Drawing on his childhood exposure to the world, he developed a repertoire of mental scenery to enhance his reading experience. He retrofitted settings as necessary; initially he did not take in that there were mountains in the background, but once Rowling mentioned them, he took pains to add them to his mental stage.

Matt's mother read him the first book when he was very young, and he feels he grew as a reader as he followed Harry into ever more complex situations. He focused on settings:

> But I think the most important parts when I first got familiarized with the books and with Hogwarts, as much as there was scenes inside, the scenes outside were the ones that gravitate to me more. So, they take the boats across the lake and then they play Quidditch, or go into the Forbidden Forest. It builds a better understanding rather than just a castle. And that's why I think the first two books are fairly juvenile because they do focus a lot on the castle and it's not until the third book that you really see them step out and can tell J. K. Rowling was probably feeling very contained by being in that castle. And by stepping out of it, and

including stories coming from other worlds coming towards them, or characters running off and doing their own thing it just built up the world so much more and it had such a better description.

Like several of the others, Matt is ambivalent about the movies. The first movie he saw "confirmed some things and it kind of made me rethink a lot of some stuff I was reading." Nevertheless, "It's almost detrimental to my understanding of the world because if I didn't watch those movies, or if they had more of a consistent visual of the movies, I think it would have been better, because if I didn't watch any of those movies I would have just relied on my understanding." With Matt, it always appears to be the setting that takes priority; unlike Riya, for example, he says very little about characters' faces. It is perhaps not surprising that he was not very interested in the Harry Potter video games he tried, but he says he would be intrigued by a digital game offering an open world to explore. He describes his reading processes as "definitely like concept work, it's imagining and thinking of building this landscape within your head." He builds this landscape on a scene-by-scene basis, rather than holistically, and has to work hard to locate individual settings correctly in relation to each other. He provides a helpful metaphor: "I think each individual icon I had a fairly good idea, but the relationship where they were with each other, I kind of had to look for … I would see like a sitcom where they have prepared rooms, compared to a movie." The idea of the sitcom setting, detailed but static, lacking organic connections to other equally fixed scenes in the program, provides a useful shorthand for describing a common response.

Matt played pretend Harry Potter games with his friends, running with hands between his legs to hold an imaginary broomstick for Quidditch matches, for example. But he is clear that for him, the priority was words first.

> I think as far as understanding the literature, playing didn't really enhance—it definitely was part of it, but I feel like the world of Harry Potter and imaging that gave me a better understanding of the novels I was reading, rather than playing with my friends. I got more out of imagining these worlds than I did playing with other friends.

Having invested such efforts in building a world to provide scope for the agency of Harry Potter, Matt is happy to transfer details to other worlds if they seem relevant. "Yeah, I've got a castle in my mind that I could use instead of kind of having to build it up and it made novels a lot easier to read because it's kind of like you're jumping in it with one foot already in. And it made reading a lot more fun for me." He will not necessarily transfer the whole castle to a new book if all he needs is a Grand Hall; he is happy to be selective and take simply features he has already worked out in his head. The Harry Potter books are important to him because they were (and remain) the site of much of his original world-building. "It wasn't being borrowed from another place or printed from another place, it was very much the foundation of my understanding of imaginary spaces."

I quote Matt at such length because he articulates the connections between the characters' world and the reader's world in such intriguing ways. Even so, I necessarily omit much of his commentary about his encounters with Harry Potter. The books were clearly formative in his development as a reader, and it is perhaps not surprising that his is the most explicitly fiction-oriented map of the twelve. Elsewhere, I describe in more detail the contrast between Roman and Matt, the two participants whose demographic details match most closely out of all the participants, yet two readers who approach the challenge of bringing a world to imaginary life in very different ways (Mackey, 2019a, 2019b).

The Portals

The Harry Potter stories represent a quintessential example of what Murray describes as "the deep enmeshment of print with other media, whether film, radio, television or the internet ... the deeply intertwined relationships between books and other media, and the legal, commercial and consumptive practices that sustain these" (2021: 2). Black, Alexander, and Korobkova refer to a contemporary form of "transmedia ecology" in which people's "literate engagement is distributed across time, space, media platform, mode of representation, and micro (e.g. at-home gameplay, conversations with friends and family) and macro (e.g. mass media) contexts of use" (2017: 2). I did not plan to interview participants about Harry Potter in particular, nor, when participants mentioned the topic themselves, did I pursue how many entry points to this story world they accessed. Any mention of how the story of Harry Potter is distributed across their personal mediascapes, therefore, comes directly from their own observation of its place in their lives. We have already seen how participants move in different ways between the world of the books and the world of the movies, and some of them refer to playing Harry Potter games with their friends. Amy comments on the different readerly invitation proffered by a hardback as opposed to a paperback edition, and Riya and Suleman make observations on the authoritativeness of their copy. But there are other references, often made in passing, that demonstrate the ubiquity of Harry Potter's multimodal manifestations in their lives.

Rahina is the only participant who refers to writing her own short fiction and posting it on Tumblr under a pseudonym. (Halia posted fan art, but she talks less about writing and she does not mention Harry Potter.) From Rahina's description of this writing, it is not exactly fan fiction, but she draws on a particular repertoire of British writers, including Rowling, to help her establish the tone of her writing: "They're all British, so that helps me not only speak the way they do accent-wise, but also the expressions they use; they sound very uppity and queen-like, and I like it."

Rahina also makes the most sweeping observation about Harry Potter's place in contemporary culture: "It's everyone, it's ubiquitous. In movies, TV shows, references outside of it. Merchandise sold all over. You go online, people are still talking about fandoms. You cannot get enough of that."

Riya and I hold an extended conversation about her need to build accurate images from descriptions of characters, and I ask her what she would do in the face of a discrepancy—say Hermione had brown eyes in one book and green eyes in another book. Riya would be very disturbed by such an error. As a child, she would have asked her mother to explain it, but, at the time of the interview, she would take her concern to the internet and go straight to the author. "Right now, I would tweet at her or something." She expands on this theme very readily.

> I'd go online and see if there's already a conversation happening about that. So if someone else has already noticed it, and it's a common discussion, people are talking about it, then okay, other people have noticed it, this is a thing, the book writer or whatever have probably already noticed too, so I'm fine with that. If there's nothing about this and this is an obvious glaring error, and it's something like Harry Potter which, when I was reading it I was super invested in, I would reach out to J. K. Rowling herself or something like that. I don't think I'd engage in a discussion about it with other people.

Matt has played a number of Harry Potter video games, though he found them stilted and unappealing in general. He has also sampled the pleasures of Pottermore, the official site now called Wizarding World (https://www.wizardingworld.com/news/discover-your-hogwarts-house-on-wizarding-world). On at least one occasion, he went online to the site with a group of friends, who enjoyed taking the test for which house they belonged to and generally reminiscing about the books. Indeed, he considers that the market for Pottermore is more likely to be adults.

> I think it's more of something that is used as a supplement of reading the books. It's not used by itself. But I think it's successful because I guess I had fun with my friends using it. I don't know if I would have as much fun using it by myself because it's kind of the idea of like, oh, I got into Hufflepuff, oh, I got into Slytherin. I got into Hufflepuff, so I was a little bummed out. For whatever reason I thought I was going to get into Slytherin.

Matt is also the only participant who mentions acquiring a piece of merchandise: a Gryffindor mug. He makes an illuminating comparison: "I do think there's reasons people buy it; it's the same thing with buying a hockey jersey. It does nothing more to your enjoyment of watching the game whether you're watching in a hockey jersey or not, but people still buy it and buy into it ... I think it just speaks to their commitment to the world, I guess."

I suspect that I would have retrieved more information about diverse access to the Harry Potter story world if I had gone to the interviews with a specific question on this topic. Even so, there are passing references to books, movies, video games, merchandise, fan fiction, the Pottermore website, online discussion sites where questions of content and interpretation may be raised, and the option to tweet a question to J. K. Rowling directly. And, of course, we should acknowledge Rahina's comment about "references outside of it"; Harry Potter is a cultural counter with a recognizable exchange value in daily conversation.

And yet, although I am certain that, if I had organized a group discussion involving the twelve participants, the subject of Harry Potter would have been comfortably familiar to all of them, the variation and individuality in their responses remains striking. The text is constant but the reactions are distinctive.

The seven books of the Harry Potter sequence, the play script sequel, the eight movies, and a host of media support systems offer an invitation to open a broad reading space that all the participants in this project would probably recognize, in all its (im)material variety. But even the limited insights offered by individual readers and viewers suggest that the personal reading spaces are distinctive in both their possibilities and their limitations.

Ying Yu's space is occupied purely by the images of the films; she has not read any of the books. Suleman's space is also largely film oriented but includes two efforts at reading Rowling's books. One was a failure (*Harry Potter and the Chamber of Secrets*); it was too big and it frightened him. The other (*Harry Potter and the Cursed Child*) was a success, and represented a personal reading triumph for Suleman. When Laura read some of the Harry Potter books, her reading space was dominated by images from the film; she specifically mentions checking the book against the movie as she read.

Amy's reading space usually provides little more than blanks in terms of setting, and when she finally watched a Harry Potter film before the publication of the final book in the series, she found the visual information very invasive and destructive. Her reading space also includes at least some tacit awareness of what she is holding in her hand, and reading the hardback also disrupted her usual automaticity. Similarly to Amy, Rahina's reading space is explicitly devoid of imagery; at one point she says that the events of a book might as well take place against a white wall for all the attention she pays to setting. She also finds particular faces "limiting" and, like Amy, explores her reading space from the perspective of being inside a character.

Amani, on the other hand, provides herself with a setting, sometimes flashed through with details of local scenery. Lily's Harry Potter reading space also features elements of local setting, only in her case that background was Chinese, even when she read the books in Canada. Only the play script (*Harry Potter and the Cursed Child*) admits any local color specific to her current home. Liang does not mention Harry Potter, but she observes that her default setting for anything she does read now is Canadian. Halia also does not make reference to Harry Potter, but she specifies her background setting according to the language in which she reads the book, and some of her Canadian backgrounds come across as hybrids, sketchily composed in her mind on a basis of satisficing the need to have some kind of representative scenery in the background.

The reading spaces of Roman, Matt and Riya all include visual details of setting. Riya and Matt specifically mention attending carefully to the written description; Roman "know[s] what it looks like," but he is less explicit about how carefully he reads all the details before assembling his mental image. In each case, these readers also observe that they tend to build up ideas of the setting on a scene-by-scene basis and pay considerably less attention to the relationship between one backdrop and another, unless the book requires them to attend to the general layout of the territory.

In this cross section of personal reactions, we can see how readers mix available information (both from the book and from their own experience) with personal reading priorities in different ratios. Rahina and Matt could undoubtedly discuss many elements of Harry Potter to good effect, but Rahina's blank background and Matt's care and delight in building an accurate story world represent very different experiences.

There is not really enough information in the transcripts to discuss a reverse phenomenon: the ways that the "palimpsestic" Harry Potter world infuses the life spaces of the participants. Matt played Quidditch with his friends but Roman robustly blocked any fictional component from his liminal path into the ravine. Rahina calls Harry Potter "a gemstone of her childhood," but does not elaborate. Nevertheless, the set of transcripts reflects the ubiquity of the Harry Potter universe in ways that indicate I would be remiss if I did not at least raise the question: to what extent, if any, is the material world of some or all of these child readers of Harry Potter imbued with its fictional magic? To what degree may the life spaces of some of them incorporate a fictional overlay imported from the reading or viewing space they have created with and for this significant story? At a minimum, it seems fair to assume that Harry Potter serves a role as cultural currency, inflecting their interactions with other members of their own generation. They assume that "everybody" has read these books and/or seen these movies, and so a connection created in the reading space is felt in the life space.

As it happens, my participant pool contains no reader who ever lived in Britain and could thus bring a relevant repertoire of the ordinary daily culture in which the Harry Potter books are set. The contrast might have offered some interesting perspectives, but the data presented here suggest that accurate and detailed quotidian background is not essential. What is striking about many of these responses to the series is the emphasis on what, for brevity's sake, I will temporarily label as atmosphere. Roman and Amani describe experiences of liminality that they bring to the shift to the magic world of Hogwarts. Matt and Amani refer to the kinds of adventures enabled by the atmosphere of the Forbidden Forest. Amy and Rahina evoke the implicit pleasures of inhabiting somebody else's point of view. Lily discusses the appeal of a hybrid setting composed of ingredients from both the book and her earliest childhood experiences.

Can we reframe these experiences in terms of movement, of different kinds of *stepping into* (Langer, 1989: 7)? The notion of the liminal space (the entrance to the ravine or the park in the river valley, the train to Hogwarts) makes a ceremony of that step. Stepping into the Forbidden Forest activates certain kinds of challenges and demands in a reader's mind. Stepping into the interiority of Hermione's perspective entails an active commitment to the fiction of a character. Even Lily's account of setting Harry Potter in a Chinese landscape seems to me to involve a mix of stepping into the story and stepping back into her own early childhood. All these readers create a space for the characters to move in, working with the raw materials of their own lives and the "cooked" materials (so to speak) of the words on the page. With this blending, their efforts provide an arena for their readerly selves to foment energy in the static and abstract words of the story and bring them to life in the mind. Yet, as Riya, Matt, and Roman make clear, the imagined landscape is also artificial, in that it can be limited to set-piece singularities on the "sitcom" model. They do not necessarily feel a need to establish how the scenes relate to each other until the story actively calls for such knowledge.

The Harry Potter lens permits us to compare readerly experiences to a greater extent than is possible with some other elements of this study. The points of similarity are not universal, but they are certainly striking. The points of individual variation are equally illuminating. In the next chapter, I investigate that diversity in greater detail.

Psychological Spaces

Interior Worlds

9

Diversity Inside and Out

This group of readers is manifestly diverse in many ways that are readily apparent on the most perfunctory inquiry. Much of this book so far has addressed differences in their life experiences as these pertain to their literacies (and, to a lesser extent, vice versa). In this chapter, I look more intently at some kinds of differences that are not apparent to the eye.

Much of what happens with reading, especially silent reading, occurs invisibly. Give any two readers the same piece of writing and it is striking "how swiftly and casually readers' experience of these sentences and the entire episode typically diverge" (Gerrig, 2011: 88). We largely take for granted that interpretation is an individual exercise; the invisible divergence of textual experience that Gerrig describes is part of a contemporary working schema of reading.

Emily Fox describes a different kind of reader variation, diverse manifestations of affect. What kinds of emotional response do readers expect and achieve with particular texts?

> Individual readers can differ in the level or intensity of affect they tend to experience, and in the type or valence of the affect evoked by what is encountered in a given reading experience; they can also differ in their control over their own affective or emotional response. They can differ as well in the typical affect with which they approach both reading in general, and different types of reading experiences. They can differ in their preferences, attitudes, interests, and beliefs. A final important type of individual difference between readers that also needs to be considered here is that readers can differ in *how* affect and cognition are related for them, and in their ability to control or regulate that connection. (2020: 181)

The strength of affective responses is not a territory I specifically explore in this project, and I cite it here simply as another example of the complexity of the private world of reading. I do, however, question participants about some invisible aspects of their reading experience.

Most of this discussion looks at routes to understanding the concealed processes taking place in our minds, utilizing two major routes to inquire about that interiority: applying brain science to complex questions of reading behaviors and actually asking readers to talk about them. Much exciting contemporary research into reading processes is scientific, producing statistical insights into eye movements, brain processes, and the like. I read this literature as a disciplinary outsider and I certainly appreciate the perceptions newly offered to us. At the same time, I continue to value the simple activity of talking in depth with readers, of gaining their perspectives on what happens as they read, of finding prompts that help them to refine and articulate their own knowledge of what they do with print.

An interesting parallel I discover in the course of researching this project provides reinforcement for this doubled approach. Mary Leonhardt is an English teacher with a passion for connecting school children with books. In the course of talking with many readers and reading many books, she discerns a helpful pattern, observing that there seem to be

> two basic kinds of action. There is interpersonal action, which usually involves solving personal problems, and learning about life. Then there is good versus evil action, which usually involves fighting something or someone outside an immediate circle of friends and family—such as wars, monsters, killers. This kind of action is adventure-type action rather than interpersonal action. Kids, and maybe adults, seem to have a lasting preference for one of these two types of action. (1996: 112)

Books, she goes on to say, can be roughly divided into three categories: those that feature interpersonal relationships, those that feature action and adventure, and those that offer a mix of both. This observation has implications for both applied practice and basic research. Certainly, the vital work of advising readers about what they might enjoy reading next is assisted by a practical opening question: do you prefer books about action and adventure, or do you prefer books about relationships? Likewise, our theoretical understanding of how reading works is also enhanced by reports of close observations of readers in the field.

Almost twenty years after Leonhardt published her book, an fMRI study confirms the pattern she observed back in the 1990s. Measuring neural activation while people listen to excerpts from literary stories, Nijhof and Willems discover a divergence between mentalizing and motor simulation. They explain the distinction clearly. "First, *sensorimotor simulation* is evidenced by activation of motor and visual cortices when people comprehend language related to actions and scenery. The second component relates to our ability to understand thoughts, intentions and beliefs of others, sometimes called *mentalizing*" (2015: 2). Nijhof and Willems find a negative correlation between a preference for mentalizing and a preference for sensorimotor response in the brain scans of their participants. They say,

> This suggests that there is a gradient among people in the way they engage with a narrative. Some rely mostly on mentalizing, others rely more on (sensori)-motor simulation, and yet others rely on both ... Some people are moved into a fiction story by mainly focusing on the thoughts and beliefs of others, whereas others

pay more (implicit) attention to more concrete events such as action descriptions. (2015: 10)

To see Leonhardt's qualitative observations confirmed by the technological and statistical approach of brain science is intriguing. Nijhof and Willem's assessment that there is a continuum accords with my own experience in research, in teaching, and in working with readers directly (Mackey, forthcoming).

As neuroimaging develops subtler interpretive powers, and as researchers are able to pose more imaginative questions as they collect brain measurement data, it is possible we will see more of the kind of overlap that is apparent between Leonhardt's careful attention to what readers say and Nijhof and Willems' scientific tallies. If nothing else, this confluence of observations is a reminder that reading researchers need to work hard at talking to each other across the technological and disciplinary boundaries.

To an ever-increasing extent, both neurotechnology and personal interview data highlight the issue of diversity among readers. The participants in this project differ from each other in a variety of ways: cultural, ethnic, disciplinary. They also diverge in more invisible and implicit ways; how they describe what goes on in their heads as they read also provides a very diverse set of portraits of reading processes at work. In this chapter, I look at how their self-perceptions of such invisible attributes may illuminate our growing understanding of the implications of scientific findings.

Varieties of Visualization—and the Nonvisualizers

"The felt experience of thinking varies greatly from one individual to another, and each head houses a distinct mental world," says Laura Otis (2015: 505). As with thinking, it seems the felt experience of reading is highly variable. In this section, I present the observations of these readers about their preferences for visualizing or not, and then explore some scientific findings that offer correlate accounts of readerly variation. I begin with a summary table and then use its six headings to group common responses and highlight the outliers.

Table 9.1 offers a basic overview of participants' claims about the kinds of mental imagery they produce. The categories are coarse rather than granular, but the overall impact of the table lies in its visual presentation of cognitive diversity. In most cases, participants are responding to an explicit question about if or what they "see" when they read. It is clear that many of them had never thought about this topic before, but they are all able to answer readily and the variations they articulate appear in the distribution across this table.

Specific Visuals

Seeing mental images as you read is taken as a relatively commonplace event, but even those participants who take this facility for granted offer a varied range of experience. Some describe a capacity to shift visual perspectives within the world of a single text. Some offer examples of hybrid image-making on the fly and others describe a process

Table 9.1 Habits of Visual Imagery as Described by Participants

	specific visuals	transient visuals	"make-do" visuals	culturally specific images	transfer from film/TV/other books	"just know"
Amani	x	x			x	
Amy					x	x
Halia	x		x	x		
Laura					x	x
Liang	x			x	x	
Lily	x			x		
Matt	x					
Rahina						x
Riya	x		x	x		
Roman	x					
Suleman	x		x	x	x	
Ying Yu		x		x	x	

of careful world-building that they plan to retain through further reading (more books in a series, for example). Some provide accounts of a relatively static world where the setting of any particular scene is detailed and clear, but the spatial relationship between one scene and another is vague and unimportant. Some read almost entirely on a text-to-text basis, importing images from one text into another; others draw on lifeworlds for detail, for background, for atmosphere. Many of them describe a capacity for taking multiple stances.

Liang, for example, sees "not pictures but more like a movie. There would definitely be visuals." Her characters have faces, but sometimes she sees at a distance. And sometimes she abandons both face and long-distance perspective for a "first person" point of view, looking out from behind the character's eyes. She suggests that her reading involves 90 percent text-to-text transference rather than life-to-text. For the most part, she infills a Canadian background rather than a Chinese one, unless a book is specifically set in China—and even then, she is cautious about the limited value of her memories of China because it has changed so much.

Lily, as we have already seen, inserts background information not according to the setting of the story but as a reflection of where she was when she first encountered it. She sees "very, very vivid" images when she reads, but her images for a generic setting may be hybrid in nature. "I would always picture it if somebody is going down the street, I would kinda picture that one [the Chinese street of her first neighborhood], but I'm not sure if the one in Scarborough kind of blends in with that. It's kind of hard to tell sometimes, but [the street in Zheng Zhou] is the main one I would say."

Roman is another visualizer. When he reads, "I don't really see the words anymore, it's mostly just images." But his images of setting are discrete: "I have a hard time with spatial areas. I'll have the book leading me through and then I have to go back and check the map at the front, because I don't know where I am. But I know what it looks like."

Amani creates faces. "I guess when I read I don't like facelessness … I like to really make sure I understand description, just so I have that face going forward." But she says nothing substantial about setting.

Riya begins with generic images and adds details as the text supplies them, a textbook example of improvising a simulation. She sticks with the generic if no description is supplied, though she will add a few details if they come readily to mind:

> If it's about a specific place and I know things about that place, then I put that over it. So if I read a book set in Switzerland, I imagine green, like valleys and hills and stuff like that. I read books set in Russia, and I would imagine stuff from old videos from World War Two or whatever. So, yeah, if it's a place that I know something about, then I would put something over it.

I am intrigued by a phrase Riya uses twice in this short account: putting something over it. She says she does not notice herself adding these impressions, it just happens. The idea of "putting over" seems to refer to an accretion of detail "over" a very generic setting, and she is very consistent in her references to a kind of layering up of imagery as the words become available or, as we see here, where she has some general text-to-text input to offer.

Riya is bothered by discrepancies and also by situations where the author is deliberately indeterminate. She assumes characters are always white until the author specifies otherwise. Her scenery also starts off as generic until specifics are supplied by the author. Her default island, for example, seems to arise out of a schema supplied in her geography book: a smooth semicircle rising from a body of water. She takes trees for granted but needs to be told by the author to add rocks. She is another reader who sees individual sites but does not trouble to figure out the relationship between places; "I'm not very good at bearings."

Suleman takes setting imagery from the movies he has watched.

> If it's something related to English, something like English characters with English names … I would switch in the background of a wooden house; we have a concrete house in Pakistan. So I would include that landscape, the clean environment there [he had commented earlier on the absence of litter in the West]. I would actually incorporate the movie scenes there.

The inner lives of the characters, however, is based on his own experience. "But the people, the psychology—I haven't met English people before—would be of my own people, the way they react."

For Matt, building the visuals of a fictional world is one of the great pleasures of reading. He is delighted when a movie confirms his personal rendering of a world, and finds it annoying when movies contradict his own ideas, or contradict each other. Matt also initially sees separate scenes, but he takes more care than Roman or Riya to make the connections between these scenes and he produces the very helpful metaphor of the discrete and static sitcom settings to describe what he does. Matt is rare in both specifying the visual details of a scene and "looking for" the relationship between these sites as he reads.

Matt sees in three-dimensional detail: "It's pretty vivid. I mean, there's a little bit of: everything within the foreground is very vivid, and as it continues to go, it kind of gets that atmosphere perspective and everything blurries a little bit."

Transient Visuals

Some readers produce more fleeting images than others. Ying Yu is very explicit about the provisional nature of her mental images. She says,

> I usually have flashes. I don't like to go into the details of the pictures. Because if there's some changes in the plot then I won't be able to change it as fast. Then I'd have to stop and rethink about how everything works. So I usually have the general layout, and then have, oh yes, there's a lot of green, there should be lots of mountains. Just quick images that flash through.

She articulates her scene-building processes very clearly, describing a sequential approach that involves both adding and deleting as needed:

> I notice when I read a book, I kinda put my shoes, I mean I put my feet into the main character's shoes, and then I kinda leave everything blank for a while and then there's the context of, oh, the setting, so I just put that into my image, into my mind, of those imageries, images, and then along the way I'd read, oh, they're the only kid, then, okay, they don't have any family, so I'd cut everything off. And then, oh, they have a mother too, okay, then link some experience with mothers and how they treat each other and keep reading. So I kinda just build on, I guess. And then sometimes if I add a little bit too much and then I read that, oh, okay, what I imagined was wrong, then I'd be like, okay, let me just fix that, kinda thing.

Making a transition from one working supposition to another as she improvises a simulation in her mind does not seem to trouble her: "I think I kinda just shift it. Yeah, I can just transform it in my mind, kind of … Yeah, I'd slowly fix that and I'd kind of get the hang of, okay, yeah, it's fixed."

Ying Yu's images are often fleeting and unformed ("oh yes, there's a lot of green") and even when she adds details, she is not committed to them if the text provides a contradiction. Her reading approach is very flexible and adaptive. Reading about fairies and nymphs, for example, she scales her forest imagery to a closer perspective and provides more details of fallen logs and the like, while maintaining a strong "nature feel."

Amani's visuals are transient on a different basis. She says, "I don't think I think of the same thing every time when I read." Matt, in contrast, finds that one of the drawbacks to rereading is that he has already worked out the landscape. "It's boring reading a book where the landscape's the exact same."

150   Space, Place, and Children's Reading Development

Figure 9.1 Halia's little stand of trees.

Make-do Visuals

We have already observed Riya's importation of stereotypes from the geography book and Suleman's mix of Pakistani psychology with Western wooden houses. Halia is more explicit in describing her approach, especially during her early years in Canada before she had seen very much of the city or the Canadian countryside. Reading in Arabic, she pictured her story taking place in Iraq; reading in English she drew on the shallower repertoire of her limited local experience in Canada. In this extended quote, she is pointing to the trees behind her house, as presented on her map (Figure 9.1):

> So here this is a very shady Google images kind of—this is my house, and this is the actual place, and there was a whole concrete area where you can play soccer and things like that, and there was a tiny amount of woods in there, and that was basically it, I didn't see much besides that. I saw the Rocky Mountains once, and that really stuck with me. I would read a lot of fiction about animals. I think there was this one book called *The Raven's Quest* by Sharon Stewart. It was very descriptive the way it described the Canadian landscape, and it was just a mixture of the Rocky Mountains that I saw very briefly and what was outside of my house. I also found myself mixing up, like I said, I was reading a lot of rural—about forests and things like that, but I would mix that up, I would mix up urban with rural. Like I'd assume, they'd be, oh, okay, there's a stream and the raven was drinking from the stream and I'd imagine a street right beside the stream.

Halia's account reminds me of Malpas's observation that we require some kind of space in order for agency to occur. The raven needed a space in which it could decide to drink and then follow through, so Halia cobbled up a make-do setting, an improvised response that sufficed to keep her reading.

What we see here is a very clear example of what scholars of information-seeking behavior call satisficing—in Denise Agosto's terms, "choosing decision outcomes that are good enough to suit decision makers' purposes, but that are not necessarily optimal outcomes" (2002: 17). We see examples of child viewers satisficing in Chapter 6, as they attempt to make sense of television animations. The term was first developed by H. A. Simon; Agosto offers this paraphrase of his thinking: "Due to time constraints and cognitive limitations, it is not possible for humans to consider all existing decision outcomes and then make fully reasoned, purely rational, choices. He suggested that humans operate rationally within practical boundaries or within the limits of bounded rationality" (2002: 16). Satisficing is a term used less often in relation to personal reading, but recreational readers in particular will often settle for an interpretation that is good enough to keep them going, without worrying too much about whether it is optimal. It seems to me that we underestimate the potency of this approach in many reading activities: young children making do rather than grinding to a halt; or readers of any age working their way through chapter 1, trying to balance a lot of new information; or, as we see here, readers who, for whatever reason, build up a better repertoire by keeping going, even if some of their initial reactions are not entirely satisfactory. The raven drinking from the stream alongside the urban street is exerting his "ravenly" agency as the story requires, and, even if the scenery sounds rather like a partial and inadequate stage flat, it still conveys enough of the requisite background schema that the story is rural.

Halia's efforts to supply Canadian scenery in her early years as an immigrant child reader were arduous enough that she can remember and articulate them. I suspect that many readers experience more fleeting moments of creating an understanding that is good enough to enable them to keep reading without being optimally worked out. And often, it probably doesn't matter. Renate Brosch suggests that it is not necessary to fill every blank when we read:

> The concept of "gap filling" has attained common currency in descriptions of the cognitive activity of the reader. But in terms of visuality, gaps for the most part do not need filling in. On the contrary, readers often relish the suggestiveness of visual blanks left by a text. It may even be this fragmentary suggestion of a larger whole that makes the experience of reading fiction so compelling. (2018: 138)

It would be useful to understand more about the cognitive enigma of the impact of a fragment of information that sometimes resonates more strongly than the whole. Matt offers an account of making do in the early stages of a story, a mix of striving to comprehend the nature of the story world and trying to create a visual scenario to accord with information that is manifestly insufficient in the early stages of reading.

> The first part is just about Hogwarts itself and how the first book, it kind of tells you a story of a lot of things you don't really know. Obviously, witchcraft has been around for hundreds of years, but this idea of a school for it and some things that

you don't really know, the idea of this castle and things, when you're reading it, it's a lot of new things.

Matt, perhaps the reader in this group most dedicated to accuracy in his scene-building, here testifies to the need to start with a good enough image and good enough comprehension, using inferences to move from the level of satisficing to a more complete sense of the story world.

Culturally Specific Images

In terms of considering imagery that reflects particular cultural information, it is important to begin with some observations about the readers who do not articulate an awareness of being culturally informed, and who therefore do not appear in this column. Four of them are local and do not think of their images as culturally specific since they are ubiquitous and taken for granted—at least "around here." Of these readers, Amy does not visualize at all. Amani, Matt, and Roman almost certainly draw on imagery that is Western at least and frequently local as well. They simply do not highlight this kind of thinking as culturally specific. Rahina also does not visualize at all. Laura prefers not to do so, though she often, willy-nilly, picks up images from her movie viewing rather than from her own life, and it would not be surprising to learn that she sees these film images more as universal than as operating out of a particular cultural framework.

The remaining six participants are immigrants themselves or have very strong links with a culture different from that of Alberta's mainstream. They have at least two settings in their repertoire, and so they are better equipped to distinguish what they know and how they know it. Riya and Suleman, for example, both separately mention a curious feature of their arrival in the West: they solved the interpretive mystery of how people can put their fist through a wall, a feat impossible to visualize with the concrete walls of the Indian subcontinent. The discovery that Edmonton walls are made of wood and plaster would seem to represent a simple substitution, but many of the images described by these participants are more complex and subtle.

When Ying Yu imagines a dragon, it is red and has "lots of scales and long whiskers;" it is not hard to perceive a Chinese influence at work. Her beach is more of a mix of elements. She mentions the pom-pom trees and very fine sand of Beihai Beach in China (Figure 9.2), which she visited as a child, and says when she reads mermaid stories, this is the beach she imagines. But if her mermaid needs a beach house, the one she mentally introduces is an image from *Hannah Montana*. Her base map mixes these real life and fictional images in a way that no other participant lays out so explicitly.

Similarly, her mental castle is very specifically described. Her opening image is a montage of square fortresses (Figure 9.3). In the links, she provides many specifications: the castle is square and built of brick, it has a flat top and an inner courtyard, there is frequently a moat, it towers over the surrounding countryside.

As antecedents to these images, she cites the Great Wall of China with its square turrets, and the movies of *Shrek* and *Scooby-Doo* (from which some of her specific images are taken). In keeping with the general fluidity of her mental scene-shifting

Diversity Inside and Out 153

Figure 9.2 Ying Yu's beach—Beihai Beach in China.

Figure 9.3 Some of Ying Yu's ideas of a castle.

capacities, Ying Yu says she can switch between Chinese and Western imagery "any time I want."

Transfer from Films/TV/Other Books

Liang says she develops mental imagery 90 percent text-to-text. Matt says he deliberately imports scenery created in the reading of one book where he finds it appropriate for another book, and he finds this process helpful. But for the most part, when speaking of intertextuality and mental imagery, these participants talk about concrete images from movies and television. Many of them find themselves drawing on the film version of what they are reading, but not all are happy when the movies colonize their reading experience.

At one extreme we have Amy. Amy normally does not visualize and takes in the story from the perspective of being inside the characters. When she lost patience waiting for the final Harry Potter book to be published, she allowed herself to be talked into seeing the first movie; up to that point, she had successfully resisted. Seeing Hermione from the outside spoiled her reading of Book 7 when it finally appeared.

At the other extreme, Laura almost invariably sees the movie before she reads the book; indeed, she will only read the book at all if the movie appealed very strongly to her. As a result, she finds herself almost using the book as a memory prod for the movie experience:

Laura:	I kinda disregard the text in a way. I'm just thinking of the movie and the characters and—.
Margaret:	So, it's a chance to re-live the movie in some ways.
Laura:	Yes, exactly. But in greater detail.
Margaret:	Yes, the book's almost always bigger, isn't it?
Laura:	Yes.

Yet when asked whether she prefers to read the book first, with no input of any kind from a movie version, Laura says she does. "But I probably wouldn't just give that character an actual face, or how that person looks like, I would just connect with the character." When I point out that she could resolve this difficulty by simply reading the book ahead of going to the movie, she laughs and says, "But then again, I never do that!"

Amani's favorite book is *The Perks of Being a Wallflower*, and she is actually rereading it at the time of our interview. She saw the movie before she ever read the novel, so she naturally gave the characters the faces of the actors. Now she is sorry. "I think at first I found it helpful just because you have something to think of, but now that I've re-read it so many times, it kind of irks me because I would have imagined them differently."

Matt, who so enjoys mental world-building, also likes the process of seeing how well his setting matches that created by a movie or fan version—"kind of seeing how close I got, it was really fun." But when the movies contradict each other, he gets annoyed.

All these participants, of course, are talking about a singular movie adaptation of a singular book, so contradictions are clear and aggravating. Movies and television also

Figure 9.4 Ying Yu's oceanic imagery.

provide a broader kind of visual slush fund of images and details, which readers use differently.

Ying Yu is an interesting witness to this process, as her approach to describing image formation is highly forensic. We have already seen a partial reference to her extended account of assembling a castle setting out of assorted sources. For her mermaid stories, she creates a nautical setting, and her sample image of boats, once again, is plural. Ying Yu attaches four labels to this composite image, citing the following sources: her viewing of Chinese dramas as a child; her trips to China, which give her not only a notion of the boats but also a sense of ocean colors; the movie *Finding Nemo*; and cartoon images of fishing boats.

She selects, in part, based on the origin of the story and the setting it suggests. If there are lots of green mountain surroundings or a possible Asian reference or "even an olden day setting," then she opts for the kind of boats pictured top left. If the setting is Western or industrial, she is more likely to fall back on *Finding Nemo*. On the link to the bottom right image (Figure 9.4), she says, "As the story continues, there may be flashes of images along with the boats I also pictured. I may have flashes of pictures that show the process of fishing, of the large amount of fish that is caught. But the main focus is usually the boat."

Not every participant is as explicit as Ying Yu about the ingredients that create a mental image, but it is striking in this account how she supplements life experience with information from movies and TV. Liang is far less detailed, but she makes a similar point when she talks about reading Western books while she still lived in China (Grimm, Andersen, and the like). She imagined "white characters who spoke Chinese" as she read, and she supplied a good enough Western background from her television viewing: the little documentary snippets from *Teletubbies*, information from the Discovery Channel. She is describing a kind of satisficing.

Just Knowing

Probably the sharpest distinction comes between the majority who take visualizing for granted and the minority who reject it. This distinction is summed up by the differences between Laura and Amani, who both object to having their imagination overridden by a cinematic image. On the rare occasion that Laura reads a book without any movie influences, she connects with characters rather than seeing them, and creates a fairly vague persona rather than a picture. Amani, however, though equally wistful about the imperious takeover that movie images achieve so relentlessly, attends carefully to descriptions when she is reading and says she "doesn't like facelessness" in her characters.

The two participants who are most definite about not visualizing are Amy and Rahina. Amy says flatly,

> You know how lots of people are like, you paint a picture in your head of what a character would look like, and someone makes a movie and they make the character completely different than what you think. That doesn't happen for me because I don't have a person in my head, of what they should look like. I don't have any—I don't make any visual connection.

At most Amy has a vague awareness: "Kind of, like—Peter shape or, like—bedroom silhouette."

Rahina is equally committed to reading without visuals. She provides many versions of the same reading stance:

- "Because if I put a face on someone, what does that face mean?"
- "I could give the same character face and then have a variety of names."
- "How do I say this? People's faces do not map onto what they're like."
- "Faces are limiting."

She is even less wedded to providing any kind of visual setting. "They could have a white wall behind them, it doesn't really affect me."

It is worth noting that a nonvisualizing stance does not interfere with reading pleasure and success; both Rahina and Amy were inveterate child readers. Amy arrived at her grandma's house with a backpack full of books every day and describes book-trawling visits to Value Village; Rahina solidly read her way through the public library. Neither woman shows any signs of an overall syndrome of aphantasia, the inability to picture objects that are not present (and, for the record, nor do I, and I also read without visualizing). Rahina offers a lengthy description of the view of trees in a park behind her Toronto apartment, and the enormous detail of Amy's visual reconstruction of a house she has not entered for eight years speaks for itself. The absence of pictorial images that they describe with such conviction is an attribute specific to their reading.

Visualization and Readers

Laura Otis, who is interested in how human minds operate differently, reports on a thought experiment with thirty-four eminent creative professionals: authors, scientists, artists, scholars, designers, and more. She asks these people about their response to the word "bridge," and garners a broad variety of responses. Some perceive no visual image and speak instead of the word's metaphoric connotations of making connections. Some describe a highly particularized bridge in great visual detail. Others provide a schematic image more like a line drawing or a model, emphasizing the relationship between parts.

Otis also talks to her respondents about how they read and finds she can group them into three categories of reading preference, more or less equivalent to the responses to the single word bridge:

> (1) little or no visual mental imagery; (2) vivid, detailed imagery; or (3) schematic imagery focused on spatial arrangements. Some readers don't consciously experience imagery, or it is so dim and vague that they can't describe it. If they do form visual mental images, they tend not to regard these internal pictures as essential for appreciating the story. (2015: 512)

For some readers, says Otis, visualization "isn't always a key part of the process ... it arises like noise in a restaurant, where the real business at hand is savouring language. For other readers, visual mental imagery offers the food that sustains the reading process" (2015: 513).

This kind of variation certainly shows up in the self-assessments of the participants in this project. Otis's qualitative work also entails talking to readers; when we shift disciplinary focus, what does neuroscience have to offer to our understanding of these distinctions? How much—and for whom—do the differences Otis describes actually matter?

An intriguing study by Kozhevnikov, Kosslyn, and Shephard establishes three categories: verbalizers and two types of visualizer. They describe the "two qualitatively different types of visualizers," in the following terms:

> Object visualizers use imagery to construct high-quality images of the shapes of individual objects, whereas spatial visualizers use imagery to represent and transform spatial relations. Furthermore ... people who score high on spatial imagery tasks tend to score below average on object imagery tasks, and vice versa for people who score high on object imagery tasks. No such dissociation was found among verbalizers. Verbalizers did not show a clearly marked preference for any particular type of imagery. (2005: 722)

These two ways of looking—in detail at the object as a whole, and in passing at dynamic spatial relationships—actually take place in different parts of the brain. The ventral pathway is responsible for object vision (the "what" factor) and the dorsal pathway takes care of the spatial (the "where" factor) (Kozhevnikov, Blazhenkova, and Becker,

2010: 29). Visualizers would thus seem to have a preference for one part of the brain over another, while verbalizers are more neutral.

In two articles published in 2017 and 2018, Renate Brosch links these findings to literary reading. She contrasts a default mode of fast and underdetermined reading with the kind of reading that produces a sense of vivid and detailed images. The default mode occurs via the dorsal or spatial area of the brain (the "where" function) and all readers make use of it when simply moving into or through a story. Its very vagueness is a virtue. "Thus, the primary advantage of the incompleteness of default visualization lies in its adaptive potential, in the ability to merge and fuse images, constantly creating new ones, so that they qualify and condition each other in the temporal succession of the reading" (2018: 137).

Readers do not perceive the lack of detail in this dorsal imagery as a problem, says Brosch. Indeterminacy permits flexibility as new information is added, and some readers do not ever look for more detail.

Mak and Willems confirm this distinction with their recording of the behavior of readers when measuring eye-tracking. "We found that motor simulation was associated with shorter gaze duration (faster reading), whereas perceptual simulation and mentalising were associated with longer gaze duration (slower reading)" (2019: 529). It is tempting to paraphrase this finding as follows: the "where" track with its spatial information processed in terms of motion is faster than the "what" track, which includes both objects of perception and the implications of other people's minds at work.

But even object visualization (the "what" function) is more dynamic than a simple snapshot effect. Emily Troscianko suggests that what we reproduce in our heads is not a simple object image but an act of seeing. We never see every detail when we look at a scene in real life; we make many working assumptions about object permanence, for example. If a rock occludes part of the river, I do not think I am looking at two rivers, one on each side of the rock. I do some active extrapolating; and I move my head if I want to see more. Troscianko says we simulate this kind of exploration in our minds (2013: 185). Some people will produce more detail than others, she says, but it isn't necessary, and the indeterminacy of language means that we can keep going without knowing every particular about a character or a setting. Philosopher Evan Thompson, working from a "phenomenological analysis of visual mental imagery," confirms this insight: "According to this analysis, visual experience is not pictorial in the way many theorists assume … Visualizing is rather the activity of mentally representing an object or a scene by way of mentally enacting or entertaining a possible perceptual experience of that object or scene" (2007: 143). Such a reworking of the experience of looking neither requires a pictorial input nor rules it out, Thompson says, and it is certainly compatible with the idea that some readers' mental images are more vivid and detailed than others. What seems to be a common element is the idea of perception as embodied motion. (And, of course, a setting occupies a sonic as well as a visual space, and some readers may "feel" the dimensions of a space using nonvisual approaches. I did not pursue these alternatives in any detail.)

Among the twelve participants in this study, we clearly have examples of verbalizers and each of the two kinds of visualizers. Rahina and Amy respond more to the words and "enact" the story by moving inside the characters. Ying Yu provides the most explicit account of a fleeting and spatially oriented approach with her talk of "flashes." Riya, Amani, and Roman all articulate a set piece form of visualization that accords with object vision. Matt does the same thing, but, unlike the others, he also takes pains to check the spatial relationships between and among his sitcom sets.

In different ways, many of the participants describe a process that resembles the kind of improvised simulation I introduced in Chapter 3. They get the simulator up and running, often with minimal early information, and then they improvise how to incorporate the revisions that become necessary as they keep reading. If their early input includes a sense of the grain of the text, they may find it easier to keep going, whether their idea of keeping going includes the ability to "look" at a detailed visual scenario or a particular face that conforms accurately to the author's description—or whether the pleasures of forward motion and/or the cadences of the words themselves are sufficient.

These neuroscience studies reinforce the idea that reading spaces are not simply furnished out of different repertoires; they are actually set up by means of different processes, involving different mental priorities. When we talk about diversity, it is important to realize that it is more than the variation of experience and/or cultural priorities; it also exists at the level of brain activity. The range of ethnic, cultural, geographical, and disciplinary backgrounds of these twelve people is readily apparent. I certainly do not wish to undervalue the significance of their diversified experiences and priorities; I simply want to underline that this variation is augmented by differences in their individual cognitive proclivities. The building blocks with which they construct a reading space are themselves diverse.

The varied observations of these twelve readers, linked to my own personal sense that nonvisualizing readers seem to be strangely absent from many discussions of reading, led me to undertake a preliminary exploration of the scientific, literary, and educational literature about visualization. What I discovered was that the scientific reports had a place for me as a verbalizing reader. The empirical literary studies are mixed. The pedagogic material, however, is far more monolithic and highly prescriptive about the necessity of visualizing. In a 2019 publication, I summarized some of my findings as follows:

> A large literature, frequently addressed to teachers, assumes that people read better by creating mental pictures as they process the words. Searching the term 'reading and visualizing' on Google in February 2019, I turned up a list of more than three million links. Checking all the links in the first three screens of this huge set, I found many very categorical assertions about the necessity of creating pictures in your head as you read. (Mackey, 2019c: 39)

In my 2019 article, I supply a number of quotations to indicate the definitiveness with which undoubtedly well-meaning people pronounce that visualization is essential to comprehension. I will not repeat those quotes here, but I will reiterate that it is dismaying to think of the reading lives of Rahina and Amy being so discounted by so many educators. "What you don't see won't hurt you" is a catchphrase, but, in this case, what these educators *can't* see about what such readers *don't* see can have destructive consequences.

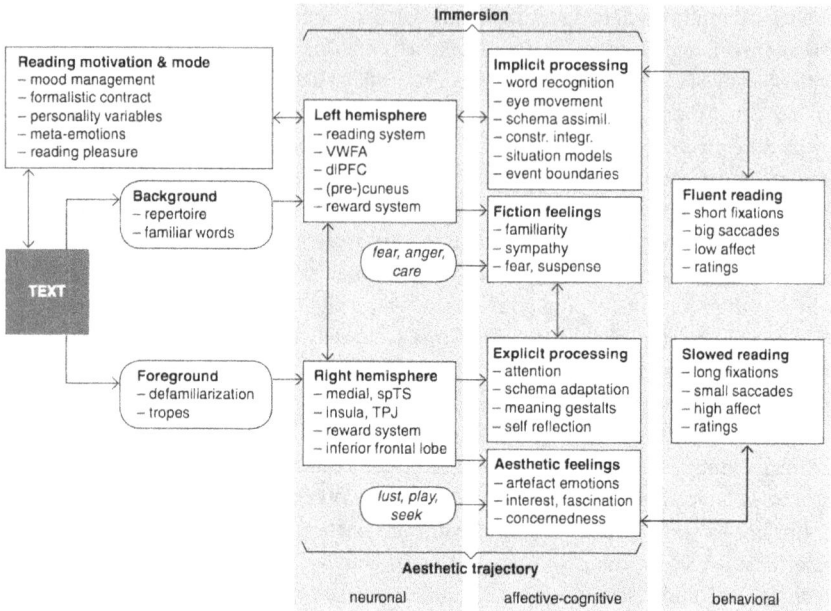

Figure 9.5 "Simplified neurocognitive model of reading literary books" by Arthur Jacobs © Cambridge University Press, from *Cognitive Neuroscience of Natural Language Use* ed. Roel M. Willems, Cambridge University Press, 2015. Reproduced with permission of The Licensor through PLSclear (142).

The Bigger Picture

I conclude this chapter by returning to a fertile interaction between neuroscience and the soft science of talking with readers.

Arthur Jacobs is a neurocognitive psychologist in Berlin. In a chapter entitled "Towards a Neurocognitive Poetics Model of Literary Reading" (2015), he offers a broad view of distributed reading processes in the brain. He contrasts immersive with aesthetic response. Immersive reading is familiar and fluent, moving forward easily. The aesthetic trajectory offers more surprises, catches the attention, and invites a reader to slow down and ponder. Both pathways are available to all readers.

Jacobs's model is expressed in diagram form in this chapter (Figure 9.5), and it repays a careful and detailed perusal. Even without being fully at home with the scientific vocabulary in the neuronal column, I find it illuminating in three ways. The first lies in how it aligns this technical language of brain science with the felt experiences of reading. It is relatively straightforward, in following this array of technical and literary language, to imagine two different readers, each activating options that are accounted for on this diagram but each manifesting a distinctive distribution of brain activity. Such divergence, alongside separate life experiences, distinctive intertextual repertoires, and individual personal identity priorities, contributes to the overall uniqueness of a reader's response to a text.

The second takeaway from this diagram is the very clear perspective it offers on a brain in motion, moving between immersed and aesthetic trajectories, via the crossways arrows. Alternative actions are available at the neuronal, the affective-cognitive and the behavioral levels.

In this overview, we can spot particular jobs for specific areas of the brain, involving implicit and explicit processing, fiction feelings and aesthetic feelings, fluent and slowed reading. Big saccades (a saccade is the measurable movement of the eyes between resting spots) and short fixations coincide with feelings of familiarity; small saccades and long fixations involve attention to novel adaptations of schemas, the development of meaning, and a kind of fascination. The diagram certainly offers a sense of action and movement; we still need to learn more about the role of agency in this brain's activities during a textual encounter. Can we purposely decide to be immersed in a text, or is it more a case of being *captured* and swept along? An aesthetic stance is probably more deliberate overall, but are there moments when the text takes a role, perhaps jolting us out of our immersed forward march through the text by means of some kind of surprise that knocks us out of our feeling of familiarity? Is there an equal but inverse process whereby a reader who normally pays close and careful attention to every detail is temporarily swept away by the momentum of the plot? There remains much to be learned, but this diagram offers a lively perspective on the complexity of our neurocognitive activities.

The third element in this diagram that I find very useful is that it includes some of the "beforehand" of reading that my own project addresses. In the top left box, we see attributes a reader brings to a text, and, in at least one of them, we may catch a glimpse of one portal between the life space and the reading space. "Mood management" is a consideration in selecting what to read—so says Jacobs from his review of a wide range of scientific and literary studies, and so also say Catherine Sheldrick Ross and Mary K. Chelton on the basis of a set of careful interviews with avid readers. More than twenty years ago, these readers articulated a process illuminated by scientists many years later. Ross and Chelton report,

> The bedrock issue is the reader's mood: What do I feel like reading now? What will I feel like reading in the future that I should borrow or buy now? (Mood was more critical for choosing fiction—which most in the survey read—rather than for choosing nonfiction.)
>
> Mood, of course, varies. When readers are busy or under stress, they often want safety, reassurance and confirmation. They will reread old favorites or new books by trusted authors. When life is less stressful, they can afford to take more risks. They may want to be amazed by something unpredictable and might pick books on sheer impulse, even through random selection of an author's name.
>
> Readers adopted various strategies to establish the right balance between safety/certainty and novelty/risk. (2001: 52)

Perhaps we will one day establish that "safe" reading features more brain work on the immersive pathway than on the more startling and confounding aesthetic route.

Or perhaps, as is often the case, readers are not so predictable. In any case, we have come full circle from the beginning of this chapter. Readers can tell us a great deal about reading. The increasing subtlety with which we can examine readers' brains at work can also provide much information, and we should not really be surprised that these two data sources confirm each other (though it would be good if the pedagogical proselytizers for monolithic visualizing would take to heart the lesson that it is possible to trust what readers tell you). In this project, the readers behave differently as they process words in their minds, and this diversity is as great as all the other manifestations of individuality that this work uncovers.

Both researchers and practitioners can benefit from asking themselves a few questions about their interactions with readers: What am I not seeing through the filter of my own internal assumptions about how reading works? What am I failing to hear because of my limited knowledge? How can I even notice my own lapses (which feel so familiar) and where can I find information to augment my understanding in productive ways? At least preliminary answers to these and many more such questions may be found within a broad range of disciplinary frameworks.

Literary Spaces

Ongoing Worlds

10

Opening a Lifelong Reading Space

There are two kinds of sentence: "I'm reading 'X,'" and its intransitive counterpart, "I'm reading." Do these linguistic variants reflect a real cognitive distinction? We can perceive the condition of reading X as it is enacted by the reader. Is there an equivalent, more permanent, ongoing condition, roughly summed up by the concept of simply "reading," a condition where the identity of X is relatively unimportant? For some readers at least, I suspect the answer is yes. A project like this one with its general focus on a reading life, rather than on particular reading experiences, is well placed to elicit some examples of the effects of constant reading.

So far, I have addressed the idea of a reading space as a kind of singular mental "opening" prompted by a personal reaction to the invitation of a particular text by an individual reader. It is an opening that incorporates cognitive and emotional responses as well as acknowledging the material conditions that feed into that encounter. Many reading spaces open temporarily and more or less close again after the book fades from memory. But this project has also uncovered a different manifestation of the reading space, an ongoing thematic fascination with some elements worked out through the fusion of life and reading experience. Birkerts says reading necessarily creates such spaces: "Apart from giving me ideas, books have forced me to create a space for reflection; they have made certain kinds of thinking inevitable" (1994: 106). Focused as he is on his own internal processes, Birkerts, I suspect, underestimates the multiplicity of different ways in which such spaces develop.

Waller talks about the "lifelong reading act":

> The kernel of the lifelong reading act is a first encounter with a book, but this act spreads beyond the initial moment of reading (or being read to) into other points of engagement in the following hours, days, months, years, and decades. Sparks of involuntary memory, conscious attempts at recollection, and instances of textual recognition; imaginative re-enactments and the incorporation of books into real or virtual environments; feelings reignited through glimpses of character or atmosphere; rereading projects and autotopographical reminiscence: all these activities play a part. The lifelong reading act can also contract as books are lost, misremembered, or forgotten. (2019: 190)

In this case, she is talking about lifelong associations with a single book, and she quotes J. G. Ballard to good effect about how a book can wind its tendrils into an individual mind and memory:

> Ballard suggests that books such as *Robinson Crusoe* departed from the page and have taken on a "second life" inside his head, not only in the sense of the virtual entity that reader response theory posits as being set in motion when reader and text meet, but also as an ongoing narrative space that plays out again and again over time and via memory. (2019: 78)

Ballard's "ongoing narrative space" remains related to a single title, but I believe it is possible to think of ongoing mental spaces that are more promiscuously linked to a lifetime of reading an assortment of books. A constant reader has a constant reading space in the mind; to conceive of that permanently open space as porous to associations from books other than the one being perused in the present moment is not an enormous stretch. Such a lifelong reading space is a positive feature of inveterate reading to many people.

Ongoing Reading Spaces

In this chapter, I present and consider three very different forms of a more open-ended kind of reading space.

Rahina's map offers an extraordinary view of several expanded versions of that space. Rejecting the idea of presenting any one landscape as too narrow to encompass her response to reading, she develops an abstract representation of how aspects of her reading life are juxtaposed and jostle together in her mind. The result of her effort to think through the impact of reading on her life gives us a multifaceted view of one person's ongoing associative reading space, expressed mainly in words with some modest support from images. Rahina's account of her mental life as a young reader provides access to a much more complex kind of reading space than is normally visible, and her frequent references to libraries establish that the tangible condition of ready access to more books to read is a vital part of that space. She is not a rereader, so having a library in her world means she can relax about finding something new to read. Her experience in Africa, with much poorer access to libraries, sharpened her awareness of how crucial they are to her well-being. She regularly has multiple books on the go at once.

The reading spaces that Rahina describes from her literate youth are idiosyncratic and quirky, though profoundly meaningful to her. She links these different states of mind to particular reading experiences. In contrast, Roman's maintenance of an ongoing reading space takes effect through a repeated life experience in his childhood: recurring exposure to a separate and clearly special geographic space. His time in the local ravine acts like a force field, charging his young reading life with an energy that links separate reading experiences in illuminating ways. Both Rahina and Roman are looking back on their youthful reading lives, and Birkerts makes an observation that I think may be helpful to keep in mind. Comparing his own adult and youthful reading, he says, "Now when I read a book that matters I feel that I am carrying it around inside me. Then it was the reverse: I was living my life inside the enclosure of the work" (1994: 102). Roman learns how to be in a charged space within the ravine and carries some of that charge into his reading.

Ying Yu describes something much more provisional, temporary, and hybrid. Her map offers a set of juxtaposed images, mingling local Edmonton scenery, Chinese landscapes and landmarks, and fictional sites such as an image relating to *Hannah Montana*. When she reads, she invokes temporary images that she edits on the fly as required, and she draws on a large range of sources for input. Her preference is for stand-alone texts rather than series materials ("it ends faster and I get to pick something new"); and change is something of a motif in her account of a reading space in flux.

This chapter will not present an orthodox kind of compare and contrast between the mental states of these three participants, however; rather, in Mol's terms, it will attempt to "articulate silent layers" (2010: 262) as part of enriching our larger understanding of reading. Its main finding can probably be summed up in a single phrase: "how different readers are." My own interest lies in exploring the hugely varied ways in which readers can articulate the sense and significance of an intensely private mental landscape, wound around and through their reading experiences. My intent is to expand our idea of the "footprint" of our reading lives, with three divergent examples to illustrate the diverse and personal nature of these ongoing spaces.

Living in Other Worlds: Rahina

Rahina is twenty-four years old at the time of our encounter. The Canadian-born daughter of Somali immigrants, she is the oldest of ten children, and a secondary education student with a major in English. She is an observant, hijab-wearing Muslim woman, who regularly speaks of the impact of her beliefs on her life and her reading. In her early years, she spoke only Somali and participated in an ESL program in Grades 1 and 2. I ask her about drawing on life experience as she read particular books, and she replies:

> That's the thing, I think the reason that I turned to books, like, from a young age is because I don't have much life experiences. I grew up quite a strict lifestyle, which is home, school and religious services, but that's it. You don't really, like, go camping, hanging out with friends, it's a very traditional lifestyle. So, the fact that I got not only an escape but also education, and a common-sense connotative view of Western culture—even though I was born and raised here, [reading] definitely helped me see through a lens, that I would not have seen if I were myself out there. So, I don't really have much life experiences to draw upon, but these [books] sort of act like my life experiences.

Rahina describes herself in hybrid terms. She lived for ten years in Toronto and fourteen years in Edmonton, interspersed with spells in Africa.

> I'm ethnically Somali ... I spent one year in Somalia when I was twelve, and then one year in Kenya, which is the country right beside it, for one year when I was eighteen. I genuinely loved staying in Africa, even though it's not as rich and as beautiful [as] here in the West. I definitely felt closer to the people there 'cause, well, there's more black people in the world than I thought there was [laughs] and I was not stared at in the street for once, so I'm like yes ... here I feel like, in the West intellectually more comfortable, but in Africa I feel like, visibly and religiously more comfortable, so I'm literally torn in between. So, if you ask me where to live, I don't know, 'cause the books—that's one thing also, they don't have libraries in Africa. Not as common as here, where you could just lend books, giving them to someone, and then not pay to have a library card. So, I definitely appreciate that.

Rahina refers to the cognitive dissonance of growing up inside an Islamic perspective and reading many Western books. Reading, she says, has broadened the gap between her parents and herself. But creating her map causes her to question what her life would be if she were not literate, or could read but chose not to do so. Her Islamic upbringing requires her to avoid "going dancing, being part of theatre, arts, basically a lot of things that would be considered immodest. So, reading and writing is the one place that you can't argue someone with."

Rahina is a nonvisualizing reader, not interested in faces or settings. Her map (Figure 10.1) makes use of visuals in a very different way, illustrating what might be called the backdrop of her mind-wanderings rather than sketching any details of the texts she has read. Her initial map is completely abstract.

Rahina titles her abstract map, "Memories: From Innocence to Familiarity," and she provides a variety of different icons. The blue book images represent books read. The green crosses link to idiosyncratic mental landscapes that Rahina associates with particular times in her life. The black drops explore Rahina's best efforts at understanding the connection between the books she read and the imaginary landscapes she fostered in her mind. The hearts represent ongoing priorities: one heart stands for libraries and the other one links to books that have made an indelible impression on her. The yellow light bulb leads us to a reflection on what reading has meant to her throughout her life, and the big black "t" opens a discussion about where she is today. The blue camera connects to a discussion of media. A printout of her comments from all the links on this map runs to seven and a half single-space pages.

The mental landscapes, which Rahina once or twice refers to as "imaginations," are dreamlike in their surreal qualities and their unique peculiarities. In her discussion of her online life, Rahina provides some clues to the kinds of experience that fuel this very personal reflection on how a person's interior life connects in and out of their reading. She makes considerable use of Facebook, Reddit, and Tumblr. Additionally, she joined Goodreads in 2015 and compiled a list of the books she had read up to that point, which was very helpful as she developed her map two years later.

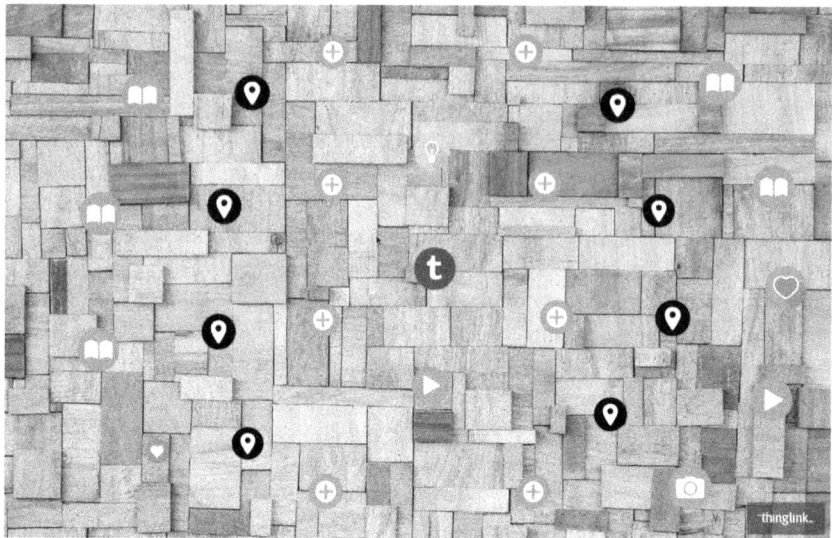

Figure 10.1 The initial screen of Rahina's map.

Rahina's distinctions between her three favored social media sites are illuminating. Facebook "is very social and has real social conventions embedded" in it.

> Reddit is more like a newspaper where you can comment on in real life. There are no adults, per se. I mean we are all adults, but none of us act like adults. So we can be childish or snarky, we can be very informative and nerdy. At the same time we could act like a jerk and no one will care. There's no—there's adults there, but there's no authority, I'm trying to say. It's run by the commenters and the posters … the more talented you are at articulating yourself, the more you're more likely to be liked.

Tumblr, unlike Facebook, is anonymous and Rahina says,

> It's a very underground place for almost any interest. I would not recommend for adults over thirty to go on, because it's very—I don't know how to say it? It's a pretty horrible place. I don't know how to say it, instead of being happy about being there, it's like that one room you have in your house, I think it could be the basement or the attic, where you just stuck things in there. They're useful, but you wouldn't exactly like spending time there. So, it's like that. It's a good reservoir of stuff.

Rahina finds Tumblr a useful outlet.

> So, it's a great way to be. It's like an intimate diary, but it's exposed to everyone, but no face or name on it, so that's awesome. And it's like sharing a hive mind, if

that's the right word for it. It's like we all have our thoughts together in one place. I post so many major events in life, without obviously using people's names. Lots of poems that come to my mind, lots of short stories that come to my mind. Things I've realized in life, awkward dreams I had, all that stuff. You just go there, and no one will judge you.

Rahina makes these observations about her online reading and writing experiences at the very end of the second interview. I believe her comments illuminate some of the dreamlike qualities of the associations she draws out in her map. With the purposes of the map in mind, she has obviously organized and shaped her thinking more acutely than she is likely to do in the stream-of-consciousness Tumblr writing she describes. She is used to thinking about and articulating these internal spaces in her mind, however, and that kind of recording offers access to mental territory so private that many of us might be hard pressed to describe it even to ourselves.

For example, Rahina draws a connection between the books about Junie B. Jones and a confusing imaginary mosque setting that lingered in her mind (Figure 10.2). Of the books, she writes:

> **Books: Junie B. Jones series.** A young girl's life from kindergarten to grade 2. She is sarcastic, loud, hilarious, witty, curious, bold and confrontational. The large text, repetitive language, strong emotions, and crazy adventures of Junie B. had sparked my imagination while still teaching me about the unwritten social rules concerning school behaviour. Parents, teachers, neighbours, and other classmates ensured that Junie B. was not left off the hook from her words and actions, no matter how well phrased her excuses were. Her world informed what I expected from mine, specifically adults who know how to help develop children's reading interests by relating to this quirky character in a safe setting.

The mosque that she links to this reading is more disturbing:

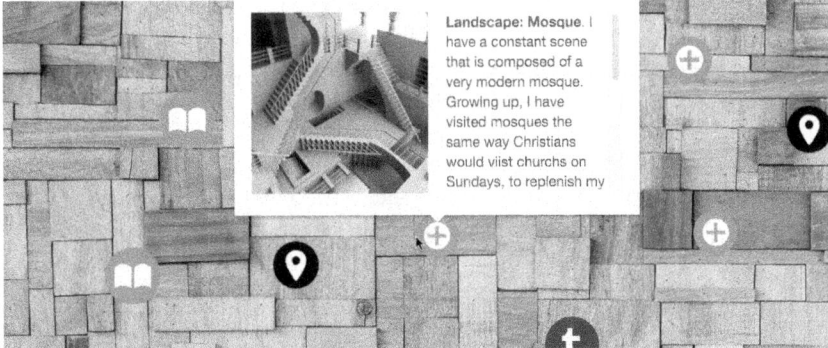

Figure 10.2 Rahina's imagined mosque.

Landscape: Mosque. I have a constant scene that is composed of a very modern mosque. Growing up, I have visited mosques the same way Christians would visit churches on Sundays, to replenish my connection with God via regular reminders and lectures. In my imagined mosque, there are confusing internal features such as maze-like hallways, blindingly white walls, 2 prayer rooms, a few bathrooms, random multipurpose rooms, and a preschool. People I knew were also scattered about in random corners.

The mosque also draws on the world of Harry Potter because the stairs keep changing. Rahina explores potential connections between this created landscape and the antics of Junie B.:

Connection. The link between the landscape of the mosque and the Junie B. Jones books are how they are both wild, unexpected, and foundations to my understanding of the world. Junie B. is a 5-year-old child who barely is kept in check with her louder than life behaviour, and this particular mosque was a confusing entanglement of stairs, hallways, floors, and rooms that don't represent a typical mosque at all. This one didn't contain many inhabitants, but I could accurately remember how magnificently decorated and impossibly large it was. The whiteness of all the walls represented how curious, innocent, and open to exploration Junie B. was, although to adults, she must be messy and cunning. Her excuses and motivations, when later on revealed, can't help but make the reader appreciate her thinking processes. So the connection between these two is that I was exposed to mosques and Junie B. really young, and found delight in the two of them, as normal behaviour for a 5-year-old, and an extremely huge and confounding interior of a place of worship, calm, and contemplation.

In our conversation, Rahina elaborates on this idiosyncratic connection:

Rahina: Well, this mosque is sort of a mess, let's just be honest. It's a mess of stairwells and hallways and random people scooting everywhere. Junie B. Jones herself, if she was a person in real life I would not know how her parents deal with her, because how much energy she has. She has curiosity, she befuddled even her kindergarten teacher. Other students had to constantly put her behavior in check with how much trouble she got in.

So, I could imagine her running around in this mosque having a swell time, and finding corners and secret doors and traps, I guess.

Margaret: Stop me if I'm putting words in your mouth; what I'm hearing is that Junie B. Jones has this wild energy, and you channeled it through a channel that was available to you in your culture, which was a mosque. So, the connection there is through the sort of wildness.

Rahina: Imagine if I was her, I would go out of my way to run around in this place. It'd be a lot of fun. I think a theme for most of my books is that

> there's just so much fun within these ... not only fun in the boring sense of just generally running around, but also fun things you can contemplate that are not normally available to you through your culture or your background. So, mentally it was a lot of fun, not only physically. You can imagine running around in these landscapes and having a good time, right? With the people you meet and the aspects of this Western culture you're exposed to, it's very new for you.

Using the character of Junie B. Jones to turn the orderly nature of the mosque on its head is certainly a personal and individual example of hybridization of influences, but the thread that connects them is discernible in these terms.

A second example makes a similarly dreamlike connection between the world of the *Goosebumps* series and Rahina's mental recasting of the portable unit at her school where she was frequently sent for detention. To this portable, she mentally added a huge tunnel and "a troll or monster of some sort that knew all my secrets."

Rahina also connects a mental image of a skate park with a giant ramp, her early viewing of television series that offered her very first framing of a world larger than the one she inhabited and her year in Somalia learning Arabic and the Quran.

> I learned how to read, how to understand Arabic, but I don't know how to speak it because I never practiced with someone. I learned to speak Somali, and the interactions that come with it, and also, like, the mental, what do you call it, the mental framework that comes with it, the mindset that comes with speaking a language so different.

She describes the skate park ramp as a good metaphor or analogy: "Cognitive dissonance feels like going from a high ramp all the way down, and then not being afraid, and then going right back up that ramp."

Rahina's reflections on the connections among the three elements lead her to an extended observation about the role of television in the life of a child becoming acculturated to a world that is not the same as that of her parents and a conceptual link to the time when she moved more closely into her parents' culture:

> TV is where I learned about the world before I cracked open my first book. It taught me about nursery rhymes, jokes, family constructions, kids up to no good, school from different children's view, what everyday activities meant to cartoon characters that were not humans (think aliens, ghosts, and vampires), and culturally significant holidays like Christmas and Easter without the religious overtones. The skatepark landscape is from my visit to Somalia at the age of eleven to thirteen where I acquired the Arabic language as well as the capacity to read and understand some of the Quran. These two experiences, my first impressions of the world via the TV programmes, and learning Arabic in a new country were very— disorienting, especially because I have never thought that there was more to the world than what I saw at home in my apartment, with nothing to do other than go to school, come home, eat, play with toys, and go to sleep. These two experiences

overlap in their impact upon my learning processes, a framework in which I view the world, and the potential they have in instilling values and character into their pursuers, i.e. myself being a pursuer of horizon-expanding ways of learning. In short, these two are a big deal in my life, visually represented in the enormity of a skate ramp.

Rahina also writes and speaks at length about the significance to her life of the Alice books by Phyllis Reynolds Naylor.

This series was the most instrumental in keeping me up to date with puberty-related matters including boys, dating, parties, parents, friendships, emotional and mental maturity, and finally, independence. It was my way of living vicariously through characters that were thoroughly Western subjects. The cognitive dissonance created from being a TCK (Third Culture Kid) was at once heightened and mitigated through reading this series.

The impact of Alice on Rahina's life was marked. "She's like a friend I've had for a long time, except she has no physical manifestation, but she's a real person." Rahina thinks of Alice as a cultural guide. "What I like about this girl is, it's an accessible way to get to know about her, and what I'm growing up in, the landscape that I'm growing up in. So, if I had to say, what is your quintessential Canadian character, I'd say Alice McKinley."

The landscape to which she connects these vital stories is a "cartoony" and "VERY condensed" Europe over which she is flying (Figure 10.3), alone in a low-hanging plane with a man who resembles a mad scientist. Lights on the ground make it difficult to discern many details, though she spots a Chinatown without knowing which city it occupies. She flies over a body of water in which many boats are also sporting lights. "There is a celebration going on of some sort and either the whole world or only Europe

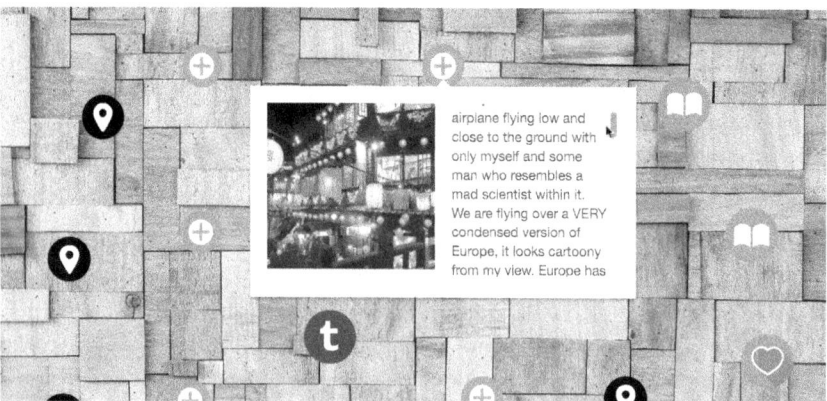

Figure 10.3 Rahina's imaginary flight over Europe.

is celebrating. There seems to be a Chinese festival in session. Did I mention that this is all happening at night? I think my dad is in this landscape somewhere."

Rahina connects these books and this confusing scenery, saying both relate to acculturation into the Western mainstream. She has actually flown over Europe on the way to her African destinations and landed in Denmark, Italy, and Britain.

> Europe has a selection of experiences, cultures, and people that tap into the experiences I had in reading the Alice series. Europe from the combination of visiting it for even a few hours with the Europe that I had imagined with the Chinatown in it, celebrating Chinese New Year, stemmed from Alice, a happy, courageous, and responsible person. These two were the bridge between childhood and adolescence.

These mental spaces are clearly significant to Rahina, but her favorite connection lies between what she calls rich and satisfying reads (series such as The Hunger Games and Harry Potter, the three novels about Afghanistan by Khaled Hosseini, Jane Austen's books, and more) and a fantasy she developed around the age of twelve. She was going to collect all the orphans of the world and house them in "a multifunctional palace for children," loaded with amenities. Rahina brings her dream landscape up to date in her reflection on the connection between the two:

> The link between the Rich Orphanage landscape and the Rich and Satisfying Reads are my absolute favourite. If I had to pick which books could be described as scrumptious, fulfilling and fragrant foods, it would be the series books I read in my teens and early twenties. These books were hefty, engaging, promising, challenging, wonderful and completely transformative reads. The Rich Orphanage was the biggest dream I had at the age of twelve because it stemmed from a well of empathy I had for those less fortunate than I am. The connection between these two is that although I had a financially burdensome hope to build a multifunctional orphanage, these books immersed me in what was at the time, a very magical and impressive array of characters who took what the world gave them and used it for their dreams of becoming either a) heroes, b) wizards, c) compassionate friends, d) inspiring independent women, e) fighters for justice, et cetera. I can now definitely see myself willing to be one of these characters because that's how much they have come alive and off the page. Rich, beloved and passionate, they are indeed cherished for their noble motivations.

Rahina refers to almost no real-life landscapes, apart from the forest behind her Toronto apartment, about which she speaks in relatively symbolic terms. She reads in a very nonpictorial way. Her inner landscapes are more visually specific than anything else she mentions, but the visuals are distorted and dreamlike, and the connections between these visions and Rahina's reading life are very personal.

For the most part, Rahina reads with a default that characters are white, which permits her a certain detachment: "I'd be like the wall observing the characters." That stance changes if she sees any point of identification.

Once I saw there's some representation of me, I'd probably be more like, "Oh my god, don't do anything dumb or stupid." Because there's so much involved in making sure that they get through things, not doing something dumb. If you've noticed in movies, the Black person is always the first person killed, because they're acting hysterical, and they're not used to it.

Representations of Rahina may be cast in different forms: "The Muslim, the Somali, and the female." She applauds fair representation under any of these headings. "If it's done inappropriately or wrong, I'll be holding it far from myself and just ignore it and try to appreciate the rest of the book." She will nevertheless finish the book.

I quote very extensively from Rahina's map, but I also omit a great deal, out of simple considerations of space. Rahina says that it is inadequate to say that she loves reading, "it's more like I breathe reading." She finds it difficult to think of a life without reading: "It's like you take my soul out and put it into another human being when I wake up in the morning. That's how much of a difference it would be. You'd be taking my memory." Her approach to describing the internal landscapes created by her reading activities is highly individual and affected by many ingredients of her life story as well as her reading tastes. No doubt the very act of creating the map, with all the autotopographical work it entailed, strengthens Rahina's memory of these odd and lively mental spaces. It seems clear, however, that the spaces are larger and more long-lived than what might open through the simple act of reading a single story. The books twine their way into Rahina's mind and carve room for very personal forms of expression and reflection that she now draws on to shape her map. The austere orderliness of her initial design is undercut and transformed by the surreal unruliness of the mental landscapes she invokes.

Exploring and Imagining: Roman

Roman is twenty-one at the time of our interviews, a student of industrial design. The younger of two brothers by rather less than two years, he has lived in the same house throughout his entire life. He describes himself as half French and half Ukrainian, but gives no information about when either branch of his family arrived in Canada.

Roman chooses a very singular focus for his map: a ravine in his neighborhood. Like others in the city, this ravine is a relatively wild area surrounding a small tributary to the North Saskatchewan River. Roman says it has shrunk considerably since his childhood, with more and more housing developments confining the natural space. It is also not as safe as it used to be: more addicts use the space and people drop garbage there. Roman says he has recently seen a flat screen television dumped in the creek.

Going to the ravine has been part of Roman's life for a long time. When he was young, particularly between Grade 1 and Grade 6, he and his brother played there; sometimes their mother came along and joined in. "Sometimes my dad would come and take pictures of random stuff." The ravine began to fade in importance as he started junior high. The adventures

> kind of just got more realistic, like we'd go paint in the woods, or we'd go—I had one of my birthdays there, and we took canvases out there and we just painted the tree, the autumn leaves and stuff. So, I guess as they progressed, they got less imaginary—Imaginative? Don't know the proper word for that, but it became more rooted in enjoying the actual space and enjoying that nature.

Unlike most of the participants, Roman manages to maintain a reading life as a student ("I still make sure to read all the time."); he reads a lot of science fiction and at the time of our conversation is in the middle of *Red Rising* by Pierce Brown.

Roman is a visualizing reader; he knows how things look, though he is not always entirely clear about the spatial relationship between one scene and another and sometimes has to check the map at the beginning of the book if he wants to ascertain the overall geography of his story. He hears character voices; the narrative voice is distinct as well: "If there's a narrator, I think it would default to a classic baritone dude." He does not think this voice is his own. "Also, I think I do hear the ambient sounds of the places that they're in." This effect can be diminished if he listens to music as he reads. Unlike Rahina's "white wall," his internal reading space is full of sensory information.

Roman snapped the photographs in this collage (Figure 10.4) with an analogue camera on black and white film—a deliberate decision, explained in his final slide:

Why the medium …
  I wanted to shoot these pictures in B & W and on film because of nostalgia. As I remember the mind-scape of my childhood, it felt right to have them be not clear,

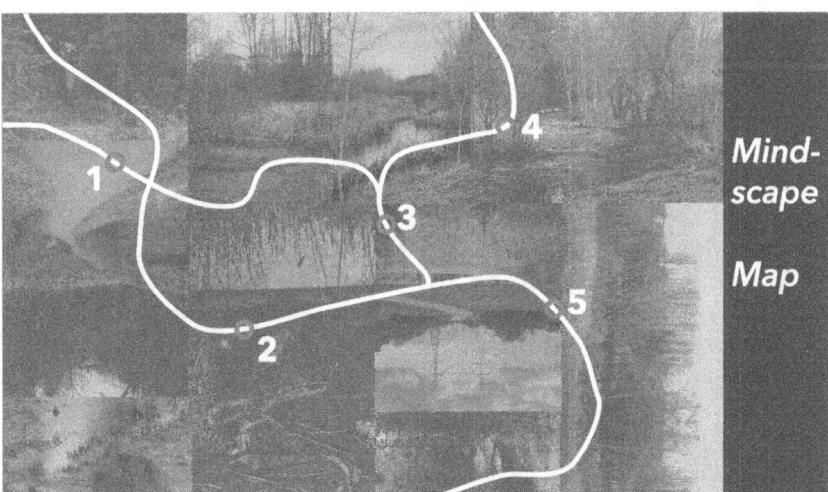

Figure 10.4 The overview image of Roman's map.

but muted and grainy because they are more than just images, they evoke feelings, sounds and smells. To have something extremely clear, well lit and in full color would overwhelm the visual and not let the imagination and memories fill in the rest of the details that were developed in so many different narratives.

High-resolution digital images seem to him to be inappropriate to the kind of sensory and emotional impact of the ravine that he wants to evoke. He numbers five particular sites on the overlaid map of the ravine pathways, and says these photographs are accurately sited on the map, but with some other pictures, he takes some artistic license in placement with a view to designing his collage of images to best effect.

In his five reflections, Roman suffuses his memories of reading particular books with recollections of experiences in the ravine. It could be described as a relatively clear-cut case of life-to-text, and it is certainly the case that the space of the ravine manifestly contributed to the reading space in each case. Roman makes very definite connections between his ravine knowledge and particular moments in his reading. It might be tempting to consider the ravine a singular space with a parade of book experiences moving through it. But that is not how Roman renders his map. In light of Rahina's associations, it is striking to observe that his pictures are not collected and placed in a monolithic way. Some are upside down; others are sideways-on. Given how carefully he envisaged the role of the black and white film photographs, it seems likely that, at least at one level, this overview image outlines a somewhat more kaleidoscopic reading space. Roman remembers and represents the ravine in a more free-form way than simply as a one-way channel for helping him visualize a sequence of one story after another.

Roman lays out his individual photographs on a black background, and for each image he adds a book or series title and image, plus a brief comment. His interview observations expand on the connections he marks so clearly.

Roman's first caption links the series Deltora Quest to a long shot of a prairie field, fringed by trees, with a housing development in the background (Figure 10.5):

> Deltora was one of my very first series that I read all by myself. It is set in a fantasy medieval era world, with forests, plains and mountains and the occasional desert. My neighborhood was a perfect example of what some of that world would look like and was a big part of shaping the world in my mind.

In the interview, he adds, "In this book, there's the plains and the plains kind of go into a forest, based on their travel … So when I pictured, like, the surrounding forests and stuff, I pictured the ravine and the grasslands kind of mixing with the forest areas."

The second shot shows a dip into a treed valley, with a path ascending up the hill on the far side; Roman makes a connection to the Ranger's Apprentice series. The caption reads:

> Ranger's Apprentice is my all time favorite series that I have ever read. It is set in the mid-evil [sic] times and primary in the forest. In this section of my ravine, there is a huge divide between two neighborhoods and I never really ventured

Opening a Lifelong Reading Space

Deltora was one of my very first series that I read all by myself. It is set in a fantasy medieval era world, with forests, plains and mountains and the occasional desert. My neighborhood was a perfect example of what some of that world would look like and was a big part of shaping the world in my mind.

Figure 10.5 The first scene in the ravine.

across it because it was the boundary of my imaginary world, similar to Will the main character in this book.

Roman expands on this idea in the interview:

In these books, the main character has his own little kingdom, or, not kingdom, but his area where he lives and he knows it all really well, and that's what I connected with in this part. Because in this part of the ravine, the river cuts off and you can see to the other side and there's a whole different world over there. So, I knew this side of the ravine, my neighbourhood, and the other side is the unknown, that's what I pictured. And these emotions were recollected when I read this book … I empathize maybe more with home and the character's feelings because I draw from what I've experienced.

The third image (Figure 10.6) shows a slope, though it is rather steeper than the picture would indicate, according to Roman. The caption reads:

This hill in the image was the scariest part for me as a kid. Because it was so steep on the way down, when I rode my bike, I would pick up a lot of speed and for a moment it would feel awesome till you start losing control a bit. This experience helped me formulate a connection to young James Bond as he, in his world would do crazy adrenaline stunts just like me facing the hill.

Roman adds in the interview:

So, this hill was always steep, and I learned to ride my bike in this neighbourhood, and whenever I got to this hill, because I was pretty young, it was pretty intense to go

Figure 10.6 The third ravine image.

down. And they used to have a dividing bar between, for some reason, maybe to stop vehicles, but it was down on the ground, laying down, and it was super sketchy to have to bike past it. And you're always going pretty fast, and so that kind of adrenaline rush is what fed into this series of books that I read, which was Young James Bond.

As we saw in Chapter 8 (Figure 8.1), the fourth image includes the path between the pylons into the ravine, creating a liminal zone that Roman connects to his reading of Harry Potter and the train ride from the regular world to the magical world of Hogwarts.

The final image (Figure 10.7) presents a layer of fallen logs on the ground, linked to the series of Magic Tree House. The caption reads:

> This was where the tree house in my ravine use to be. It is now a weird assortment of sticks but playing the tree house developed an [sic] world for me to imagine as I read through the Magic Tree House series.

The interview makes it clear that the role of this tree house is symbolic, as is this pile of sticks.

> There used to be a tree house up in the tree just to the right of it, but when I went to go look at it again, it was gone, and I just found this pile of sticks like someone was building a fort or something. [The tree house], I think, was just plywood. I kind of thought of this as the graveyard.

In other words, this pile of sticks is not the tree house in collapsed form. The tree house was plywood; the proximity of these piled logs to the original site of the tree house is probably

Figure 10.7 The final image from the ravine.

coincidence. Furthermore, Roman did not actually play in the tree house itself—in part because he was very young when he was reading the Magic Tree House books and in part because he was concerned about safety: "No, I never went up in it because it was super sketchy ... a couple planks going up and then there was a rope hanging off it for swinging on. It was pretty rickety. And I was afraid of heights as a kid." Yet the tree house was a potent force in his early childhood: "But knowing about tree houses, and seeing them and walking by them, it was kind of, like, look—deep in the woods there's a random tree house. It could whisk you off somewhere ... there's some sort of emotional connection. It helps build the atmosphere when you're reading these books."

Roman has been a big reader all his life. As well as the different series he associates with the ravine in the ways explained above, he also read books about science: astronomy, space, geology. He read books about art and the biographies of artists as well. He was a particular fan of the Eyewitness books published by Dorling Kindersley, and he read an online encyclopedia. None of this material was particularly associated in his mind with the ravine.

And yet connotations of the ravine link much of his childhood reading. The reading space created is like a number of different rooms, all connected by the fact that their windows look out onto the same view. Or perhaps the different rooms share a common source of light. The ways in which ravine experience illuminates his reading are exceptionally varied, given the size of the set, yet there is a discernible pattern: Deltora Quest + the ravine; Ranger's Apprentice + the ravine; Young James Bond + the ravine; Harry Potter + the ravine; Magic Tree House + the ravine.

To some extent, this result is simply an artifact of the approach to mapping that Roman decided to take. But his ready explanations of how the ravine experience fed into his reading spaces are convincing. The ravine let him appreciate the potential for magic in a tree house that might whisk you away, or the ritual of liminality in moving from one ontology to another, or the surge of adrenaline that leads you to take risks and find adventures.

Roman says explicitly and more than once that the ravine was a life space on which he drew to illuminate assorted reading spaces. Unlike Amani, for example, he did not import experiences from the reading space back into the life space of the ravine, though he did so elsewhere. The life experience of the ravine was complete in its own right and supplied a geographic, experiential, and affective repertoire for his reading. The emotional and aesthetic charge of this experience has suffused his reading over many years.

Merging Many Worlds: Ying Yu

Ying Yu is twenty-two years old and a student of electrical engineering. She has an older sister of twenty-six and two younger brothers of seven and four. She was born in Edmonton and has lived in about ten different homes in the city, mostly apartments. She speaks Cantonese to her parents and English to her siblings. Her family visits China every two years or so, and the longest visit was about two or three months. She reads in both English and Chinese (the latter mainly in school and mainly shorter pieces); she thinks she is better at reading and listening in Chinese than in actually speaking it "because my tones are wrong." She is a much more fluent reader in English than in Chinese; only in English does she have mental images of the story. "I can't really grasp Chinese too well, so it's only words. If I'm just reading Chinese, it's just gonna be like reading words and I can't really express—."

Ying Yu does not do much reading at present; her study obligations dominate. She has a few books at home waiting to be read (or, in one case, at least, waiting to be finished; she says she will have to start from the beginning again in order to finish it). A substantial amount of her reading occurs on her phone; everything she has read by Morgan Rice is on her phone, for example. She watches whatever television family members happen to be viewing, but not much of that either, although her viewing of Chinese programs from Hong Kong (drama and detective series) does appear to be rather more extensive. Her comprehension of Chinese is sufficient for viewing purposes, though she thinks she would not be able to recap the full story afterward. She does not game, and she rarely goes to movies, though she will watch them at home.

Ying Yu visualizes what she reads in the form of provisional flashes, always open to amendment—though whether she troubles to edit in part depends on her assessment of how important it is to get it right. We saw in Chapter 7 that she can add detail if it becomes important. When she needs a "stronger nature feel," for example, her forest image moves to a close-up focus with details of fallen logs, tall trees, and bushes. She attends to vocabulary when required as well, sometimes checking a word on her online dictionary, especially if she is reading on her phone.

Ying Yu's map (Figure 10.8) juxtaposes images of Edmonton (several of Chinatown) with shots of nature, images of castles in general, and a more specific fortification on the Great Wall of China in particular, a representation of the fictional *Hannah Montana*'s beach house and a picture of the very real Beihai Beach in Guangxi, China, where she

Figure 10.8 The home screen of Ying Yu's map (edited to remove two stock images).

went as a child. Of her seventeen images, two are Google Earth overviews of Edmonton settings, six are of Edmonton scenes, and a triple image of a forest is generic. Four involve castles (in total, she provides nine discrete castle images on her map), and one is a collection of four images of boats. The *Hannah Montana* shot and a scene from *Shrek* are purely fictional; and the Chinese beach rounds out the set. As a set of static images, this motley collection may initially come across as eccentric. What Ying Yu describes, however, are reading processes that resemble a kind of cognitive dance, in which she draws on this varied repertoire to illuminate her internal vivification of her stories, sometimes in very fleeting and temporary ways. There is, however, some consistency to these flashes; for example, the crenelated shape of her castle images is reliably square.

Ying Yu moved many times during her childhood, but her early years were spent near Edmonton's old Chinatown (Chinatown itself has moved and changed since those days because of new roadworks). "This is my childhood," says Ying Yu. "My childhood was filled with bustling people, adventure, colours, and fun." It also included walks in the river valley and outings to local parks. Ying Yu maps herself onto an area of central Edmonton and speaks of it with affection, describing a supermarket (Figure 10.9), for example:

> This supermarket is one I went to very often as a child. The inside of the store was very cute and filled with colour. They had everything in my opinion. As a child,

Figure 10.9 A Chinese supermarket in Edmonton.

> I remember always being very excited because I could see the fishes swimming and because my parents could potentially buy us snacks. This is my childhood. Food is life. Snacks are just the cherry on top of the icing.

Ying Yu here describes a grounded connection to a particular space, one that has lasted—with some local changes—throughout her life so far.

Yet Ying Yu consistently describes another way of thinking and reading, one that invokes "flashes" of imagery that are woven out of a mélange of fiction, known territory, familiar images, and a mix of Chinese and Western iconography. She provides instances of how her mind creates these fleeting images.

For example, we have already seen how she readily places *Hannah Montana*'s beach house on Beihai Beach, in Guangxi, China, which she visited as a child. Her concession to the requirements of the mermaids she is reading about is to add more glass to Hannah's house. When she needs a castle, Ying Yu flashes to a highly elaborated composite image. As sources for this imagery, she cites *Shrek* and *Scooby-Doo*, childhood picture books (unnamed), and a family photograph of the Great Wall of China. She attaches the following comment to Figure 10.10:

> While I didn't get to go to the Great Wall of China when I was a child, I did get to see pictures of it. There was this very beautiful picture of my parents and my older sister at the Great Wall. I wasn't born yet so I was not in the picture. But from the picture, you can see how the top is flat so people can walk on it, and the walls above have the up and down patterns to it. Also, there is a lot of square shapes incorporated into it. The image of the Great Wall is incorporated into my image of how a fortress is supposed to look—strong, protected, and surrounded by nature in the form of mountains and trees.

Figure 10.10 An image of the Great Wall of China.

Another image incorporates four pictures of boats. Her approach of entwining an assortment of visual inputs into a single "flash" is a recurrent motif in all these accounts.

In both her map and her interviews, Ying Yu is consistent in the use of the term "flashes" to describe her mental imagery. In one of the map comments attached to a picture of an Edmonton park, she expands on this description in intriguing ways. Here is her description in full:

> This park is very vibrant in colour. I love colours. When reading books or stories, if the plot is interesting and I actually read through it, I like to incorporate colour into the story. I like to make the story symbolic by using colour. Example: (Morgan Rice adventure book) When Thor, the main character, needs to travel from one place to another in order to retrieve information about his birth and identity, that is usually imagined with flashes of different colours like green and grey. Accompanying colours are flashes of image of how adventures and journeys should be like. I don't focus too much on the detail of the image. These flashes usually just have typical shapes. If I focus too much on a specific image, I will become confused because the story doesn't explicitly state what things look like. Unless it does, otherwise I won't imagine in that way. Also, I don't imagine too much on just one image but a flash of images, because this way I will be less confused as to how the story can go. If sudden changes happen, it is easier to accept.

Ying Yu's flashes are more than visual, as she explains in an interview comment.

> I think I notice, when I read—sometimes, for example, they're talking about apartments, I'd have the apartment smell … I kinda like that apartment smell, it

feels really homey, because we moved from a lot of apartments to apartments. So, I would have that smell. And then there was small images maybe. Like stairs, or it's a little bit dark, like the hallways.

Unlike Roman, Ying Yu does not hear voices, though she does sometimes register a narrative voice that seems to be her own.

Ying Yu attaches symbolic weight to her flashes of color. "So dark would be evil or mysterious, and then bright colour means, oh, there's hope, or there's sunlight coming in, there's hope. Or for example, if you're in the ocean and then it's just pitch dark blue, then I think, oh, we're lost, kind of thing." She says more than once that she likes to think about the symbolic impact of what she reads.

At the same time, there is a certain element of "easy come, easy go" about Ying Yu's low detail and flickering mental imagery. She does not describe a life of complete commitment to reading, even though she would like to be reading more; between her student obligations and her two small brothers, her time is largely accounted for. She is far more likely than Rahina or Roman to lay down a book without finishing it, and there is a sense of incompleteness in some of her description of what I would term her ongoing reading space. Flickering can happen when a light bulb starts to fade, but, even though her reading is now spasmodic, the swift transience Ying Yu describes is an active ingredient in how she always reads, not a symptom of how she is currently reading less. She has spent her life in Edmonton, but her Chinese experience is also very significant to her. Perhaps more than any other reader, she provides an analytical description of a kind of oscillation between sources of imagery from many elements in her life. She draws on one reading space to illuminate another, as well as flashing onto moments from her life space to create a fleeting combination that meets her temporary needs in a story. It is perhaps no accident that "flash" is both a noun and a verb.

Lifelong Reading Spaces

Rahina and Roman and Ying Yu are all very different readers. They have distinctive life experiences and also their minds work variably when reading. For example, Rahina's indifference to visuals and Roman's detailed manifestations of image and sound provide a contrast that might not be apparent in an ordinary conversation between them about books they have both read. Ying Yu's vague flashes of "mountains" or even simply "green" might seem like too much imagery for Rahina and nowhere near enough for Roman, but it is highly unlikely that either of them would even think to ask her about the degree of specification in her head as she reads.

The readers in this study are very different from each other, but their examples by no means exhaust the potential for variation; and Suleman and Laura, in particular, serve as a reminder that the concept of a lifelong *viewing* space may be more salient for some young people. No doubt there are also those whose "ongoing narrative space" in their minds is filled with the resonances of a lifetime of gaming, but none volunteered for this study.

In my initial exploration of the idea of the reading space, I drew on a personal memory: my own childhood and then lifelong experience of reading Rumer Godden's *The Story of Holly and Ivy* (Mackey, 2021b). This exercise was productive for developing my thinking about the concept, but its singular focus directed my attention to a particular kind of one-off reading space. What Rahina and Roman and Ying Yu are describing through their different experiences seems to be more plural, more diffuse, and more of an ongoing phenomenon in some normally unattended part of their brain. Alison Waller is perhaps venturing into the same territory with her description of the lifelong reading act:

> Affective traces cause textual encounters to resonate across the life space, connecting individuals and their reading scenes. Bundles of emotional response work according to the theory of mood-congruent recall, allowing specific moments from the past to chime with the remembering present through affective vibrations. Since paracanons are by definition made up of texts that are emotionally significant in some way, remembering and rereading accounts are often saturated with affect. Passionate responses can be found most often when readers recall experiencing "make-believe" attitudes that mimic the emotions felt by characters within a childhood book. More pervasive than these are moods and ambivalent feelings, such as anxiety, desire, and boredom, that emerge in childhood and in digging down the reading memories in childhood. (2019: 191)

Perhaps, that well-known anxiety about running out of reading material experienced by avid readers indicates a concern that a reading space kept open through the constant application of literate actions will shut down without fuel to keep it operational. Conceivably, readers of series books maintain a particular kind of ongoing reading space. Maybe, rereaders keep a space open for any potential returns. Imaginably, fan writers feel more proprietorial about a reading space they plan to readjust. There are many questions to contemplate. But just as the idea of a lifelong reading *act* supplies new ways of thinking about readers' relationships with single titles, so I think the notion of a lifelong reading *space* offers the option of exploring the impact of simply being a person who reads.

A. S. Byatt designates such a space in two different ways: as developing a way of thinking and also as a route to storing up content. She quotes Samuel Taylor Coleridge as saying his early reading habituated his mind "*to the Vast*" (Byatt, 1992: 127), and goes on to describe the residue of her own childhood reading:

> The roots of my thinking are a tangled maze of myths, folktales, legends, fairy stories, Robin Hood, King Arthur, Alexander of Macedon, Achilles and Odysseus, Apollo and Pan, Loki and Baldur, Sinbad and Haroun al Rashid, Rapunzel and Beauty and the Beast, Tom Bombadil and Cerberus. I have no idea now where I got all this, except for the Norse myths ... the tales and myths and legends did, I am now more sure than ever I was, exactly what Coleridge said they did. They made it clear there was another world, beside the world of having to be a child in a house, an inner world and a vast outer world with large implications—good and

evil, angels and demons, fate and love and terror and beauty—and the comforts of the inevitable ending, not only the happy ending against odds, but the tragic one too. (1992: 127–28)

Byatt is describing a long-term accrual of time spent in a reading space, and also exploring how it sets up a particular kind of relationship with a life space.

Rita Felski, in her extensive account of the mysteries involved in how we become attached to particular works of art, provides a cameo portrait of the way characters may become inextricably lodged in our minds. She reminds us that the characters do not exist until we bring them to life: works of art, she points out, "are *constituted* via the act of reception" (2020: 147). Although she does not use the term, her description of how we constitute characters is dense with elements of (im)materiality:

> Characters, in short, are portmanteau creatures, assembled out of disparate materials drawn from fiction and life. Rather than being restricted to a single text, they often serve as nodes in many networks. They are distributed, adapted, and mediated. Their presence can be exceptionally vivid, yet it is painstakingly composed … They are fabricated out of many things working together: the texts that house them; random scraps of knowledge about authors or actors; acculturation into ways of reading and habits of response; the diligence and devotion of publisher, producer, agents, reviewers, fans; the fictional objects with which they are associated (Sherlock Holmes's pipe; Jane Eyre's gray dress) and the real objects they bring into the world, from Harry Potter wands to Don Quixote prints. (2020: 91)

Having cocreated these beings out of such (im)material factors, readers then live with them; and, in some cases, the relationship is very extended. Felski continues:

> To live in this fashion, characters must rely on the kindness of strangers; without the input of readers or viewers, they are naught. Yet the latter are also obligated to the fictional beings that take possession of them, infiltrate them, speak through them. Stripped of the sediments of the novels I've read, the films and TV shows I've watched, I would be another person entirely. Fictional beings serve as alter egos, ideal types, negative exempla, moral guides, objects of desire, imaginary friends. They depend on us yet also engender us. (2020: 92)

Roman and Rahina and Ying Yu and A. S. Byatt and Rita Felski have read X and X and X. But they have also spent a lifetime engaged in the activity we colloquially call simply "reading." The residue of that "reading" may be more of a dreamlike jumble than any account that they might offer of reading one X or another would ever indicate. The territory opened up by such considerations (Rahina's hallucinatory mental spaces; Roman's strong sense of the affect of the ravine; Ying Yu's vague, colorful, and transiently flexible flashes; Byatt's mythological vastness; Felski's brain full of imaginary people) is profoundly private and personal, and these hints of somebody else's ongoing reading space are provocative and tantalizing rather than definitive. The differences between their distinctive accounts strongly suggest that the space created by anyone's residual reading afterlife is composed on disparate principles. Even a glimpse is a privilege.

If ongoing reading nourishes an ongoing reading space, what I have described so far are different reading lives that foster highly private manifestations of such a phenomenon. But there are many ways that such "ongoing narrative spaces" in the mind may occasionally, as it were, throw open a window onto a more public view—either life spaces or, perhaps, sometimes, other people's reading spaces. Matt and his friends playing Quidditch or sampling Pottermore are continuing to furnish the reading space that contains their ongoing relationship to Harry Potter. Rahina writes forms of fan fiction; Halia produces fan art and plays book-related role-playing games with her junior high friends at recess time. Lily takes notes about her neighborhood, enacting the most potent form of agency exhibited by Harriet the spy. Not all such spaces are purely based on fiction; Liang's ongoing reading and thinking about ancient Chinese ways of fortune-telling clearly lingers in her mind, as does Suleman's hopeful engagement with successful entrepreneurship. These reading spaces connect to life spaces in ways that make room for exchanges with other readers.

In some cases, however, we can see a window being closed and a reading space that might have been public instead restricted to a purely private experience. Changing the home culture and the language of reading is often a swift route to such closure. Here is Lily's account of losing access to a community that helped to sustain her active engagement with a series of participatory mystery books:

> *A Mystery for You and the Tiger Team* by Thomas Brezina, this series is written by an Austrian author. It was hugely popular in China, but its popularity never reached North America ... I remember playing games with other kids pretending to be the book's main characters as a child, but that stopped when I moved to Canada because nobody has heard of the series here.

Ursula Le Guin calls the shared experience of books "a genuine bond," and adds, "a person reading seems to be cut off from everything around them ... that's the private aspect of reading. But there is a large public element too, which consists in what you and others *have read*" (2008). The loss of that shared reading community, whether through immigration or for other reasons, is often a blow visible to readers themselves but not necessarily to anyone around them.

Almost by definition, invisibility is a tricky theme to pursue. But the interviews raise questions of repertoire, and they display moments where I failed as an interviewer because of the inadequacy of my own international cultural literacy. These instances do provide some brief examples to demonstrate how a potentially public conversation may of necessity stay at the level of private experience. One involves Lily again, and the other, Suleman. I present them here, not as a form of self-flagellation but as a reminder that the public side of our ongoing reading spaces is both something we may deliberately curate and something that depends on interactions with other readers. Some forms of reading diversity remain invisible even though they are in plain view. The incapacity of one conversationalist to recognize and resonate with the observations of another shapes more discussions than we probably like to think. The examples I present here do me no great credit, but they probably represent a commonplace situation.

One way and another, I have taken an informed interest in children's literature for more than fifty years. As a result, I was both appalled and intrigued by my ignorance of the lively worlds of children's reading in non-Western countries, as presented by some participants in this study. I was also horrified to realize how much more powerful and useful were my initial reactions to those titles that I did recognize: the Western classics such as Grimm and Andersen and Sherlock Holmes at a primary level, and the less well known (to me) but still recognizable world of Japanese anime in a kind of secondary way.

The readers, of course, speak of their childhood favorites with affection, regardless of whether the titles are meaningful to me. Only when I begin to investigate the maps in detail do I start to register how much I missed in my initial response. My research into the titles they mention with enthusiasm is not extensive, but it is enough to confirm huge blind spots. I share these blind spots with many monolingual readers of English. Translation *from* English is widespread across the globe; translation *into* English is notoriously less likely to occur. We readers of English are the losers in this lopsided arrangement, but the point I want to make here is slightly different.

Lily is an avid reader, and Suleman, the reverse. Lily mentions many books that I recognize from her childhood in China, but she is also enthusiastic about a number of other titles, including *Girl's Diary* by Yang Hongying. A swift search informs me that Yang Hongying has sold something like 160 million copies of her books (https://publishingperspectives.com/2019/11/china-childrens-book-author-yang-hongying-unit-sales-160-million/). She has been called the J. K. Rowling of China, and her Chinese sales massively outstrip the figures for the Harry Potter books in China. Her work is not lacking in international recognition; in 2014, she was nominated for the Hans Christian Andersen Award. Had I taken the trouble even to follow those award nominations more assiduously than I do, I could have known about her a long time ago. That point is not exactly the issue that interests me now. I want to consider the impact of the different resonances in my conversation with Lily. She mentions reading Harry Potter and I not only have a reaction on the spot, I feel some connection with Lily as a reader. When she draws my attention to Yang Hongying, however, she meets silence and ignorance from me, and has to take the lead in explaining the importance of this author.

A similar situation arises with Suleman. He talks about the novels he sampled in his brief fling with reading. The titles are familiar to me and I can discuss his response to them. When he mentions *Hamdard Naunehal*, the little monthly magazine to which he actually had regular access, I have nothing to offer in reply.

I mention these exchanges as potent examples of invisibility. Yang Hongying and *Hamdard Naunehal* are significant ingredients in the intertextual experiences and lifelong reading spaces of Lily and Suleman (and millions of other children). My complete lack of familiarity with them means that when Lily and Suleman comment on their importance for their reading lives, there is none of the interpersonal reverberation that accompanies other aspects of our conversation. Because I am actively engaged in research, I chase every reference to acquire at least some minimal and basic information. If I were a working librarian or teacher with many other priorities to deal with, I would not have time for such research, even with the impetus of an identical conversation. Almost inevitably, I would resonate with Sherlock Holmes and *Black Beauty* and let the unfamiliar references evaporate. The consequence would be a very skewed sense of Lily and Suleman as readers—and the skew would be invisible to me but almost certainly not to them.

The mapping project gives the readers in this study some chance to educate me about authors and titles that mean a great deal to them. They know that when our discussion is over, I will be studying their responses further. Obviously, such an exercise cannot be part of every reader's advisory conversation, but it is salutary to keep in mind that the warm echoes surrounding a conversation about familiar authors create a risk of ignoring what may be vital to one person and devoid of resonance to the other. Listening for what we do not automatically hear is important with any reader; with readers from a cultural background to which we have little detailed access, it is even more important.

Educator Sabine Little supports this perspective in an article about the need for multilingual libraries. Starting from a British perspective, she says,

> Children readily adapt and edit their identities in ways that they consider most suitable for particular environments, and they do so from an early age. In the current English education policy context, multilingual children appear mainly from the perspective of being children with English as an additional language (EAL), creating a duality where English is on one side (specifically, the side of the curriculum, formal assessments and measures, etc.), and all other languages (unspecified and unnamed) are on the other side. This is natural in a monolingual country, but this duality automatically leads to a deficit model, which essentially asks "is their English good enough?," rather than "what are the language skills of this child?" (2020: 10–11)

Punday usefully reminds us that the normative sense of future-oriented mainstream fiction we currently take pretty much for granted is in fact something quite specific and relatively local: a modern development in the West. If I were to adapt Little's question and ask: "What are the literary skills of these participants?," my answer would undoubtedly highlight the forms of literary skills I am myself equipped to recognize. I am not always able to interpret right to the edge of the maps these readers chose to produce; but I can at least recognize that my limits and theirs are differently outlined.

Rahina's elaborate mind map of the connections between her reading and her daydreams is built on a core of Western children's and adult literature. She knows of almost no Somali literature, and is not familiar with much fiction based on Islam either. Nevertheless, it is very clear that her dreamscapes draw from a rich mix of cultural input. Liang describes a feeling of rootlessness and a sense that her education has Westernized many of her reactions, but she also feels some ownership of the ancient ways of fortune-telling in China. Ying Yu's red dragon resonates with Chinese imagery. In the personal zone of an ongoing private reading space, different sources of cultural information may jumble together more or less comfortably, but they are difficult to share because of their hybrid and idiosyncratic nature. I believe this invisible dilemma is an important one, particularly for readers with experience with more than one cultural background. But I think it is also worth asking to what extent all readers may be tongue-tied when it comes to expressing the muddle of personally peculiar and culturally conventional responses that reading evokes for them.

One force that may keep a reading space open in the back of a reader's mind is the allure of agency. Children's agency may be fettered for many reasons. Roman, for example, seems to have been relatively autonomous in his access to the ravine; Amani had reasonably free rein in her local parks; but, in both cases, their engagement with the challenges on offer was sometimes limited by their own fears. Fictional child agents are not so restricted; nor (apparently) are the heroes of financial success stories such as Elon Musk. Riya's wistful notion that, somewhere in the world, white children occupy a role of supreme agency in their own lives gave her a mental zone to occupy, in which she might be in charge of her own choices. Today, a version of that agency is something she relishes about living far from home. Readers with strong connections to countries outside of Canada observe how Alice McKinley or the heroes of *High School Musical* move with authority within a culture that may still be opaque to them, and they gradually assume some of that power of self-government (sometimes marked by official events such as being promoted out of the ESL class).

An open reading space for the language left behind provides a different form of agency. Obviously, conversations with family, religious observations, media exposure, maybe Saturday language school, and many other forms of support system may keep a person's mother tongue alive, and the sense of maintaining a reading space in the first language is a source of power for some readers.

To keep a reading space open so that you can move in and out of it, rehearsing forms of agency that may not be available to you in your daily life, just makes psychological sense. I have neither the expertise nor the wealth of data that would be needed even to begin to wade into large issues of identity, but the views of childhood encapsulated in these maps do offer fascinating hints of child priorities and purposes, and these immaterial elements pervade the reading spaces we see here, weaving through the material conditions and contingencies of each reader's life space.

A lifelong (or even a temporarily ongoing) reading space is a locus for continuing imaginative rumination, inflected by the resonances of other people's thinking as presented in texts that have made an impact in both obscure and obvious ways. The role of this reading space in the larger world of the mind may shift between a vague background awareness and a more actively alert focus. It is not always helpful; we have seen how Halia describes a period in her life where she could almost be said to have lived inside an ongoing reading space, and she found this condition was not good for her mental health. With Rahina, Roman, and Ying Yu's accounts, however, we see many hints and suggestions of a state of simply being open to the shaping that reading can offer. It is highly idiosyncratic and personal, and manifests (im)materiality in different forms.

There is no way of telling how many readers would even recognize the concept of a lifelong reading space; the oblique and fleeting perspective on some readers' minds that I present here is really a route to raising questions rather than supplying any definitive answers. Nevertheless, I find the questions compelling, and I believe they demonstrate the potential in asking readers not just to talk *about* what they read, but also to talk *around* that experience of reading. What does it mean to read X—and what does it mean, in more abstract terms, simply to be a reader?

Life Spaces and Reading Spaces

Conclusions

11

Reading Minds in Motion

A space contains many juxtaposed trajectories, and the stories it includes are "stories-so-far" (Massey, 2005: 9) rather than completed and closed narratives. A space provides the necessary conditions for active agency (Malpas, 2018: 138). A space, in short, teems with open-ended activity, as a moment's reflection on our own busy life spaces will remind us. Although a text begins by offering a finite space, our minds oxygenate and extend it with the active energies of the life space. And our minds themselves, as Jacobs' diagram in Chapter 9 illustrates, are in constant motion as they process the written symbols.

This project begins with the creation of maps as marked spaces, as mnemonics. My conversations with the participants use these spaces as a reference point, a process that, at least to a degree, resists the paring down imperative that comes into play when shaping a narrative about the past. Carolyne Van Der Meer, in consideration of life writing, quotes Brian Henderson, director of Wilfrid Laurier University Press, which sponsors a life writing series. Henderson makes a significant point: "Truth, strangely, becomes harder to achieve because once the writing process begins, it becomes more about the written word than the truth," he says. "Psychologists and psychoanalysts believe that as soon as the narrative begins, memory ends—because it's no longer a straight-up story—it becomes influenced by the moment, the current moment, which alters the truth" (Van Der Meer, 2006: 27). Van Der Meer uses Henderson's observation to address issues of "this blurring of lines between truth and narrative, between craft and story, between living memory and unmoving words" (2006: 27), and her comments raise a useful reminder. The nature of this project greatly reduces the quotient of "unmoving words." In contrast to the stillness of the written word, digital maps can make greater provision for messiness, and these maps become fixed only as I print screen captures. The interviews move between our spoken words and the images on the screen that shift as each participant darts the cursor around their map and its links. Only at the point of transcription are the oral discussions pinned down in print. Obviously, the mapping and interview operations act reductively on the surplus of experience that constitutes everyday life, but the layering up of the maps and the improvised elements of the spoken conversations make room for miscellaneous or fragmented developments that may be smoothed out of existence when a story is shaped in words.

Bearing in mind the fluidity of the responses made possible by this approach, let us return to the initial focal question: what can we learn about processes of private reading from the individual specifics presented in these diverse and inherently personal maps? The maps permit participants to display some of their own particular "richly situated knowledge" (Preston, 2003: 26). It is rare to be able to "situate" readers in their personal background setting as we talk about their reading experience. Does this extra knowledge about these readers illuminate the transfer from life space to reading space?

My own words in this book are clearly "unmoving" and my straight-arrow organizer highlights the rigorously artificial qualities of my presentation of the information these participants convey. In the next section, however, I call on a metaphor that introduces some potential for "movement" back into this account.

Drawing Conclusions

When I planned this project, I did not anticipate that it would offer a definitive account of reading behaviors, and indeed it does not do so. I did hope that it would open doors and windows on to new ways of thinking about reading, and it is these insights I address in this chapter, making use of an evocative metaphor from the work of Tim Ingold and Norman Bryson.

Ingold, an anthropologist, offers a useful way to value an incomplete account. Citing the work of Bryson, an art historian, Ingold contrasts the oil painting with the pencil drawing. The conventional oil painting is a bounded surface, usually rectangular, which must be filled in, shaped by what Bryson calls the imperative of the "all-over" (2003: 150). "Every element that is added—every trace of the brush—has to anticipate the totality of the complete picture of which it will eventually become a part," says Ingold. A line drawn with a pencil, in contrast, "can unfold in a way that responds to its immediate spatial and temporal milieu, having regard for its own continuation rather than for the totality of the composition." Ingold observes further, "Whereas painting moves to completion, drawing carries on, manifesting in its lines a history of becoming rather than an image of being" (2011: 220–1). Bryson testifies to the open-endedness of the pencil line, in terms I have taken to heart for this study: "However definitive, perfect, unalterable the drawn line may be, each of its lines—even the last line that was drawn—is permanently open to the present of a time that is always unfolding" (2003: 150).

This fascinating and illuminating contrast is very liberating for anyone trying to represent the full breadth and subtlety of the exercise of reading. I have not filled the whole canvas with an "all-over" explanation of how readers move from their life spaces to their reading spaces and back. I have used my pencil to delineate what I have observed in the data offered by the readers in this project—partial outlines, occasional feathering, even some crosshatching. But eventually, I simply lift my pencil from the page and leave open the prospect of further pencil marks, hoping that my lines and shadings add up to a workable representation with vital scope for others to continue the work. Even my artificial preference for the present tense wherever possible is a gesture toward open-endedness rather than closure.

Despite their many infilled and rectangular qualities, the maps produced by the participants are also partial and tentative—and dynamic in ways that Bryson ascribes to the pencil rather than the paintbrush loaded with oils. Rahina, with the aid of a compilation of titles she created for Goodreads, and Suleman, drawing on a list composed in high school of all the cartoons he remembered watching, come closest to any kind of "all-over" representation of even one corner of their reading spaces. Even they, however, are nowhere near to covering every square inch of space with a comprehensive image. The maps, the linked commentary and imagery, the interviews, all compound to a sketch rather than a complete landscape.

In my opening chapter, I say that the straight line I used to designate the direction of the organization of this book is fantastical and misleading. The formal chapters, which present the data as clearly as I can manage, represent, as it were, the actions of a pencil reined in by a ruler—in some cases literally, in the organization of tables. In contrast, in this final chapter, I take the reader maps as my starting point and explore where a pencil licensed to wander can take us. What have I learned through investigating the annotated maps and the interview conversations? How have my questions been further extended by exploring observations on reading processes by scholars in many different disciplines? My default in the following discussion will address issues in the mental life created by narrative fiction, since the richest conversations arise in that context. But my own construct of a reading space is not limited to one kind of writing; and, where the maps and the readers take me outside the territory of fictionality, I will specify that I am taking a detour.

Reading as Reflection

The idea of reading as a form of repose has deep roots in our ways of thinking. Reading is restful and restorative. It calms us. It opens a private space of intensity and evokes deep memories. Punday speaks of "a long tradition that imagines reading as a disembodied, intellectual, and frequently spiritual experience" (2003: xvii). Murray confirms this popular perception: "Indeed, the general public still regards reading as predominantly a silent, solitary, private and passive activity that leaves no record" (2021: 163). The act of reading looks backward, drawing on our prior encounters with the world, including our first efforts to make sense of a great deal of inchoate information.

We unavoidably read from the position of where we are now and where we have been. As anthropologist Clifford Geertz puts it, "No one lives in the world in general. Everybody, even the exiled, the drifting, the diasporic, or the perpetually moving, lives in some confined and limited stretch of it—'the world around here'" (1996: 262). Nobody *reads* from the perspective of the world in general either, and one potent source of input is our first place, where we begin to make sense of the world through the terms of our own location in it. The straightness of my arrow is a fiction, but its unidirectional pointer does represent a key element of the life space. Reading may be more recursive than life, but our reading experience also cumulates in one direction over time. Our interpretive capacities increase (even if irregularly) as our intertextual repertoire compounds and our life knowledge offers us insights into previously enigmatic situations. And yet, even as we may rejoice in the positive impetus of that forward arrow, reading continues to draw retrospectively on the heart of our early experience of life.

Perhaps nobody is more eloquent on the imaginative force of the first place than George Eliot, who comments on the "elderberry bush overhanging the confused leafage of a hedgerow bank" that offers great delight because it is "no novelty in my life, speaking to me merely through my present sensibilities to form and colour, but the long companion of my existence that wove itself into my joys when joys were vivid" (1965: 164). While reading invites us into new worlds, the abstract nature of the words means we must animate them with the energies of our own lives. Again, Eliot captures the power of our earliest associations:

> These familiar flowers, these well-remembered bird-notes, this sky, with its fitful brightness, these furrowed and grassy fields, each with a sort of personality given to it by the capricious hedgerows—such things as these are the mother-tongue of our imagination, the language that is laden with all the subtle, inextricable associations the fleeting hours of our childhood left behind them. (1965: 48)

It is difficult to imagine a more potent recipe for evoking response than words deliberately and artfully arranged on the page for the express purpose of being brought to life via the "mother-tongue" of our own imagination. The force of that imaginative dynamism includes the powerful energy of childhood "when joys were vivid" and when we acquire our first starter sample kit of the ways of the world.

This kind of description of reading might be summed up with the full range of meaning of the word "reflective"—but reading does more than invest past energies into a set of new thoughts (somebody else's thoughts) that occupies our mind, courtesy of the words presented to us by an author. Such ingredients are certainly part of the appeal of reading, but what takes place when we read is a far livelier and more complex event than what I, with Eliot's eloquent assistance, describe so far. But it is important not to ignore the deeply felt roots of association, the power of that childhood vividness. In terms of the readers in this project, we can probably see the clearest traces of that kind of energy in the varied and affectively powered significance they attribute to the experience and the conceptual force of the forest.

I have not done much drawing since I was a little girl, but I still recall the significance of placing the line of the horizon on the page. I do not want to outwear my metaphor, but it is this kind of "grounding" in childhood landscapes that I initially envisaged exploring when I set up this project. I have no doubt that the felt experiences of childhood, emplaced in one or several specific locations, do indeed "earth" our reading lives. But this vocabulary has a bias toward reading as static and/or backward-looking; and what these maps and transcripts offer is insight into a much more dynamic phenomenon. In real life, the horizon moves as we move; it does not fix itself as a single line in space.

The idea of polysituatedness (Kinsella, 2017) may help here. Paradoxically, my language of grounding and earthing and rooting both describes one key aspect of reading (the power it draws from lived experience) and simultaneously outlines a scenario that is inherently portable—transferrable into another setting, capable of animating a world invented by somebody else. That power of transfer calls for many different and lively mental activities.

And indeed, our life spaces today are themselves dynamic, their (im)material elements in flux. Even as our feet traverse the ground, our heads may be active *somewhere else*. Jessica Dubow reminds us,

> Every person has a place of their own, even if it is unclear where that place is and what forms of attachment it entails. In the simplest sense we inhabit places (sites, positions, settings, and locations) but those places are themselves inhabited by mental happenings (dreams, phantasies, memories, ideations), in which the present is sliced together with other moments of time, whether with a past that is incompletely or vaguely regained or with the imagined locale of a future. Place, as a spatial phenomenon is also a temporal one. (2015: 39)

George Eliot would have understood that idea of a first place shot through with memories and anticipations, and certainly the pace of technological change during her lifetime was daunting (the disruptive impact of the railways is a recurrent theme in *Middlemarch*, for example). Our sense of space today, however, is more porous, more open to *elsewhere*, than anything Eliot would have recognized. Joshua Meyrowitz makes the point succinctly:

> Individually, of course, we each need to be *some*where, even as we interact with images, sound, and people not co-present. And yet the meaning of local space is nevertheless reshaped. The spread of personal mobile communication devices small enough to fit in a pocket has a major impact on where we are when "at home" and seemingly "with" family members (who may be on their own devices that connect them to other places and non-present people) as well as exactly "where" we are socially when in public space … [M]any of the once-fundamental differences between being in one place versus another place are diluted by digital mobile media. (2015: 114)

Rahina's story provides one extreme example of this contemporary version of place. Speaking of the extended time she spent in Somalia and Kenya to further her religious education, she observes,

> Over there, I just spent time with my family; we're not really allowed to leave our household because there are so many security guards. Theft is a huge issue, and corruption, in Kenya. In our own household we had maids stealing things, so we're not allowed to leave our household. So, I would say nothing really happened in Kenya that I would say increased me in any way, I just spent time there. Most of the time on the internet, on web forums, Facebook, Reddit, Tumblr, Snapchat, Quora, all those websites, I'm just spending more time.

The conditions of Rahina's Kenyan home shaped her behavior during the months she lived there, and so did the attitudes she brought with her from Canada, as she explains:

> I need to be constantly mentally stimulated, I can't sit, clean, cook, take care of the family, just talk to neighbours when they come over, that seems very Africa-lifestyle, just chillax and relax and not think about heavy topics. I grew up here [in Canada], I need to be constantly mentally stimulated, even from just me going through like a feed, a Facebook feed, anything.

It is interesting to observe how Rahina's capacity to gain access to her familiar reading spaces alters her relationship to the new life spaces she encountered in Africa, a very contemporary paradigm of (im)materiality. Reading itself becomes a form of agency in such a situation, though conditioned by some very material considerations: limited access to electricity, as little as an hour a day, and "garbage internet." Even so, her web forums offer Rahina at least some escape from the physical constraints of the household.

Ying Yu, born in Edmonton and a frequent visitor to China, likes to check out Chinese news on Facebook. "I kinda like to get an idea of what's going on too, because I feel like the lifestyle there is, like, pretty interesting, it's pretty cool." Again, we see a doubleness of place, a capacity to keep in touch (as we say) with places not present. Connections can be sustained through technology or through simple memory, throughout our daily existence. This double perspective bears many similarities to the process of inhabiting a fiction.

Reading in Motion

In this chapter, my pencil also outlines my own processes of thought as I work through this project, developing a livelier concept of reading as mental action. The reader's body settles into the chair, but the mind shifts from active assessment and agency in the surrounding world to a virtual movement engendered by the words on the page. The same neurons remain active as we improvise a dynamic simulation of the actions and agencies of the characters. But the participants do more than set the characters in virtual motion. Their minds dance around the words on the page in complex ways.

The participants speak infrequently and often elliptically about their focused interpretation of a singular title. What they show more clearly is the mind's scope for peripheral activity, around and through the reading event. Below, I provisionally label this approach a kind of counterpoint, and investigate some of the examples provided in this study.

In the early stages of reading a new book, before we can swing into action with the characters, we are aware of fumbling with the setup of the new world we are creating. Surely, part of the appeal of rereading and/or series reading for aficionados is that this scramble to "move into" the story is reduced. With entirely fresh reading material, as we decode, assemble, and evaluate new information, our minds are restless, trying to decide how to focus our attention, a process articulated by Daniel, a participant in my doctoral research, many years ago:

> I know I have, before I start reading a book, in any context, not just this one, some anxiety about being interested in this book. And I always think about that when I start. Okay, when's it going to be that I get it, that I catch on to what's going on? When's it going to be? You know, I always know two or three pages into it where I'm more relaxed and all of a sudden, I'm really reading for understanding. (Mackey, 1995: 216)

In Ingold's terms, our initial improvised responses need to take account of the grain of the material we are working with. The artist, says Ingold, must

> join with and follow the forces and flows of material that bring the form of the work into being. The work invites the viewer [or reader] to join the artist as a fellow traveller, to look *with* it as it unfolds in the world rather than behind it to an originating intention of which it is the final product. (2011: 216)

For many readers, it is a relief to get past the initial barrier of uncertainty, to achieve the dorsal activity of default reading, in which the eye scans the provided information with increasing fluency, and, at least temporarily, the brain does not worry about indeterminacy. Some readers accomplish this kind of reading while being alert for detail and particularity; some are happy to keep just gliding along. As we improvise a simulation of character behavior and motivation, our own mind is itself active, alternating between dorsal and ventral paths as the text and our own predilections seem to demand. The mind is in motion, noticing here, skimming there, getting a feel for the cadence of the words on the page (itself an activity with embodied implications) and a sense of what might matter later for the plot. Of the readers represented here, it is probably Suleman who most clearly acknowledges the importance of this initial submission into the movement that the text requires, although he discusses it in a kind of negative relief, in terms of his own difficulties in aligning himself with a text.

Acclaimed fantasy author Ursula Le Guin sums up the need for readers to invest their own mental movement into a text:

> In its silence, a book is a challenge; it can't lull you with surging music or deafen you with screeching laugh tracks or fire gunshots in your living room; you have to listen to it in your head. A book won't move your eyes for you the way images on a screen do. It won't move your mind unless you give it your mind, or your heart unless you put your heart in it. It won't do the work for you. To read a story well is to follow it, to act it, to feel it, to become it—everything short of writing it, in fact. Reading is not "interactive" with a set of rules or options as games are; reading is actual collaboration with the writer's mind. (2008)

This requirement for readers to "keep moving" as they meet a text has also been expressed in more cognitive terms. Literary theorist Anezka Kuzmicova addresses the issue of motor enactment as part of the brainwork of reading and as essential to creating a sense of readerly presence within the text. "A higher degree of spatial vividness, arousing in the reader a sense of having physically entered a tangible environment (presence) is achieved when certain forms of human bodily movement are rendered in the narrative, as compared to when they are not" (2012: 25). Mentally enacting movement delineated in the text is a much more direct route to such spatial vividness than any amount of detail in spatial description, she says; "presence arises from a first-person, *enactive* process of sensorimotor simulation/resonance, rather than from mere visualizing from the perspective of a passive third-person observer" (2012: 24).

Essayist and English professor Elaine Scarry takes the idea of minds being activated by accounts of motion a step further, by exploring the extra impact when the movement being described parallels the actual motions of a reader's hands or eyes. "Reaching, stretching, and folding are the actual motions the hand carries out—like a spell of hand motions performed over the book—as one reads," she says (1999: 147). When characters reach or stretch or fold, our own minds are doubly active. Similarly, readers and characters make use of their eyes:

> The eyes, meanwhile, are also in motion, rolling from left to right and back again, skating down the page, darting back to a detail missed, then forward again. The actual motion is incorporated into the motion of fictional persons so that our somatic mimesis of what is happening in the book works to substantiate and vivify motions on the mental retina that are wholly imaginary. (1999: 148)

In language that is by now familiar to us, Kuzmicova says, "In fluent reading, imagery is mostly spontaneous and pre-reflective … it is not consciously controlled by the reader—once the reader has made the initial choice to treat the narrative conventionally as narrative literature, i.e. to immerse" (2012: 26). She is also firm that imagery does not necessarily involve pictures, offering the same kind of full list as Nikolajeva.

> By imagery, I do not mean visual imagery only, as has been the case in nearly all theoretical work on perceived vividness in literary narratives so far … Imagery encompasses any vicarious experience whatsoever of what is most commonly referred to as perception, i.e. exteroception (sight, smell, taste, touch, hearing), but also proprioception (e.g. pain) and, crucially, the senses of bodily movement (the proprioceptive, or kinesthetic, senses, e.g. the senses of limb and organ position, velocity, effort, acceleration and partly balance and touch). (Kuzmicova, 2012: 26)

To create that internal sense of movement, our minds also need to improvise at least a minimal inner space where it can (as we say) take place.

Learning How to *Be* in Space

Let us return to George Eliot's invocation of childhood for a moment, and consider whether there are different ways of thinking beyond the visual in terms of "the mother-tongue of our imagination, the language that is laden with all the subtle, inextricable associations the fleeting hours of our childhood left behind them" (1965: 48). Many of the subtle and inextricable associations from the fleeting hours of our childhood encompass just the sensations Kuzmicova lists: sight, and also smell, taste, touch, and hearing, and that feeling of a body in motion. When I think back to my own childhood, one of the elements of my young life that I remember most clearly is the sensation of my body's relationship to the ground. I am standing upright, I am falling, I am jumping, I am rolling on grass, I am thrashing through deep snow, I am skidding on ice. I also recall the sensations of the air: it is warm, almost tender in its gentleness; it is chilly, with a raw and penetrating dampness; it is hostile, as a strong wind forces the freezing rain that Newfoundlanders call "icy pins" hard into any exposed part of my face. In Malouf's terms of the "first place," I learn about this world "from inside, from my body outwards" (1985: 3).

I do not consciously call up such details as I read unless an author particularly induces a specific connection, but my general sense of spatial vividness, as I move *inside* a text world, includes a bodily relationship both to the ground and to the air, one that arises from my own early experiences. For me as a reader, at least, this sensation is more important than visual details. Ingold confirms the significance of placing our body in the world, most commonly on our feet, saying,

> A more literally *grounded* approach to perception should help to restore touch to its proper place in the balance of the senses. For it is surely through our feet, in contact with the ground (albeit mediated by footwear), that we are most fundamentally and continually "in touch" with our surroundings. (2011: 45)

That sense of *being* in a space is essential for any character who is going to matter to a reader. As a rule, the character has feet, ground to place them on, and a working connection between the two, even if readers are oblivious to the importance of these facts. A narrative agent with beliefs, hopes, fears, and the like must occupy and be "in touch" with some kind of space for that agency to be meaningful and for both purposeful and accidental actions to be possible. Action words evoke a parallel reaction in the mind that serves to vivify the space and animate the characters with a capacity for movement, economically sponsored by the reader's own.

One big difference between being in a space and running a simulation of being in a space is that the simulation involves a reduction of consequences. If I am out in a winter landscape, it behooves me to be extremely alert for black ice because a sudden slip may break my bones. If I am simulating such an excursion via a narrative of a winter outing, I need not be so hypervigilant; the characters will come to grief only if the author decrees it—and, in that case, no amount of care on my part will avert the catastrophe. Indeed, I can even notice the black ice only if the author puts it there and then mentions it—and, regardless of the hazards and perils of the story, I, as reader, remain safe in my chair.

We are highly selective in how we import live knowledge into our improvised response to a text. Daily life provides an unceasing stream of stimuli, always surplus to requirements for any given moment; we must choose where to direct our attention.

Readers, by and large, do not add such excessive layers of distraction and irrelevance to the information they infuse into a text as they bring it to mental life. The characters we vivify are more able to focus on the events of their own lives than we are often able to do ourselves as readers, embedded as we are in a twenty-first-century cacophony. But, in life, a constant flow of distraction hovers in my peripheral vision and inhabits my personal soundscape. Characters do not have to expend energy blocking out the aeroplane overhead, the dog barking across the street, the motorcycle screeching round the corner; we eliminate these distractions on their behalf before we even begin to engage, and an author has to introduce them back into the text for us to take account of them. And, of course, when that happens, their appearance is not random but something that happens on purpose.

So the text streamlines and the reader edits out the superfluous noise of the real world, and, although response is fluid and multifaceted, it is still organized around a stimulus that is shaped and crafted. As a result, even after donating awareness to the characters in my story, I often have attentional capacity in the form of what we might call brain energy to spare, and it is interesting to see how the participants in this project speak of dispensing that surplus mental capacity.

Counterpoint

Our minds do not simply activate the characters and simulate their movements in a kind of virtual lockstep. One of the pleasures of reading lies in keeping our balance between what the text permits us as readers to know and what the characters know. Sometimes, readers are more knowing because the narrator provides information to them of which characters are not aware; more often, characters assume the knowledge of a full-sensory world around them while readers make do with and/or extrapolate from a few snatched details. Let us look at the implications of Matt's account of how an author presents a forest scene:

> I mean, authors don't write a chapter where they are all of a sudden at this landmark. They're going to talk about walking there and maybe some conversation and build up to the landmark. And it helps contextualize maybe where it is and maybe the feelings surrounding it. And so, I think all of those—it's crazy how much it's not just description of the landscape that makes you understand it, it takes characters in these novels talking about the landscape or how they're feeling around these landscapes builds into the entire feel of it. If they're talking about being worried and scared, you're going to kind of picture it to be darker, you're not going to picture a bright, sunny forest.

The characters are *in* the forest. Their virtual beings have visual, sonic, olfactory, tactile, exteroceptive, and proprioceptive information about the forest. They have a developed sense of their own bodies in this particular space. We as readers have the author's words, organized to present us with selected details. Matt provides a sharp description of a careful reader's interpretive processes, drawing on those words to illuminate which inferences may offer the fullest, most dynamic sense of that setting, those characters, their subjunctive take on the world expressed in feelings, wishes, and so forth, and the relationship among all these elements. Some of this reader's mind is pulling up "forest" imagery in general, seeing, feeling, smelling, hearing the forest, invoking a sensation of being in, and moving through a forest. Some of that mind is trying out alternatives to see which version best accords with what the author has chosen to show.

We as readers invest one particular and vital characteristic of "ourselves in the world" into these characters by default, presuming that, as "live" people, they need only look around to get a full-sensory impression of the forest they fictively inhabit. The characters breathe the air of that forest as they chat in such illuminating ways about the atmosphere of this particular corner of it. The reader, in contrast, is mentally moving around this textual space, looking for clues: is this forest bright and sunny, or dark and spooky? A reader brings a more or less fleshed out sense of "forest" to bear on the words—in Matt's case, his embodied experience of the trees behind the school soccer pitch. But "forest in general" is only an initial stepping-stone, a starting place for assessing what this moment in this text demands of its readers. Much of the appeal of reading lies in this kind of balanced mental activity: the plot-driven and/or character-driven sense of moving in and out of alignment with the events on the page and, at the same time, what we might call its verbal counterpoint—an awareness of the words on the page with their denotations and connotations, local cadences, and larger rhythms. The active work of collecting and assembling clues of all kinds—affective, intellectual, atmospheric, and more—includes visual details for some readers, more kinesthetic pleasures for others, and so forth.

At the same time, readers are, to a degree, bound by the writer's potent powers of omission. Life requires putting one foot ahead of the other with no shortcuts. In contrast, art can short-circuit. Riya talks about what is not present in a story. She is a reader who likes to be accurate when the author supplies direction, but who can readily revert to the generic or skip altogether, if that is how the writer places the playing pieces. Here she is discussing how much she attends to the geographic relationship between the location of Kirrin Island and the town where George lives with her parents, that is, between one scene in the story and another connected one:

> If I had to think about it like that, I could. If something in the book made it, or if they put all of that in one sentence, then I would think about it like that. But usually it's like, they spent some time here, they make their way there; unless something eventful happens in the journey it's not really important. And then they get there and then something happens there. So, unless there's something specific [about the journey] that forces me to think about it like that, I usually won't.

Whether the story itself moves straightforwardly into the future or shuffles sideways into diversions and retrospections, there is a sense in which the orthodox reader makes forward headway through the book—the pages pile up on the left-hand side, the percentage mounts on the screen; the arrow points in one direction. Even if the reader moves back and forth, it is in the cause of reading *more*. Readers may deliberately choose to subvert the tyranny of the forward progression, but there is a very real sense in which, even if the reader obediently moves from one page to the next in the orthodox order, the mental activity of reading is never completely in lockstep with the actions of the characters or the details of the set-piece scenery. What we might call the dance that assembles the clues and fragments on the page in ways that make sense to a reader is a major component of the concept of reading as movement, an essential counterpoint to the activities of the characters and the descriptions of the settings. Matt makes inferences about setting from clues supplied by dialogue as characters walk through the forest; Riya floats over moments of textual elision in which all movement from one scene to another is eliminated from consideration. Both readers must take account of what the words supply or omit as they build their sense of the story.

Other kinds of mental movement are more specific to particular situations. Revisiting a textual world that is presented in new form is a commonplace of contemporary life, and these readers move among versions in entirely taken for granted ways. In the next section, we explore the importance of adaptation to the reading lives of these participants.

Moving Around and Between Versions

As dwellers in the twenty-first century, the participants in this project belong to a world in which stories are frequently and heavily reworked, and their reading spaces are furnished with multitudes of versions and a large variety of formats. They have much experience of being what Linda Hutcheon calls a "knowing audience" (2006: 120), familiar with a story from previous encounters.

Participants' most explicit conversations about mental movement arise in relation to such versions, particularly in relation to the movement between books and the movie reworkings of those books. Matt watches the Harry Potter films and compares the world-building of the movies with his own. Laura, in something of a reverse process, reads books to recapitulate moments from the movie version that she has invariably seen first. Amani at first appreciates having actor faces to populate *The Perks of Being a Wallflower*, but, as the book grows on her, she finds this level of specification "irksome." Suleman tries to use his comprehension of the film of *Harry Potter and the Chamber of Secrets* to propel him into the considerable challenge of the print version, but in the end is overwhelmed by the sheer quantity of words in the book. Amy finds that seeing Hermione from the outside warps her capacity to return to her favored reading position on the *inside* of that character.

The pleasures of following a known story are complex. Certainly, many readers and viewers succumb to the subjunctive, as it were, and recenter themselves in deictic terms in the position of people who do not yet know the outcome of the story. But at some level, in the most minimalistic sense, they may sustain an idea, buried somewhere, of what will *not* happen. I do not have to worry that a particular character will die—is such knowledge ever completely subtractable from a subsequent encounter? I am not sure if any kind of brain study could establish the nuances of how a rereading or a reviewing

Figure 11.1 Cartoon version of *Journey to the West*, as placed on Liang's map.

differs from a first meeting with a story. Does even a small part of the mind relax or, alternatively, brace itself for bad news to come later in the story, somewhere beyond the scope of conscious attention because the surprises have had the edge taken off?

We also know very little about how familiarity with a text may free parts of the interpreting mind to wander into different kinds of territory—anticipatory, comparative, technical, and much more. The participants in this study offer hints of such roving minds, but hints only.

Different versions of stories sometimes provide cultural information that might not be acquired otherwise. Liang, for example, provides a link on her map (Figure 11.1) that addresses issues of versions and translation, saying in her caption:

> I watched many animes and cartoons on TV during the lunchtime. The picture is "Journey to the West" in cartoon. The *Journey to the West* is one of the four masterpieces in Chinese literature along with *Outlaws of the Marsh*, *The Romance of the Three Kingdoms*, and *Dream of the Red Mansions*. These are amazing books that speak for the culture. Because of the difference in grammar and words it's hard to directly translate word to word. I searched for the English names online. I found them nowhere close to the beauty of the original name.

Liang's cartoon version is one of multiple incarnations of this story over many centuries. Britannica.com offers a terse digest of its epic history:

> *Journey to the West* … foremost Chinese comic novel, written by Wu Cheng'en, a novelist and poet of the Ming dynasty (1368–1644). The novel is based on the actual 7th-century pilgrimage of the Buddhist monk Xuanzang (602–664) to India in search of sacred texts. The story itself was already a part of Chinese folk and literary tradition in the form of colloquial stories, a poetic novelette, and a six-part drama when Wu Cheng'en formed it into his long and richly humorous novel. Composed of 100 chapters, the novel can be divided into three major sections. (https://www.britannica.com/topic/Journey-to-the-West)

Liang speaks of the difficulties of translation, ascribing them to differences in grammar and vocabulary. To appreciate this work, her mind must move between languages, and the cartoon helps to promote a feeling for her Chinese culture and way of thinking. She makes no reference to reading the 100-chapter novel, but, whatever its literary merits, the classic version is only one instantiation in an ongoing cycle of retellings. Liang's viewing of the animation clearly brings her into the force field of that cycle. It is an experience that operates on a different basis from the perspective of individual characters addressing an unknown future, the core structure of most contemporary mainstream Western literature (though, of course, Western mythologies also often operate on a similar basis of implied familiarity with a very old story).

Lily describes an encounter with the classic Chinese novels through the form of a parody (see Figure 4.8), which she describes as follows: "*You Mo San Guo* (no translation found) by Zhou Rui. This is a humorous book that makes fun of the four Chinese classic novels. The author has written parodies of all four of the Chinese classics and this is my favorite out of all." She sends a link to a website, but it is in Chinese, since she could find almost nothing in English (nor could I, apart from listings on a few bookselling sites). Her selection of her favorite out of the quartet suggests some familiarity with the series and is neutral on how much she knows of the originating classics.

Halia describes a movement in the other direction, when her enthusiasm for unicorns is validated by a story in Arabic about the Prophet meeting a magical horse. Her childish reaction was electric as she connected unicorns to the Prophet and to a text valued by her father, and she struggles to express her delight in this moment, even as an adult. What she seems to be describing is a moment of joy as her different worlds cohere rather than pull in different directions.

In these examples, participants describe minds moving both through and around the stories, making connections that are both culturally based and highly personal in nature, and this movement accompanies the processing of the narratives in question, via watching the cartoon, reading the parody or listening to the Arabic audiotext.

A number of participants talk about making more deliberate cross-cultural connections between different kinds of social experience, by means of book reading and film viewing. A list of materials serving as cultural translators would include stories featuring Junie B. Jones, Alice McKinley, Hannah Montana, the *High School Musical* heroes and heroines, the characters of *Malcolm in the Middle*, Sherlock Holmes, the Secret Seven, and the Famous Five, characters presented by Grimm and Andersen, the protagonists created by Judy Blume, and, of course, Harry Potter. In addition to following the adventures and introspections of these characters, readers actively made use of information from these stories as a way of illuminating a culture. Rahina, for example, found that Junie B. and Alice offered a framework for comprehending the actions and decisions of her Canadian classmates. Riya, on the other hand, read Blyton books in her Indian tea valley in order to savor a "not here" quality; she later used the insights provided by these and other Western books to mitigate the strangeness of her new life in Canada when she arrived at the age of eighteen. Halia drew on the LGBTQ books recommended by her junior high friends to help her reconsider the restrictions of her home culture. In all these cases, we can see them both processing and enjoying a particular story and thinking around and through that story at the same time. In all these cases, some of such ruminations occur post-reading, but it is clear that sparks are initially ignited during the ongoing reading event. In such cases, a reading space becomes a working element in an ongoing life space.

The narrative text that triggers the opening of a reading space is shaped and crafted. The life space of a reader of that text teems with surplus stimulation and manifests aspects of "throwntogetherness" (Massey, 2005: 140) that exceed the options available to the most capacious text imaginable. The vast heterogeneities of a life space must somehow be pruned and refined to provide a useful charge for the organized world of a text; and I suspect the energies of that refining process also fuel movement inside the reading space.

Much texting and some forms of stream of consciousness writing in sites such as Tumblr and Reddit provide some counter-opportunities to read text that is much more like conversation in its lack of careful shaping and its surplus of life details. It would be very interesting to find a way to explore if and how readers approach such materials with different cognitive tools and strategies. What could neuroscience tell us if we could find a way to measure brain activity in settings of such naturalistic and often under-edited writing?

The minds that encounter the shaped and edited world of a published text and that refine the excesses of the life space to enliven that text world in useful ways do not settle down meekly to follow the train tracks of the words and to reduce all other activity to the lowest order of mere maintenance. Brains continue to buzz, with verbal connotations and more personal affective associations, with questions, with hypotheses, and more. And of course, we, the readers in our comfortable chairs, must ourselves continue to block the extraneous stimuli that surround us in the life space—that plane, that dog, that annoying motorcycle.

These maps are all retrospective but, of course, the lives they model are lived forward. The readers represented so diversely in these documents are moving through a period of maximal learning. As a fellow Blyton reader, I invent a time traveling visit from me to Riya, set up to inform her that real-life white children also inhabit a world of restrictions. Riya responds with a phrase that sums up the attitude of many young readers to the constant flow of new knowledge that is a feature of childhood life and reading: "Wow, okay, I didn't know that."

Children themselves need to assemble their sense of the world in the tentative form of a pencil drawing, rather than laying down layers of oil paint that cannot be adjusted or realigned. (I do not want to strain my metaphor much further, but the idea that many children are provided with a mechanistic reading scheme operating as a kind of paint-by-numbers kit, rather than simply being given their own pencil, is an irresistible extension.) New readers must find ways of satisficing as they expand their repertoires; they need to figure out how to hop onto the merry-go-round of learning to read, reading to learn, and applying that learning in order to read better and to learn more. It sounds straightforward when laid out in the linear form of a sentence, but of course it is a dynamic and sometimes bewildering process. Fortunate children gain a sense of agency from these expanding possibilities; they learn that reading and writing are sources of power. They also become more skilled at assessing the grain of a new text as they begin to establish the best route to improvising a simulation of the events it presents.

Complicating the Straight-Line Arrow

In my introduction, I produced a list of the chapters in this book, accompanied by the simplest possible graphic, a straight, one-way arrow. That arrow, of course, has always been an oversimplification, a response to the need to impose some kind of legibility on an overwhelmingly diverse data set. It is time now to return to the account of reading implied by the arrow and to look anew at what the maps and the interviews can tell us about its utility and its deceptiveness.

The maps present an assortment of geographic spaces in reasonably orthodox ways, and the impact of home is primary, though not always "first" in Malouf's sense; for example, we gain no sense of Halia's Iraqi origins from her image of her first Canadian house. Overall, it is straightforward to discern a home space in which children establish a sense of the world that they are able to bring to their texts. This space is shaped by social relationships, and children find many ways to practice home range agency. They learn the essential geography of the area where they are permitted to exert some independence. Away from the domestic rules and conventions that their parents and caregivers enforce, they learn to create and negotiate this childhood space, both in terms of real-life relationships with other children and also in terms of how those relationships are inflected by physical activities, by games and by pretending. Such experience adds to the equipment they are able to bring to bear on texts. Within the scope of the textual home range, they may also acquire their first early experience of interpreting different kinds of representation without any adult scaffolding.

GEOGRAPHIC SPACES   from the outside world

    The first place
    Childhood stability and disruption
      The social space
    Reading and relationships
      The domestic space
    The home range and agency

TEXTUAL SPACES
    Border country
    The forest
      A shared fictional world
    Harry Potter

PSYCHOLOGICAL SPACES
    Interior worlds
    Diverse approaches to mental imagery

LITERARY SPACES
    Ongoing worlds
    The arc of the lifelong reading space   to the reading mind

Figure 11.2 Revisiting the straight-line account of reading.

The geographic spaces, though extremely diverse in terms of local detail, provide these general support structures for all the readers in this study. In describing and explaining some of their textual spaces, the participants supply a common core and also a very long tail of individual experiences and examples. The forest and the world of Harry Potter, the two specimens of textual space that I explore in detail, offer a look at different elements of the reading experience. In many ways, the chapter on the forest feels like the key pivot point of the whole schema. However constrained their access to trees, most of the readers recognize the psychological, symbolic, and narrative potential of a forest setting. The forest functions as a kind of basic unit of narrative space, both enabling agency and action and also fostering an extended repertoire of atmospheres. The comments on local trees and fictional forests provide the clearest glimpse in this entire study of life space material being transmuted into reading space potential. It also appears that negotiating narrative forests in a reading space can wash back into attitudes toward actual trees in the life space, at least for some readers. More than one participant provides some fictional overlays to the forests in their lives. Amani shivered away from entering the stand of trees behind the park because of reading-induced fears. Matt, in contrast, relished the opportunity to play imaginary games among the real trees.

So far, if not exactly following the straight line of my arrow, the actions and responses of the participants are comparable. Ironically, it is in their point of greatest crossover, reading and viewing Harry Potter, that they start to manifest more distinctive patterns of behavior. They avoid the movies so their reading will not be sullied by external perceptions and conflicting interpretations. Or they take the movies as the primary version, and read selectively, almost purely in order to reactivate the mental pleasures of the movies in a larger and more leisurely way. They connect online with other readers, perhaps only lurking, or perhaps taking the authoritative "Britishness" of Rowling's voice as a model for their own writing. They acquire merchandise and play in the Harry Potter zone of Pottermore. They imagine themselves into games of Quidditch. They see fragments of the Potter universe in their own surroundings—or they draw on their experiences of their own surroundings to enliven their understanding of the story. The Potterverse is large, and these participants roam around it in divergent ways.

Harry Potter is the largest example of multiple interpretations and instantiations of a core story, but this little set of readers belong to their own temporal era, however broad their geographical distribution. As readers of the twenty-first century, they are entirely used to plural versions. Amani is both pleased and annoyed to have two renditions of *The Perks of Being a Wallflower*. Liang and Lily approach vital masterpieces of their Chinese tradition through the vehicles of two different forms of retelling. Many participants are familiar with a "heritage" collection of cartoon classics, drawn from a large range of decades and cartooning styles and replete with cross-references and quotations. The internet opens opportunities for fan reworkings of favorite stories.

These examples are all volunteered by the participants. In contrast, the data supporting the concept of psychological spaces are available only because I probe. The chapter on visualization processes is the one section of this book that does not originate with ideas offered by the mapmakers; I actually ask questions about their interest in "seeing" what they read about. Everybody answers very readily, though it is clear that some have never thought about it before. I have asked many other readers this question in the past and am not surprised by the range of the answers, but, in my own further reading on the topic, I am very struck with the scale and precision of current scientific confirmation of these varied reading styles.

In his novel *Atonement*, Ian McEwan describes a naive teenage writer who assumes that readers will simply respond to her direction. Briony's authorial fantasy of readerly obedience to the writer's will throws the diversity I have been presenting into a kind of relief:

> A story was direct and simple, allowing nothing to come between herself and her reader … By means of inking symbols onto a page, she was able to send thoughts and feelings from her mind to her reader's. It was a magical process, so commonplace that no one stopped to wonder at it. Reading a sentence and understanding it were the same thing; … nothing lay between them. There was no gap during which the symbols were unravelled. You saw the word *castle*, and it was there, seen from some distance, with woods in high summer spread before it, the air bluish and soft with smoke rising from the blacksmith's forge, and a cobbled road twisting away into the green shade. (2001: 37)

Briony presumes her readers will visualize, will provide a distant pictorial scene with just one hint of any other form of sensory information in the words "soft with smoke." She assumes their vision will match her own, and that all powers of evocation lie with the author.

But the participants in this study disrupt Briony's absolutist fantasies with their commentary. For some of them, a provisional sense of a castle arises instantaneously; this image may be fleeting, or recurrent, or relatively permanent, or, for certain readers, amenable to revisiting and refining as they choose. Castles inflected by the Great Wall of China and by American animated movies may flash up as a hybrid substitute for Briony's European imagery. A reader may perhaps compose an image that has much in common with Briony's distant vista but is suffused with a life force from an Edmonton ravine. Others may not conjure up any kind of castle until they are able to inhabit a character to perceive it. And some readers simply read "through" the word, not needing to have it "there" at all, substituting a white wall or thinking, "the scenes, who cares?" They may make do with a vague "castle silhouette" and not trouble to absorb any further particularities.

We know far too little about internal reading behaviors. What makes the building blocks of cognitive approaches to reading so different for each person? Maryanne Wolf reminds us that reading is not hardwired in our brains the way language is: "No human was born to read. Literacy requires a new, *plastic* brain circuit" (2020). The brain would seem to adapt to the need for new circuits in personal ways, as attested by the distinctiveness of these participants' accounts of their own processes. Wolf is much more interested in the impact of digital changes than she is in the nuts and bolts of individualized cognitive responses. Her account of the value of reading with attention (which she claims is much more difficult to do in digital contexts) is very abstract: "These processes include connecting background knowledge to new information, making analogies, drawing inferences, examining truth value, passing over into the perspectives of others (expanding empathy and knowledge), and integrating everything into critical analysis. Deep reading is our species' bridge to insight and novel thought" (2020). Rahina, Roman and Ying Yu probably all pass muster in these terms, but the singularity of Wolf's account gives no access to the lively idiosyncrasies of their mental approaches. Brains would seem to be plastic in particular as well as general ways.

Rahina, Roman, and Ying Yu, of course, offer a segue to the final stage of my schema, one kind of end point to the directional arrow (with the necessary proviso that the arrow of the life space continues pointing forward long after our interviews end). As Wolf indicates, reading changes our brains in many ways, and also regularly helps us to change our minds as well (not quite the same thing). In their different ways, these three readers remind us that the impact of reading does not automatically cease when we lay down the book. They provide three examples of how reading can create a kind of ongoing, open-ended, and highly idiosyncratic open space. (Viewing and gaming may offer similar possibilities, but my focus remains on reading.) Wolf does not use these terms, but she seems to worry that we are turning too much of our reading space over to what she considers the fleeting and frivolous inconsequentialities of online reading and texting. J. G. Ballard's ongoing narrative space devoted to the half-life of Robinson Crusoe would presumably be much more meaningful to her, though it is not clear how much critical analysis his relationship with that text ever featured, in the moment or in the aftermath.

Rahina's example makes the strongest case for some kind of lifelong reading space as a possible outcome of inveterate reading. But in reality, none of these three participants nor any of the others offers more than a suggestive hint and a set of intriguing questions. Does the mind of a constant reader operate on the basis of a different relationship between the ongoing life space and an equivalently ongoing reading space? Does it matter what that person reads? For example, does a loyal reader and rereader of a few selected series set up a zone of familiarity, comfort, and routine, which works quite differently from the space created by a reader who operates on a basis of permanent self-challenge? Does the ongoing reading space of materials that offer a safe haven and a refuge set up a particular kind of resource in relation to the life space, as contrasted with the space created by adventurous and potentially upsetting reading? For whom does it matter? And does this connection shift if the bulk of a reader's texts are conversational and ephemeral, and, if so, how?

For much of history, the majority of any given population either did not read, or read very narrowly, confined to religious or political texts, or, in more secular times, to a largely sensationalist popular repertoire. What makes reading valuable is itself a shifting concept. My university library once acquired a large collection of Sunday school prize titles and a librarian invited me to look at them all, after they were unpacked but before they were taken away for cataloging and shelving. The experience quickly became overwhelming as I absorbed recurring patterns of colonialist virtue-signaling and virulent racism—in materials, it is important to remember, that were, in their time, cast as reading that would turn children into better people.

Although the participants in this study offer only glimpses of the potential for thinking about a lifelong reading space, they provide more direct evidence of the intractable individuality of what matters to them. Amy, for example, observes, "Most of my friends read books about how to be more successful or how to improve your life in this way, and it's literally so boring. I can't." Instead, she reads books about what to do with grey water, and, to get away from all of it, she reads fantasy. Suleman, on the other hand, is inspired to start reading more steadily by the potential for self-improvement, though at the same time he clearly maintains a soft spot for the fantastical heroics of Umro Ayar. To me, it seems crucial for literary researchers to beware of their own agendas, sometimes hidden even from themselves. No doubt it is a good thing if reading fosters empathy, for example, but that goal is sometimes imposed by the researcher rather than by the reader in question. Respect for participants and their own priorities is vital, and it calls for genuine agnosticism about the moral outcomes of reading on the part of the researcher. Such detachment is probably rarer than it should be.

Janice Radway reinforces the vital necessity of not taking the stories of these twelve participants and their reading processes as closed, concluded, packed into this book as finite case studies. "To restore to social processes their open-endedness, to conceive the subject as always a subject-in-process is to seek to preserve a future that has not been truncated but remains open to the possibilities of change" (2008: 342). It is very possible, even likely, that some or all of the twelve participants changed as a result of participating in the project. It is certain that, for a variety of reasons, they have all continued to change since they and I parted company.

Eight of these readers articulate some kind of bicultural perspective; ten of them refer to extensive global travel. For all of them, their first place is only one source of the worldly understanding they invest in their reading, though the affection they describe for the locations they mapped suggests it remains vital. Their online access to the rest of the world reduces the primary significance of their current whereabouts, as Rahina's story of her time in Somalia and Kenya vividly illustrates. And yet, no matter what virtual possibilities open up to them, their bodies occupy a particular space. For the duration of the interviews, each participant sat with a graduate assistant and me in the research center of the Education Building at the University of Alberta, in a room with large windows looking out into a big tree. Our introductory conversations referred to the dropping of the last leaves, or to the snow on the branches, or to the new buds. From Christmas week of 2017 to the end of January 2018, Edmonton was bitterly cold, and any January conversations refer to that experience. It is worth noting further that those of us who were veterans of Alberta winters and those who were newcomers to the prairies felt this frigidity very differently. The research enterprise itself, in addition to referring to other times and places, is placed in its own particular geography and time frame. We come into the center via an experience of a specific day's weather. During Ramadan, we avoid bringing coffee and snacks into the interview setting, though at other times of the year we are not so punctilious. We schedule meetings around the exam timetable.

In addition to these grounding variables, there are larger distinctions that inevitably affect the research process. For different participants, the timespan between the first and second interviews varies substantially, a disparity that almost certainly shapes the nature of some follow-up questions, and that also reflects whether the creation of the map itself is a brief and intense experience or a task distributed around the completion of course assignments, and job requirements, and family obligations.

I provide these mundane details as a reminder that readers are inevitably earthed at all points of their reading lives. Our richly situated knowledge is made up of many components. A mix of daily responsibilities and pleasures contributes to the warp and weft of encountering any text. At the same time, we bring our social experiences, our cultural priorities, our sense of aesthetic delight, our varying capacities to picture or hear or feel the written word, our past reading of other fiction and nonfiction, and many other attributes. We also bring our own bodies and our history of bodily awareness of the world.

The life space is particular, specific, finely detailed, and always in motion. Jill Paton Walsh describes its scope and singularity:

> We shall see every day, if we just raise our eyes to the hills, the movements of wind and water, and the fall of the light. There are never two moments the same, what with sky and weather and tide, the passage of time, and the random fall of the rain. To be alive is to be bodily present, to notice where and when one is. (1997: 237)

This account of a life space actually arises within a reading space, expressing the reflections of a fictional character, Madge in *Unleaving*. Madge's fictional world is based on a real-life place in Cornwall—and so the (im)material cycle rolls on. As readers of this constructed world, we bring to the passage our own awareness of wind and water and light, of sky and weather and tide. Perhaps we take our reading experience back into our lives and look at the hills more frequently while the resonance of these observations reverberates inside our minds. Life and reading inflect each other in (im)material ways and with (im)material consequences; for readers it is very difficult to detach them, one from the other.

In this small study, each map distills a few components of the rich life and reading situation of an individual reader. Their discussion of these life spaces and the impact on their reading spaces offers some illumination of the vast reach of experience that feeds into our reading processes, and sometimes echoes back into our life awareness in ways mutated by the text. Messiness is not a deficit but a feature. Into the unnaturally tidy lines of print, we bring a mental apparatus and history that allows us to suffuse and enlarge these abstractions through invoking our own experiences, in all their disarray and confusion, in ways that bring the sentences to life. We assess the grain of the text, and then we move *into* the cadence of the words or the performance of visual imagery or the atmosphere of the situation. Or all of the above. The unruly delights of reading take many forms.

References

Abraham, A., D. Y. von Cramon, and R. I. Schubotz (2008), "Meeting George Bush versus Meeting Cinderella: The Neural Response When Telling Apart What Is Real from What Is Fictional in the Context of Our Reality," *Journal of Cognitive Neuroscience*, 20 (6): 965–76.

Adolph, K. E. (2000), "Specificity of Learning: Why Infants Fall over a Veritable Cliff," *Psychological Science*, 11 (4): 290–5.

Agosto, D. E. (2002), "Bounded Rationality and Satisficing in Young People's Web-Based Decision Making," *Journal of the American Society for Information Science and Technology*, 53 (1): 16–27.

Ahmed, S. (2013), "*Kachee Goliyan* Makes Its Debut with Umro Ayar—First Urdu Comic," *Express Tribune*, April 15. Available online: https://tribune.com.pk/story/535638/lingo-revitalised-kachee-goliyan-makes-its-debut-with-umro-ayar-the-first-urdu-comic/ (accessed September 29, 2021).

Barr, R., A. Lauricella, E. Zack, and S. L. Calvert (2010), "Infant and Early Childhood Exposure to Adult-Directed and Child-Directed Television Programming: Relations with Cognitive Skills at Age Four," *Merrill-Palmer Quarterly*, 56 (1): 21–48.

Barsalou, L. (2003), "Situated Simulation in the Human Conceptual System," *Language and Cognitive Processes*, 18 (5–6): 513–62.

Bartlett, L. (2008), "Literacy's Verb: Exploring What Literacy Is and What Literacy Does," *International Journal of Educational Development*, 28 (6): 737–53.

Barton, D., and M. Hamilton (1998), *Local Literacies: Reading and Writing in the Community*, London: Routledge.

Birkerts, S. (1994), *The Gutenberg Elegies: The Fate of Reading in an Electronic Age*, Boston: Faber and Faber.

Black, R., J. Alexander, and K. Korobkova (2017), "Flows of Literacy across Corporate and User-Produced Virtual Worlds," *Teachers College Record*, 119 (12): 1–20.

Brandt, D. (1998), "Sponsors of Literacy," *College Composition and Communication*, 49 (2): 165–85.

Brosch, R. (2017), "Experiencing Narratives: Default and Vivid Modes of Visualization," *Poetics Today*, 38 (2): 255–72.

Brosch, R. (2018), "What We 'See' When We Read: Visualization and Vividness in Reading Fictional Narratives," *Cortex*, 105: 135–43.

Bruce, D. R. (2001), "Notes toward a Rhetoric of Animation: *The Road Runner* as Cultural Critique," *Critical Studies in Media Communication*, 18 (2): 229–45.

Bruner, J. (1986), *Actual Minds, Possible Worlds*, Cambridge, MA: Harvard University Press.

Bryant, P. E., L. Bradley, M. Maclean, and J. Crossland (1989), "Nursery Rhymes, Phonological Skills and Reading," *Journal of Child Language*, 16 (2): 407–28.

Bryson, N. (2003), "A Walk for a Walk's Sake," in C. de Zegher (ed.), *The Stage of Drawing: Gesture and Act: Selected from the Tate Collection*, 149–58, London: Tate Publishing; New York: Drawing Center.

Burnett, C., and G. Merchant (2021), "Returning to Text: Affect, Meaning Making, and Literacies," *Reading Research Quarterly*, 56 (2): 355–67.

Burnett, C., G. Merchant, K. Pahl, and J. Rowsell (2014), "The (Im)materiality of Literacy: The Significance of Subjectivity to New Literacies Research," *Discourse: Studies in the Cultural Politics of Education*, 35 (1): 90–103.

Butler, C. (2020), "Japan Reads the Cotswolds: Children's Literature, Tourism, and the Japanese Imagination," *Children's Literature*, 48: 198–233.

Byatt, A. S. (1992), "A. S. Byatt," in A. Fraser (ed.), *The Pleasure of Reading*, 127–32, Toronto: Alfred A. Knopf Canada.

Carroll, J. S. (2011), *Landscape in Children's Literature*, New York: Routledge.

Cave, T. (2016), *Thinking with Literature: Towards a Cognitive Criticism*, Oxford: Oxford University Press.

Cecire, M. S. (2019), *Re-enchanted: The Rise of Children's Fantasy Literature in the Twentieth Century*, Minneapolis: University of Minnesota Press.

Cecire, M. S., H. Field, K. M. Finn, and M. Roy (2015), "Introduction: Spaces of Power, Places of Play," in M. S. Cecire, H. Field, K. M. Finn, and M. Roy (eds.), *Space and Place in Children's Literature, 1789 to the Present*, 1–19, Farnham, VA: Ashgate.

Charlton, E., G. Cliff Hodges, P. Pointon, M. Nikolajeva, E. Spring, L. Taylor, and D. Wyse (2014), "My Place: Exploring Children's Place-Related Identities through Reading and Writing," *Education 3–13*, 42 (2): 154–70.

Coats, K. (2019), "Visual Conceptual Metaphors in Picturebooks: Implications for Social Justice," *Children's Literature Association Quarterly*, 44 (4): 364–80.

Cole, H. (1996), "Helen Vendler, the Art of Criticism No. 3," *Paris Review*, 141: 166–212.

Currie, G. (1995), "Visual Imagery as the Simulation of Vision," *Mind & Language*, 10 (1/2): 25–44.

Dubow, J. (2015), "Place and Loss," in J. Malpas (ed.), *The Intelligence of Place: Topographies and Poetics*, 39–49. London: Bloomsbury Academic.

Eco, U. (1994), *Six Walks in the Fictional Woods*, Cambridge, MA: Harvard University Press.

Eliot, G. (1965), *The Mill on the Floss*, Toronto: Signet Classic.

Evans, I. (2020), "OPINION: The Battle for the Soul of Hogwarts: Re-thinking 'Harry Potter' in the Wake of J. K. Rowling's Transphobic Comments," *Student Life*, June 23. Available online: https://tsl.news/opinion-rowling-transphobic-comments/ (accessed September 29, 2021).

Felski, R. (2020), *Hooked: Art and Attachment*, Chicago: University of Chicago Press.

Fox, E. (2020), "Readers' Individual Differences in Affect and Cognition," in E. B. Moje, P. P. Afflerbach, P. Enciso, and N. K. Selaux (eds.), in *Handbook of Reading Research, Volume V*, 180–96, New York: Routledge.

Gallese, V. (2020), "Brain, Body, Habit and the Performative Quality of Aesthetics," in F. Caurana and I. Testa (eds.), *Habits: Pragmatist Approaches from Cognitive Science, Neuroscience, and Social Theory*, 376–94, Cambridge: Cambridge University Press.

Garlick, S. (2007), "Harry Potter and the Magic of Reading," *Christian Science Monitor*, 2 May. Available online: https://www.csmonitor.com/2007/0502/p13s01-legn.html (accessed September 29, 2021).

Geertz, C. (1996), "Afterword," in S. Feld and K. H. Basso (eds.), *Senses of Place*, 259–62, Santa Fe, NM: School of American Research Press.

Gerrig, R. J. (1993), *Experiencing Narrative Worlds: On the Psychological Activities of Reading*, New Haven, CT: Westview Press.

Gerrig, R. J. (2011), "Individual Differences in Readers' Narrative Experiences," *Scientific Study of Literature*, 1 (1): 88–94.

Gornick, V. (2020), *Unfinished Business: Notes of a Chronic Re-reader*, New York: Farrar, Straus and Giroux.

Greene, M. (1995), *Releasing the Imagination: Essays on Education, the Arts, and Social Change*, San Francisco, CA: Jossey-Bass.

Grumet, M. (1992), "The Language in the Middle: Bridging the Liberal Arts and Teacher Education," *Liberal Education*, 78 (3): 2–6.

Gubar, M. (2013), "Risky Business: Talking about Children in Children's Literature Criticism," *Children's Literature Association Quarterly*, 38 (4): 450–57.

Gumbrecht, H. U. (2012), *Atmosphere, Mood, Stimmung: On a Hidden Potential of Literature*, trans. E. Butler, Stanford, CA: Stanford University Press.

Hartner, M. (2017), "Scientific Concepts in Literary Studies: Towards Criteria for the Meeting of Literature and Cognitive Science," in M. Burke and E. T. Troscianko (eds.), *Cognitive Literary Science: Dialogues between Literature and Cognition*, 17–34, New York: Oxford University Press.

Heddon, D. E. (2002), "Autotopography: Graffiti, Landscapes & Selves," *Reconstruction: Studies in Contemporary Culture*, 2 (3).

Hennion, A. (2005), "Pragmatics of Taste," in M. Jacobs and N. Hanrahan (eds.), *The Blackwell Companion to the Sociology of Culture*, 131–44, Oxford: Blackwell.

Hodge, B., and D. Tripp (1986), *Children and Television: A Semiotic Approach*, Cambridge, MA: Polity Press.

Hutcheon, L. (2006), *A Theory of Adaptation*, New York: Routledge.

Ingold, T. (2011), *Being Alive: Essays on Movement, Knowledge and Description*, London: Routledge.

Iser, W. (1978), *The Act of Reading: A Theory of Aesthetic Response*, Baltimore, MA: Johns Hopkins University Press.

Jacobs, A. M. (2015), "Towards a Neurocognitive Poetics Model of Literary Reading," in R. M. Willems (ed.), *Cognitive Neuroscience of Natural Language Use*, 135–59. Cambridge: Cambridge University Press.

Jaffri, T. (2017), "*Naunehal* Magazine: In Memory of Masood Barkati," YouTube video, 57, December 11. Available online: https://www.youtube.com/watch?v=ZPG9qQGeTS8 (accessed October 9, 2021).

Jameson, F. (2000), *The Jameson Reader*, M. Hardt, and K. Weeks (eds.), Oxford: Blackwell.

Jaques, Z. (2011), "States of Nature in His Dark Materials and Harry Potter," *Topic: The Washington & Jefferson College Review*, 57: 1–16.

Jones, S. (2018), *Portraits of Everyday Literacy for Social Justice: Reframing the Debate for Families and Communities*, Cham: Palgrave Macmillan.

Kinsella, J. (2017), *Polysituatedness: A Poetics of Displacement*, Manchester, NH: Manchester University Press.

Kozhevnikov, M., S. Kosslyn, and J. Shephard (2005), "Spatial versus Object Visualizers: A New Characterization of Visual Cognitive Style," *Memory & Cognition*, 33 (4): 710–26.

Kozhevnikov, M., O. Blazhenkova, and M. Becker (2010), "Trade-Off in Object versus Spatial Visualization Abilities: Restriction in the Development of Visual-Processing Resources," *Psychonomic Bulletin & Review*, 17 (1): 29–35.

Kuzmicova, A. (2012), "Presence in the Reading of Literary Narrative: A Case for Motor Enactment," *Semiotica*, 189 (1/4): 23–48.

Langer, J. A. (1989), "The Process of Understanding Literature," Report Series 2.1, New York: Center for the Learning and Teaching of Literature, University at Albany, State University of New York.

Le Guin, U. K. (1972), *The Word for World Is Forest*, New York: Tor.

Le Guin, U. K. (2008), "Staying Awake: Notes on the Alleged Decline of Reading," *Harper's Magazine*, 316 (1893): 33–8. February.

Leonhardt, M. (1996), *Keeping Kids Reading: How to Raise Avid Readers in the Video Age*, New York: Three Rivers Press.

Little, S. (2020), "Why Multilingual Pupils Need to Encounter Books in Their Language in Formal Education Contexts: Stories from a Multilingual Library," *English 4–11*, 69: 10–13.

Little, S., and V. Derr (2020), "The Influence of Nature on a Child's Development: Connecting the Outcomes of Human Attachment and Place Attachment," in A. Cutter-Mackenzie-Knowles, K. Malone, and E. Barratt Hacking (eds.), *Research Handbook on Childhoodnature: Assemblages of Childhood and Nature Research*, 151–78, Cham: Springer.

Lively, A. (2016), "Joint Attention, Semiotic Mediation, and Literary Narrative," *Poetics Today*, 37 (4): 517–38.

Lynch, K. (1960), *The Image of the City*, Cambridge, MA: MIT Press.

Mackey, M. (1995), "Imagining with Words: The Temporal Processes of Reading Fiction," Unpublished Ph.D. dissertation. Edmonton, AB: University of Alberta.

Mackey, M. (2007), *Mapping Recreational Literacies: Contemporary Adults at Play*, New York: Peter Lang.

Mackey, M. (2011), *Narrative Pleasures in Young Adult Novels, Films, and Video Games*, Basingstoke: Palgrave Macmillan.

Mackey, M. (2016), *One Child Reading: My Auto-Bibliography*, Edmonton: University of Alberta Press.

Mackey, M. (2019a), "Maps of Literary Play: Reading and the World," in Lynda Graham (chair), *UKLA National Conference July 2019: Sharing Inspiration Practice*, Sheffield, UK: United Kingdom Literacy Association.

Mackey, M. (2019b), "Placing Readers: Diverse Routes to the Cognitive Challenge of Fictional World-Building," *Children's Literature Association Quarterly*, 44 (4): 415–31.

Mackey, M. (2019c), "Visualization and the Vivid Reading Experience," *Jeunesse: Young People, Texts, Cultures*, 11 (1): 38–58.

Mackey, M. (2021a), "The Famous Five and the Autotopographical Two: Interpreting Blyton across Differences of Time, Space, and Race," *Children's Literature in Education*, 52: 271–89.

Mackey, M. (2021b), "The (Im)materialities of the Reading Space: *The Story of Holly and Ivy*," *Children's Literature*, 49: 218–40.

Mackey, M. (forthcoming), "Exploring Readerly Diversity," in K. Menarin (ed.), *Reading across the Disciplines*, Indianapolis: Indiana University Press.

Maitland, S. (2012), *Gossip from the Forest: The Tangled Roots of Our Forests and Fairytales*, London: Granta.

Mak, M., and R. M. Willems (2019), "Mental Simulation during Literary Reading: Individual Differences Revealed with Eye-Tracking," *Language, Cognition and Neuroscience*, 34 (4): 511–35.

Malouf, D. (1985), "A First Place: The Mapping of a World," *Southerly: A Review of Australian Literature*, 45 (1): 3–10.

Malpas, J. (2018), *Place and Experience: A Philosophical Topography*, 2nd ed., London: Routledge.

Marsh, J., and J. Bishop (2014), *Changing Play: Play, Media and Commercial Culture from the 1950s to the Present Day*, Maidenhead: McGraw Hill Education/Open University Press.

Massey, D. (2005), *For Space*, Los Angeles, CA: Sage Publications.
McEwan, I (2001), *Atonement*, Toronto: Alfred A. Knopf Canada.
McNally, L. (2014), *Reading Theories in Contemporary Fiction*, London: Bloomsbury.
Medina, C. L., and K. E. Wohlwend (2014), *Literacy, Play and Globalization: Converging Imaginaries in Children's Critical and Cultural Performances*, New York: Routledge.
Meyrowitz, J. (2015), "Place and Its Mediated Re-Placements," in J. Malpas (ed.), *The Intelligence of Place: Topographies and Poetics*, 93–128, London: Bloomsbury Academic.
Mize, C. J., and K. Elder (n.d.), "Hogwarts and Environs from the Books," *Harry Potter Lexicon*. Available online: https://www.hp-lexicon.org/place/atlas-wizarding-world/atlas-of-hogwarts/hogwarts-environs-books/ (accessed October 8, 2021).
Mol, A. (2010), "Actor-Network Theory: Sensitive Terms and Enduring Tensions," *Kölner Zeitschrift für Soziologie und Sozialpsychologie. Sonderheft*, 50: 253–69.
Moore, J. W. (2016), "What Is the Sense of Agency and Why Does It Matter?," *Frontiers in Psychology*, 7 (article 1272): 1–9.
Murray, S. (2021), *Introduction to Contemporary Print Culture: Books as Media*, London: Routledge.
Nijhof, A. D., and R. M. Willems (2015), "Simulating Fiction: Individual Differences in Literature Comprehension Revealed with fMRI," *PLoS ONE*, 10 (2): 1–17. Available online: https://doi.org/10.1371/journal.pone.0116492 (accessed January 5, 2022).
Nikolajeva, M. (2014), *Reading for Learning: Cognitive Approaches to Children's Literature*, Amsterdam: John Benjamins.
Nikolajeva, M. (2017), *"Haven't You Ever Felt like There Has to Be More?* Identity, Space and Embodied Cognition in Young Adult Fiction," *Encyclopaideia*, 21 (49): 65–80.
Oatley, K. (2011), *Such Stuff as Dreams: The Psychology of Fiction*, Chichester: Wiley-Blackwell.
Otis, L. (2015), "The Value of Qualitative Research for Cognitive Literary Studies," in L. Zunshine (ed.), *The Oxford Handbook of Cognitive Literary Studies*, 505–24, Oxford: Oxford University Press.
Pallasmaa, J. (2015), "Place and Atmosphere," in J. Malpas (ed.), *The Intelligence of Place: Topographies and Poetics*, 129–55, London: Bloomsbury Academic.
Picton, O., and S. Urquhart (2020), "Third Culture Kids and Experiences of Places," in A. Cutter-Mackenzie-Knowles, K. Malone, and E. Barratt Hacking (eds.), *Research Handbook on Childhoodnature: Assemblages of Childhood and Nature Research*, 1575–2600, Cham: Springer.
Preston, C. J. (2003), *Grounding Knowledge: Environmental Philosophy, Epistemology, and Place*, Athens: University of Georgia Press.
Proffitt, D., and D. Baer (2020), *Perception: How Our Bodies Shape Our Minds*, New York: St. Martin's Press.
Pullman, P. (2015), "Inside, Outside, Elsewhere," in M. S. Cecire, H. Field, K. M. Finn, and M. Roy (eds.), *Space and Place in Children's Literature, 1789 to the Present*, 215–39, Farnham, VA: Ashgate.
Pullman, P. (2017), *Daemon Voices: On Stories and Storytelling*, S. Mason (ed.), New York: Alfred A. Knopf.
Punday, D. (2003), *Narrative Bodies: Toward a Corporeal Narratology*, New York: Palgrave Macmillan.
Radway, J. (1984), *Reading the Romance: Women, Patriarchy, and Popular Literature*, Chapel Hill: University of North Carolina Press.
Radway, J. (2008), "What's the Matter with Reception Study? Some Thoughts on the Disciplinary Origins, Conceptual Constraints, and Persistent Viability of a Paradigm,"

in P. Goldstein and J. L. Machor (eds.), *New Directions in American Reception Study*, 327–51, Oxford: Oxford University Press.

Ross, C. S., and M. K. Chelton (2001), "Reader's Advisory: Matching Mood and Material," *Library Journal*, 126 (2): 52–5.

Ryan, M.-L. (2010), "Narratology and Cognitive Science: A Problematic Relation," *Style*, 44 (4): 469–95.

Ryan, M.-L. (2015), *Narrative as Virtual Reality 2: Revisiting Immersion and Interactivity in Literature and Electronic Media*, Baltimore, MD: Johns Hopkins University Press.

Sartre, J.-P. (1978), *What Is Literature?*, trans. B. Frechtman, London: Methuen.

Scarry, E. (1999), *Dreaming by the Book*, New York: Farrar, Straus and Giroux.

Schafer, L. (2015), *What I Learned from Watching Scooby-Doo: An Essay*. Kindle edition. Available online: https://lorilschafer.com/2018/10/29/what-i-learned-from-watching-scooby-doo-2/ (accessed September 30, 2021).

Schilling, D. (2014), "On and Off the Map: Literary Narrative as Critique of Cartographic Reason," in R. T. Tally (ed.), *Literary Cartographies: Spatiality, Representation, and Narrative*, 215–28, New York: Palgrave Macmillan.

Segal, E. M. (1995), "Narrative Comprehension and the Role of Deictic Shift Theory," in J. F. Duchan, G. A. Bruder, and L. E. Hewitt (eds.), *Deixis in Narrative: A Cognitive Science Perspective*, 3–17, Hillsdale, MI: Lawrence Erlbaum.

Skolnick, D., and P. Bloom (2006), "What Does Batman Think about SpongeBob? Children's Understanding of the Fantasy/Fantasy Distinction," *Cognition*, 101: B9–B18.

Slowik, M. (2016), "The Animal Fable, Chuck Jones, and the Narratology of the Looney Tune," *Narrative*, 24 (1): 146–62.

Spufford, F. (2002), *The Child That Books Built*, London: Faber and Faber.

Starr, G. G. (2015), "Theorizing Imagery, Aesthetics, and Doubly Directed States," in L. Zunshine (ed.), *The Oxford Handbook of Cognitive Literary Studies*, 246–68, Oxford: Oxford University Press.

Stimpson, C. R. (1990), "Reading for Love: Canons, Paracanons, and Whistling Jo March," *New Literary History*, 21 (4): 957–76.

Thompson, E. (2007), "Look Again: Phenomenology and Mental Imagery," *Phenomenology and the Cognitive Sciences*, 6 (1–2): 137–70.

Troscianko, E. T. (2013), "Reading Imaginatively: The Imagination in Cognitive Science and Cognitive Literary Studies," *Journal of Literary Semantics*, 42 (2): 181–98.

Van Der Meer, C. (2006), "Let Me Tell You My Life," *Literary Review of Canada*, 14 (6): 27–8.

Waller, A. (2019), *Rereading Childhood Books: A Poetics*, London: Bloomsbury Academic.

Walsh, J. P. (1997), *Goldengrove Unleaving*, London: Black Swan.

Wohlwend, K. E., B. A. Buchholz, and C. L. Medina (2018), "Playful Literacies and Practices of Making in Children's Imaginaries," in K. A. Mills, A. Stornaiuolo, A. Smith, and J. Z. Pandya (eds.), *Handbook of Writing, Literacies, and Education in Digital Cultures*, 136–47, New York: Routledge.

Wolf, M. (2020), "Screen-Based Online Learning Will Change Kids' Brains. Are We Ready for That?," *The Guardian*, August 24. Available online: https://www.theguardian.com/commentisfree/2020/aug/24/deep-literacy-technology-child-development-reading-skills (accessed September 30, 2021).

Zhou, R. (2011), *You Mo San Guo Zhi Mo GUI Xun Lian Ying*, United States: Lian Jing/Tsai Fong Books. Image available online: https://www.amazon.ca/You-San-Guo-Lian-Ying/dp/9570838183 (accessed October 15, 2021).

Index

Note: Page numbers with (t) refer to tables and pages with (f) refer to figures.

Abraham, Anna 102–3
Adolph, Karen 94–5
affect
  about 144, 185
  felt experience of reading 146, 160–1
  life and reading spaces 185
  loss of first place 73
  moods 161, 185, 200
  neurocognitive model of reading 160–2, 160(f)
  nostalgia 5, 114, 175–6
  paracanons 45–6, 185
  readiness for text 87, 89, 161, 200
agency
  about 43–4, 47–8, 94–6
  embodiment 70, 95–6
  first place 51–2, 59–60, 69–73
  home range independence 59–60, 91–2, 94, 97–8, 107–8, 209–10
  in language left behind 190
  lifelong reading spaces 190
  movement in 39, 43–4, 51
  neurocognitive model of reading 160–2, 160(f)
  reading as 199
  space for 43–4, 124–5, 150–1
  of white children 59, 190, 208
ages of participants 11(t), 12(t)
  See also research project, participants
Agosto, Denise 151
Alberta, University of 2, 4, 11(t), 12(t), 213
Alexander, Jonathan 127, 137, 139
Alice McKinley series 87, 172–3, 190, 207
Amani
  about 20–1, 20(f)
  family 20, 81–3, 98
  fears 81–3, 91, 111, 119, 210
  first place
    backyard 20, 98

    friends 21, 81–3
    maps
      generic park 20–1, 20(f), 82(f), 131
      Rundle Park 20, 81–3, 82(f)
    moves in Edmonton 81, 98
    parks
      explorations 21, 82–3, 90, 96, 98, 131
      liminality and thresholds 81, 83
Amani, reading processes
  agency 190
  diversity in cognition 145–6, 147(t), 159
  forests as reading spaces 111, 119, 124, 210
  home range 20–1, 91, 92, 94(t), 98–9, 111
  life and reading spaces 81–3, 99, 111, 131, 210
  lifelong reading spaces 164–5
  pretend games 96, 98–9
  social spaces 81–3
  subjunctive and deictic 99
Amani, visualization
  about 147(t), 148, 149–50
  faces 148, 154, 156
  flashes of images 111, 139, 149
  just knowing 152, 156
  object vision 159
  text-to-text 154, 156
Amani, texts
  books vs. movies 205, 210
  specific
    Choose Your Own Adventure 111
    Goosebumps 111
    Harry Potter 111, 131, 139–41
    The Little Prince 83, 99
    Narnia 83, 87
    The Perks of Being a Wallflower 154, 205, 210
Amy
  about 18–19, 18(f)

family 18, 53–7, 71, 98–9, 104
fear of windows 18, 53–6, 71, 72–3, 91
first place (grandmother's home) 53–7
　domestic literacy 54–5
　little milk cupboard 55–6, 73
　loss at age twelve (death) 18, 53, 56–7, 72, 73
　pretend games 55, 97–9, 97(f)
　toy room 55, 97–8, 97(f)
homes (Edmonton)
　acreage outside Edmonton 53–4, 55, 92
　grandmother's home 18–19, 18(f), 51, 53, 53(f), 92
maps, grandmother's home
　kitchen 18(f), 53–4, 53(f)
　toy room 55, 56, 97–8, 97(f)
Amy, reading processes
　agency 69, 71, 97–8
　diversity in cognition 145–6, 147(t), 159
　domestic literacy 18(f), 19, 54
　first place 51, 52–7, 72–3
　forests not mentioned 110
　formats 34, 71, 137, 139
　home range 91, 92, 94(t), 97–9, 97(f)
　(im)materiality 34
　inside characters' minds 71, 73, 130, 139–40, 205
　life and reading spaces 56
　lifelong reading spaces 164–5
　literacy sponsors 19, 54, 156
　preferences 34, 71
　pretend games 55, 97–9, 97(f)
　purposes of reading 70–3
　reading priorities 213
　subjunctive and deictic 99
Amy, texts
　about 18–19
　cartoons 104
　domestic literacy 18(f), 19, 54
　environmental books 70, 71
　fantasy 55, 71, 73
　formats 34, 137, 139
　movies 34, 71, 130, 154, 205
　science fiction 55–6
　specific
　　The Baby-sitters Club series 55
　　Bugs Bunny 104

　　Harry Potter 34, 71, 73, 130, 137, 139–41, 154, 205
Amy, visualization
　about 147(t), 152, 154, 158, 159
　just knowing 156
　nonvisualizing reader 56, 71, 73, 152, 156, 159
　text-to-text 56, 154
　verbalizers vs. visualizers 157–9
animations, full-length 103–4, 106
　See also cartoons and animations
aphantasia 156
Arabic language. *See* Halia; Rahina
Assamese language. *See* Riya
atmosphere
　about 119–21, 124, 210
　forests 112–13, 113(f), 116–18, 119–21, 124, 210
　Harry Potter 116–18, 140
　life and reading spaces 119–21, 210
　visual imagery 147, 147(t), 149
　weather 99–100
autotopography 44–6, 47
　See also research project, maps

Baer, Drake 94
Ballard, J. G. 165, 212
Barr, Rachel 101
Barsalou, Lawrence 36
Bartlett, Lesley 35, 108, 126
Barton, David 54
bilingual and multilingual participants. *See* Halia; Laura; Liang; Lily; Rahina; Riya; Suleman; Ying Yu
bilingual readers. *See* global connections
Birkerts, Sven 31, 87, 164, 166
Bishop, Julia 104
Black, Rebecca 127, 137, 139
Blyton, Enid, series 55, 58–60, 71, 114, 119, 125, 204–5, 207, 208
brain science
　confirmation of reading styles 211
　diversity in cognition 159, 162
　interdisciplinary research 32–3, 145–6
　literacy as new brain circuit 211–12
　mentalizing 145–6
　neurocognitive model 160–2, 160(f)
　provisional thinking 38–9
　reading preferences 145–6

real vs. fictional characters 103
sensorimotor simulation 145–6
simulationism 36–7, 158–9
visualization 145–6, 157–62, 160(f)
Brandt, Deborah 54, 81
Brosch, Renate 38–9, 151, 158
Bruce, Douglas 104
Bruner, Jerome 40–1
Bryson, Norman 195–6
Buchholz, Beth A. 3
Burnett, Cathy 33, 36
Butler, Catherine 128
Byatt, A. S. 185–7

Cantonese language. *See* Ying Yu
Carroll, Jane Suzanne 119–20
cartoons and animations
   about 101–8
   as cultural translators 105–8, 206–7, 206(f)
   Disney world 24, 106–8
   full-length animations 103–4, 106
   games 106–8
   home range of texts 7, 101–8
   languages 101, 105
   merchandise 107–8
   multiple versions 210
   narrative conventions 102–4
   and nursery rhymes 104
   vs. reality 103
   See also home range, textual; Suleman, texts (Urdu) cartoons
Cave, Terence 36–8, 44, 51
Cecire, Maria Sachiko 99, 128
Charlton, Emma 100–1
Chelton, Mary K. 161
childhood
   agency 94–5, 97–8
   cutoff at age twelve 6
   embodiment 28–9, 31–2, 70
   nursery rhymes 104
   plurality 29
   purposeful movement 94–5
   satisficing and making do 208
   situated beings 28–9, 31–2
   See also home; home, first place; life spaces and reading spaces
Coats, Karen 1
cognitive science. *See* brain science

Coleridge, Samuel Taylor 185–6
Currie, Gregory 36

deictic
   about 40–3, 47, 99
   body and movement 43, 96
   games 96–7, 99
   life and reading spaces 96–9
   non-Western cultures 41–2
   possibilities vs. certainties 40–1
   shifting into a story 41–2
   verb tenses 41
   words *(here* and *there; I* and *you; now* and *then; yesterday, today,* and *tomorrow)* 41, 42–3, 99
   See also subjunctive
Derr, Victoria 91
domestic spaces. *See* home; home, first place
Dubow, Jessica 198

Eco, Umberto 122–3
Edmonton, parks and green spaces. *See* Amani; Roman
Edmonton, universities. *See* University of Alberta
Eliot, George 197–8, 201–2
embodiment 70
emotions. *See* affect
Empson, William 40
encyclopedias 26, 75, 79–80, 179

Facebook 80, 167–8, 198, 199
   See also online spaces
fairy tales and folk tales 121–4
   See also Liang
feelings. *See* affect
Felski, Rita 87, 186–7
fiction
   about 29, 46–8
   actions 145–6
   agency in 43–4
   characters 43, 103, 145–6, 186, 203–5
   (im)materiality 186
   implausibility of 102
   life and reading spaces 47
   mentalizing 145–6
   narrative conventions 102
   particle-level events 110, 119

post-reading performance of 87
preferences 145–6
reading as reflection 196–9
sensorimotor simulation 145–6
settings 145–6
subjunctive and deictic shifts into 40–3
truth and narrative 194–5
verbal counterpoint 203–5
See also lifelong reading spaces; life spaces and reading spaces; nonfiction; reading

film. *See* formats and versions of texts

first place. *See* home, first place

folk and fairy tales 121–4
See also Liang

forests
about 7, 110–25
absence of certainty 121
agency 44, 121, 123–5, 210
atmosphere 111–13, 113(f), 116–18, 119–21, 123–5, 210
borderlands 123–5
characters in 125, 203–4
cultural forest 121–5
"footfall knowledge," 119–21
Harry Potter's Forbidden Forest 111, 116–18, 123–4, 140
(im)materiality 120–1, 124–5
key questions 123–4
life and reading spaces 7, 123–5, 210
link to libraries 113–14
as metaphor for text 122–3
topos 7, 119–20
unit of narrative space 210
See also life spaces and reading spaces

formats and versions of texts
about 154–6
consistency of books/movies 130, 139
as cultural translators 87–8, 206–8, 206(f)
(im)materiality 34
movement between versions 205–8
as text and object 127–8
translations to/from English 41–2, 188–9
visualization (text-to-text) 147, 147(t), 154–6
See also cartoons and animations; global connections; Harry Potter series, formats and versions; languages

Fox, Emily 144

Gallese, Vittorio 37, 45, 47
games
about 96–7, 106
agency in 100
home range 94–100, 106
life and reading spaces 96–9
nursery rhymes 104
purposeful movement 95
subjunctive and deictic shifts 96–7, 99
specific
hide-and-seek 95–6, 106
playground games 104, 106
pretend 86, 87, 96–9, 97(f), 98(f), 103, 106–8, 115–18
sports 96
tag 106
video games 136, 138, 184, 212
See also movement

Garlick, Shayna 126–7
Geertz, Clifford 196
gender
home range of participants 92, 119
LGBTQ fiction 85–6, 87, 89, 207
ratio of participants 10
geographic spaces
graphic organizer 7–8, 8(f), 209–14, 209(f)
See also home; home, first place; home range, geographic and social; life spaces and reading spaces
Gerrig, Richard 99, 144
Gilmour, Logan 3
global connections
about 52, 106–8
agency 52, 88, 190
Disney universe 106–8
glocal experiences 106–8
Harry Potter universe 52, 126–9, 137
home cultures 88–9
home range of texts 92, 101, 106–8
invisibility of non-Western texts 187–90
media conglomerates 106–7
multilingual libraries 189
multiple localities 92, 106–8
polysituatedness 52–3, 197–8
pretend games 106–8, 187
shared reading community 188–90
texts as cultural translators 87–8, 105–8, 206–8

translations to/from English 41–2, 188–9
transmedia ecology 137
travel by participants 52, 198–9, 213
See also formats and versions of texts; languages
Gornick, Vivian 87
grammatical reading processes 40–3
See also deictic; subjunctive
Greene, Maxine 28–9, 91
green spaces in Edmonton. *See* Amani; Roman
Grumet, Madeleine 74
Gubar, Marah 74
Gumbrecht, Hans Ulrich 120

Halia
  about 17–18, 17(f)
  family 17, 84–6
  first place
    house in Edmonton 17–18, 17(f), 51, 84–5, 85(f), 209
    trees 92, 111, 112(f), 150(f)
  friends 85–6, 88–9
  indoor spaces 17–18, 84, 91, 92, 150
  Islamic upbringing 84–6
  languages (Arabic, Persian) 18, 84, 105, 150, 207
  map
    home in Edmonton 17–18, 17(f), 84–5, 85(f), 150–1, 150(f)
    move at age six from Iraq 17, 84, 92, 111, 209
  travels 85, 150
Halia, reading processes
  about 18
  agency 150–1
  bilingual reader 18, 84–6, 85(f), 88, 105, 124, 139, 150–1
  deep immersion 88–9
  diversity in cognition 145–6, 147(t), 159
  forests as reading spaces 111, 112(f), 119, 124–5, 150, 150(f)
  home range 91, 92, 94(t)
  life and reading spaces 86, 89–90, 150, 150(f), 187
  lifelong reading spaces 164–5, 187, 190
  pretend games 86, 87
  satisficing and making do 139, 151
  settings 105, 139, 150, 150(f)

social spaces 84–9
texts as cultural translators 87–8, 207–8
visualization 111, 124, 147(t), 150–1, 150(f)
Halia, texts (Arabic)
  about 84–6, 85(f)
  Anne of Green Gables 105
  dubbed cartoons 105
  settings 139, 150–1
  storybooks 84, 207
Halia, texts (Western)
  about 18, 84–6, 85(f), 88–9
  character focus 88–9
  coming-of-age stories 85–6
  fan art and writing 87–9, 187
  fantasy 84, 88, 207
  graphic novels 85, 86, 87
  Harry Potter not mentioned 111, 137
  LGBTQ fiction 85–6, 87, 89, 207
  manga 85–6
  settings 139, 150–1
  specific
    Anne of Green Gables 105
    Great Expectations 85
    Naruto 86, 89
    1984 86
    The Raven's Quest 150–1
    The Secrets of Droon 87
Hamilton, Mary 54
Harry Potter series
  about 7, 126–41, 210
  atmosphere 116–18, 140
  characters
    Harry Potter 127, 131
    Hermione 131–2, 137–8, 140
  cultural currency 126–8, 137–8, 140
  Cursed Child (play) 129, 130, 139
  games
    online games 138
    pretend 116–18, 136
    Quidditch 34, 87, 96, 136, 140
    video games 136, 138
  global connections 126–30, 137, 140
  growth of characters/readers 116–18, 135–7
  (im)materiality 34, 128
  key questions 140
  life and reading spaces 7, 128, 132–3, 132(f), 136–7, 139–41, 210

lifelong reading spaces 187–8
map of Hogwarts 23, 133–4, 135(f)
participants
  interviews 126, 128–9, 137–9
  as Potter generation 126, 128–9, 210
  without mention of Potter 110, 126
settings
  castle 135
  Forbidden Forest 111, 116–18, 123–4, 140
  Great Hall 23
  Hogwarts 135, 140
  the University of Oxford 128
texts as cultural translators 87–8, 207–8
threshold experiences 132–3, 132(f), 140
transphobia controversy 127
visualization 135, 136, 139–40, 151–2
See also home range, textual; Matt, texts, Harry Potter
Harry Potter series, formats and versions
  about 127–8, 137–41, 210
  books vs. movies 136, 205
  fan fiction 137
  hardback vs. paperback 34, 129, 137
  merchandise 138
  movies 34, 126, 136–7, 139–41, 154, 205, 210
  music 127
  pirated books 129, 137
  Pottermore (Wizarding World) 87, 128, 138, 210
  video games 136, 138
  See also formats and versions of texts
Hartner, Marcus 32–3
Henderson, Brian 194
Hennion, Antoine 126, 127
Hindi language. *See* Riya
Hodge, Robert 103
home
  about 50–3, 73, 209
  age at major change 52–3, 60
  agency 51–2
  first place not always birthplace 51, 209
  as nouns and verbs 51–2
  polysituatedness 52–3, 197–8
  See also home, first place; home range, geographic and social; home range, textual; social spaces
home, first place
  about 3, 50–3, 70–3, 196–9
  agency 51–2, 60, 69–73
  birthplace not first place 51, 209
  cultural adjustment 52–3
  grounded perception 197–8, 202
  images of elsewhere 51–2
  loss of 73
  as "mapping the world," 50–1, 73
  movement 51–2
  participants' maps as 50–1
  polysituatedness 52–3, 197–8
  purposes of reading 70–2
  reading spaces 72–3
  restart of first place 51
  textual diasporas 52
  vividness of childhood 197–8, 201–2
  weather 99–100
  See also life spaces and reading spaces
home, first place, participants. *See* Amy; Laura; Liang; Lily; Riya
home range, geographic and social
  about 6–7, 91–100, 94(t)
  agency 7, 91–2, 94, 99, 101–2, 209–10
  gender divide 92, 119
  geographic 91–4
  key questions 92, 101
  life and reading spaces 96–101
  list of participants 92, 94(t)
  movement 94–100
  multiple localities 92
  purposes 94–5
  subjunctive and deictic shifts 96–7, 99
  See also games
home range, textual
  about 7, 91, 100–8, 209–10
  cartoons 7, 104–6
  glocal experiences 106–8
  life and reading spaces 100–1
  multiple languages 101
  multiple localities 92, 106–8
  parental restrictions 101
  satisficing and making do 102, 151–2
  See also cartoons and animations; forests; Harry Potter series

imagery. *See* visualization; visualization, diversity
(im)materiality
  about 33–4, 47–8

agency in 43–4
borderlands 123
fictional objects 186
forests 123–5
lifelong reading space 186–7, 190
mapmaking 33–4
reflexive and recursive 33–4
situated beings 33
See also life spaces and reading spaces
infancy. *See* childhood
informational texts. *See* nonfiction
Ingold, Tim 39, 99–100, 195, 200, 202
interdisciplinary research 32–3, 145–6
international connections. *See* global connections
internet. *See* online spaces
intertextuality (text-to-text). *See* life spaces and reading spaces; visualization; visualization, diversity
Iser, Wolfgang 40

Jacobs, Arthur 160–2, 160(f)
Jameson, Frederic 37
Jaques, Zoë 123
Jones, Susan 54
Junie B. Jones series 87, 89, 105, 169–71, 207

key terms 32–3
See also agency; autotopography; deictic; (im)materiality; life spaces and reading spaces; movement; research project, key terms; subjunctive
Kinsella, John 52
Korobkova, Ksenia 127, 129, 137
Kosslyn, Stephen 157
Kozhevnikov, Maria 157–8
Kuzmicova, Anezka 200–2

languages
culture and bodily demeanor 41
ESL school programs 67, 88, 166, 190
first-language reading space 190
home range of texts 101
invisibility of non-Western texts 187–90
multilingual libraries 189
shared reading community 188–90
texts as cultural translators 87–8, 206–8
translations to/from English 41–2, 188–9
versions and cultural information 206(f)
See also formats and versions of texts; global connections
languages, bilingual and multilingual participants. *See* Halia; Laura; Liang; Lily; Rahina; Riya; Suleman; Ying Yu
Laura
about 13, 14(f)
family 13, 64, 66
first place (Hong Kong apartment complex)
apartment complex 13, 14(f), 64–6, 65(f), 73, 88;
loss (as long ago) 73, 88
move at age nine to Canada 13, 60, 64, 88
friends 66, 88
houses vs. apartments 13, 66
languages (Chinese) 41–2, 66–7, 70, 88
maps
Hong Kong apartment complex 13, 14(f), 64–6, 65(f)
travels 13, 14(f), 64–6, 65(f), 73
move at age eighteen to Edmonton 13, 64
Vancouver 13, 66, 67, 88
Laura, reading processes
agency 70, 71
bilingual reader 13, 41–2, 64, 66–7, 71, 72, 87–8
diversity in cognition 145–6, 147(t), 159
first place 52–3, 64–7, 65(f), 73, 88
forest settings not mentioned 110
home range 92, 94(t)
life and reading spaces 130
lifelong reading spaces 164–5
nonvisualizing reader 152, 156, 159
purposes of reading 70–2
subjunctive and deictic 41–2
texts as cultural translators 87–8, 207–8
visualization 147(t), 152, 156, 159
Laura, texts (Chinese)
about 70, 88
television 67
translations 41–2
Laura, texts (Western)
about 88
consistency of books/movies 130, 139

magical and myth 66
manga 66, 70
movies 66, 130, 139, 154, 205
specific
   Can You Keep a Secret? 67
   Frankenstein 67
   Geronimo Stilton 87
   Harry Potter 66, 130, 139–41, 205
   Judy Blume 67, 87, 207
   Malcolm in the Middle 67, 87, 207
   The Maze Runner 66
   Percy Jackson 66
   The Secrets of Droon 66
Le Guin, Ursula 120–1, 187, 200
Leonhardt, Mary 145–6
LGBTQ fiction 85–6, 87, 89, 207
Liang
  about 13–14, 15(f)
  attitude to change 61, 63–4
  Chinese culture 63–4, 70, 72, 189, 210
  family 13, 71
  first place (small town in China)
    grandparents' house 61, 61(f)
    loss (as long ago) 61–2, 64, 71, 73, 147
    motorcycle store 61–2, 93(f)
    move at age nine (to city near Shanghai) 60, 61, 63–4
  friends 13, 62
  home as nowhere 14, 63, 72, 88
  languages (Chinese) 70, 206–7, 206(f)
  maps
    fairytale princess 62, 62(f)
    Journey to the West cartoon 206–7, 206(f)
    small town in Eastern China 15(f), 61, 61(f), 62(f), 93(f), 206(f)
  moves 13, 61–3
  postmodern thinker 14, 63, 72, 88
  travels 61
Liang, reading processes
  agency 64, 69, 71, 190
  bilingual reader 13–14, 35, 70–2, 87–8, 189, 206–7, 206(f)
  curiosity 64
  diversity in cognition 145–6, 147(t), 159
  first place 52–3, 61–4, 73
  forests not mentioned 110
  home range 92, 93(f), 94(t)

life and reading spaces 35, 64, 72, 187
lifelong reading spaces 164–5, 187
multiple versions 206–7, 206(f)
purposes of reading 70–2
texts as cultural translators 14, 72, 87–8, 207–8
Liang, visualization
  about 63, 72, 147, 147(t)
  like a movie 63, 71, 147
  satisficing and making do 156
  text-to-text 64, 72, 147, 147(t), 154, 155–6
  Western visuals 63, 71, 139, 147
  white characters speaking Chinese 13, 72, 155–6
Liang, texts (Chinese)
  about 13–14, 72
  Chinese texts 72, 147
  fairytale picture books 62, 62(f)
  formats 70
  fortune-telling 35, 64, 70, 71, 187, 189
  Journey to the West (literary masterpiece) 13, 206–7, 206(f)
  social media 35, 70
  texts with Western origin 13, 72, 155–6
Liang, texts (Western)
  about 13–14, 72
  Canadian settings 139, 147
  fairy tales 13, 72, 155–6
  specific
    Discovery Channel 72, 156
    Hannah Montana 14, 72, 87, 207
    Harry Potter not mentioned 126, 139
    High School Musical 14, 72, 87, 190, 207
    Sherlock Holmes 72
    Teletubbies 72, 156
libraries
  multilingual libraries 189
  Rahina's love of 23, 113–14, 165, 167
  relation to forests 113–14
lifelong reading spaces
  about 164–6, 184–91, 212
  affect 45–6, 185
  agency 43–4, 190
  cognitive diversity 166
  early experiences 164
  invisibility of non-Western texts 187–90
  key questions 212

life and reading spaces 185–6
paracanons 45–6, 185
pleasure of reading 185–7
private and personal 186–7, 196–9
series books 166, 185
shared reading community 188–90
lifelong reading spaces, participants.
    See Rahina, lifelong reading
    spaces; Roman, lifelong reading
    spaces; Ying Yu, lifelong
    reading spaces
life spaces and reading spaces
  about 34–5, 47–8, 210, 214
  atmosphere 119–21
  definitions 34–5
  examples 34–5, 185
  forests 123–5, 210
  forward movement 39, 199–201, 204–5
  games 96–9
  (im)materiality 34–5, 45, 186–7, 214
  key questions 123–4
  lifelong reading spaces 185–7
  life-to-text 30
  maps 47–8
  movement in 35–9
  non-narrative texts 35
  participants 72–3
  reading spaces 34–5, 47–8, 164–5
  reciprocal relations 34–5, 37–8,
    89–90, 210
  social relations 89–90
  subjunctive and deictic shifts 42, 99
  text-to-life 56
  See also forests; Harry Potter series;
    home, first place; (im)materiality;
    lifelong reading spaces
Lily
  about 15, 16(f)
  family 15, 68, 71
  first place (Zheng Zhou)
    age of move to Canada 67–8
    loss of urban life 67, 69, 73
    urban apartment 67–9, 68(f), 114–15
  friends 68–9, 115–16, 115(f), 125
  languages (Chinese) 68, 71, 72, 207
  maps
    Scarborough, Ontario 16(f), 67,
      68(f), 115, 115(f)
    Zheng Zhou 16(f), 67, 68(f), 114–15
    Zheng Zhou apartment floor
      plan 67, 68(f)
  moves
    age eleven to urban Scarborough 15
    to suburban Edmonton 67
  suburban Edmonton 15, 67, 69, 92
  urban Scarborough 15, 68–9, 115–16,
    115(f)
  urban Zheng Zhou 15, 68, 114–15
Lily, reading processes
  agency 67, 69–70, 71–2, 73, 92
  bilingual reader 68, 70–2, 88, 207, 210
  Chinese settings 68, 71, 72, 88, 114–15,
    130, 139, 147
  diversity in cognition 145–6, 147(t), 159
  first place 52–3, 67–70, 73, 187
  forests as reading spaces 114–16, 115(f),
    119, 125
  home range 92, 94(t)
  life and reading spaces 115–16, 187
  lifelong reading spaces 164–5,
    187, 188–9
  literacy sponsors 15
  multiple versions 207, 210
  pretend games 115–16, 187
  purposes of reading 70–2
  shared reading community 188–90
  texts as cultural translators 87–8,
    207–8, 210
  visualization 71, 88, 147, 147(t)
  Western settings 88, 130, 139, 147
Lily, texts (Chinese)
  about 70–1, 72
  Girl's Diary 68, 188
  A Mystery for You and the Tiger Team
    series 68, 187
  settings 68, 128, 129–30, 139–40, 147
  You Mo San Guo (parody) 68, 69(f),
    207, 210
Lily, texts (Western)
  about 15, 68–9, 70–1
  cartoons 71, 104–5
  mysteries 68
  nontraumatic immigration stories 15, 70
  settings 68, 128, 129–30, 139, 140, 147
  urban settings 15, 70–1, 72, 105, 147
  specific
    Bridge to Terabithia 69, 87, 115,
      115(f)

City of Bones 70
  Corduroy 71, 104–5
  Cursed Child (play) 139
  Goosebumps series R. L. Stine 68
  Harriet the Spy 15, 68–9, 96, 115, 125
  Harry Potter 68, 128, 129–30, 139–41
  The Kite Runner 70
  Madeline 71, 105
  Sherlock Holmes 68, 72, 130, 207
literacy sponsorship 54, 75, 79, 81
literary spaces
  graphic organizer 7–8, 8(f), 209–14, 209(f)
  See also fiction; home range, textual; lifelong reading spaces; life spaces and reading spaces
Little, Sabine 189
Little, Sarah 91
Lively, Adam 89
loss of first place 73
Lynch, Kevin 37

Mackey, Margaret
  Anglo-Canadian heritage 11–12
  Holly and Ivy study 34–5, 185
  interest in maps 3
  See also research project
Mackey, Margaret, reading processes
  agency 60
  close reading 30–1
  colonial reader 30
  cultural forest 121–2, 124–5
  Enid Blyton's series 59, 208
  first place 50, 60, 95, 197, 202
  folk and fairy tales 121–2, 124–5
  forests as reading spaces 121–2, 204
  games 95
  lack of familiarity with non-Western texts 187–9
  lifelong reading space 185
  settings 30
  verbalizing reader 157–9
Maitland, Sara 122–3, 125
Mak, Marloes 158
Malouf, David 3, 50–1, 73, 202, 209
Malpas, Jeff 43–4, 70, 124, 150–1
maps. *See* research project, maps
Marsh, Jackie 104

Massey, Doreen 35–6, 92, 100–1
materiality 33–4
  See also (im)materiality
Matt
  about 23, 24(f)
  family 23, 135
  first place 51, 52
  friends 136
  maps
    Hogwarts in Harry Potter 23, 24(f), 133–4, 135(f)
    Rocky Mountains 134, 135(f)
    school soccer field with trees 51, 93(f), 116–18, 116(f), 135(f)
  music 134
  travels 134
Matt, reading processes
  about 23, 34
  agency 124
  atmosphere 116–17
  diversity in cognition 145–6, 147(t), 159
  forests as reading spaces 116–18, 116(f), 119, 124–5, 140, 203–5, 210
  games 34, 87, 96, 116–18, 210
  home range 92, 93(f), 94(t)
  (im)materiality 34
  life and reading spaces 116–18, 116(f), 154, 187, 210
  lifelong reading spaces 164–5, 187
  satisficing and making do 151–2
  settings 134–6
  text-to-text 117–18, 154
  verbal counterpoint 203–5
  versions and formats 34, 117
  world-building 136, 148–9, 154
Matt, visualization
  about 147(t), 148–9
  consistency of imagery/texts 23, 148, 152, 154, 159
  object vision 159
  satisficing and making do 151–2
  sitcom settings as metaphor 136, 148, 159
  spatial relationships 134, 159
  specific images 147(t), 148–9
  text-to-text 117–18, 154
  world-building 136, 148–9, 154, 205
Matt, texts
  fantasy 118, 124, 134

graphic novels 134
specific
   Harbrace Anthology of Poetry 134
   Leonard Cohen 134
   Tender Is the Night 134
See also Matt, texts, Harry Potter
Matt, texts, Harry Potter
   about 116–18, 133–7, 135(f)
   atmosphere 117–18, 140
   books vs. movies 136, 205
   Forbidden Forest 116–18, 140
   as foundation for imaginary spaces 136–7
   games
      online games 138
      pretend 117–18, 136
      Quidditch 34, 87, 136, 140
      video games 136, 138
   growth of characters/readers 117–18, 135
   life and reading spaces 136–7, 139–41
   map of Hogwarts 23, 133–4, 135(f)
   merchandise 138
   Pottermore.com (Wizarding World) 87, 138
   settings 116–18, 134–6, 139–41, 151–2
   visualization 135, 136, 139–40, 148–9, 151–2
See also Harry Potter series
McEwan, Ian 211
Medina, Carmen L. 3, 52, 106–7
mental imagery. *See* visualization; visualization, diversity
mentalizing 145–6
Merchant, Guy 36
Meyrowitz, Joshua 51, 198
Mol, Annemarie 2, 166
mood. *See* affect; atmosphere
Moore, James W. 43
Morrison, Toni 120
movement
   about 35–40, 47–8, 199–201
   agency 39, 43–4, 51
   by characters 43
   eye movements 161, 201
   first place 51–2
   forward movement 8, 39, 158–9, 199–201, 204–5
   goal-directed movement 47
   home range 94–100

improvisation 39, 47, 159, 199–201
life and reading spaces 35–9
perception-action system 95
provisional thinking 38–9
purposeful 94–6
reading as mental action 199–201
sensorimotor system 37–8, 40, 145–6, 201
simulation of seeing 36–7, 158–9
subjunctive and deictic shifts 40–3, 96, 99
visualization 38–9
See also deictic; games; subjunctive
movies. *See* formats and versions of texts
multilingual and bilingual participants. *See* Halia; Laura; Liang; Lily; Rahina; Riya; Suleman; Ying Yu
multilingual readers. *See* global connections
Murray, Simone 34, 127, 137, 196

narrative fiction. *See* fiction
neuroscience. *See* brain science
Nijhof, Annabel D. 145–6
Nikolajeva, Maria 42–3, 102–3, 201
nonfiction
   autotopography 44–6, 47
   vs. fictional characters 103
   IKEA instructions 35
   paracanons 45–6
   subjunctive and deictic 42
See also fiction
nursery rhymes 104

Oatley, Keith 39
online spaces
   about 167–9, 208, 213
   bicultural perspectives 70, 199, 213
   fan art and writing 87–9, 137, 187, 208
   life and reading spaces 35
   lifelong reading spaces 187
   post-reading performances 87
   social relations 80
   specific
      Facebook 80, 167–8, 198, 199
      Goodreads 167, 196
      Pottermore (Wizarding World) 87, 128, 138, 187, 210

Reddit 167–8, 198, 208
Tumblr 87, 137, 167–9, 198, 208
optical detail. *See* visualization
Otis, Laura 146, 157

Pallasmaa, Juhani 120
paracanons 45–6, 185
participants. *See* research project, participants
Picton, Oliver 92
place and space
  about 47, 52, 100–1, 196–9, 201–3
  agency in 43–4, 124–5, 150–1
  being in a place 52
  digital technologies 198
  embodiment 70
  grounded perception 202
  life and reading spaces 34–5, 89–90, 100–1
  materiality 33–4
  movement in 35–8
  multiple localities 92
  polysituatedness 52–3, 197–8
  reading spaces 34–5, 47–8, 164–5, 194
  vs. simulationism 202
  situated beings 28–9, 31–2
  sonic space 40
  topos 119–20
  See also home, first place; (im)materiality; life spaces and reading spaces; movement; research project, maps
playground rhymes 104
poetry 40, 134
polysituatedness 52–3, 197–8
  See also home
Preston, Christopher 31–2, 37
Proffitt, Dennis 94
psychological spaces
  graphic organizer 7–8, 8(f), 209–14, 209(f)
  See also affect; brain science; visualization
Pullman, Philip 99, 110, 123, 125
Punday, Daniel 41, 43, 189, 196
purposes of reading 70–2

racialized characters
  agency of white children 59, 190, 208
  deracination in text-to-text 72
  representation of Black characters 174
  speech of non-Western characters 58, 72
  speech of white characters 13, 72, 155–6
  white characters assumed 148, 173
Radway, Janice 8, 46, 213
Rahina
  about 21–3, 22(f)
  family 23, 35, 105, 113, 166, 199
  first place 51, 171–2
  friends 89
  homes
    Edmonton 21, 167
    Kenya 21–2, 167, 198–9, 213
    Somalia 21–2, 41, 167, 171, 189, 213
    Toronto 21, 113–14, 167
  indoor spaces 23, 91, 92, 113–14, 119, 166
  Islamic upbringing 11, 22–3, 41, 166–7, 169–71, 169(f), 174, 189
  languages (Somali, Arabic) 41, 166, 171–2, 189
  libraries 23, 113–14, 156, 165, 167
  map (abstract)
    key to map 23, 167
    map 22–3, 22(f), 51, 165–74, 168(f), 169(f), 172(f), 189
  travels 173
Rahina, lifelong reading spaces
  about 164–74, 190–1, 212
  "breathe reading," 174
  Goodreads 167, 196
  Islamic upbringing 41, 166–7, 169–71, 169(f), 170(f), 189
  libraries 165, 167
  map 22–3, 22(f), 51, 165, 167–74, 168(f), 169(f), 172(f)
  multiple books at once 165
  nostalgia 165–6
  online spaces 168–9, 187
  orphanage fantasy 173
  series books 169–73
  texts as cultural translators 171–4
  See also lifelong reading spaces
Rahina, reading processes
  about 41, 165
  agency 35, 199
  cognitive dissonance in bicultural life 171–2

Index 233

diversity in cognition 145–6, 147(t), 159
forests as reading spaces (libraries) 113–14, 119, 124, 125
home range 91, 92, 94(t), 105
life and reading spaces 35, 89–90, 105, 113–14, 166, 171–2, 187
multilingual reader 41, 87–8, 105, 171–2, 189
need for mental stimulation 199
subjunctive and deictic 41
texts as cultural translators 23, 87–8, 105, 171–4, 207–8
as Westerner 41
Rahina, visualization
about 147(t), 156, 158, 159, 173–4, 184
abstract and dreamlike
Europe flight and cultural guides 172–3, 172(f)
mosque and Junie B. Jones 169–71, 169(f), 207
skate ramp and Islamic culture 171–2
characters as white or Black 173–4
faces 139, 156, 167
nonvisualizing reader 131, 139–40, 152, 156, 159, 167, 173
settings 139, 156, 167, 173–4
surreal and unruly images 167, 173–4
verbalizers vs. visualizers 157–9, 173
Rahina, texts (Arabic)
fiction 189
Quran 41, 171–2
Rahina, texts (Western)
about 105
cartoons 105
fan writing 35, 87, 137, 187
series books 173
TV shows 105, 171
specific
Alice McKinley series 87, 172–3, 190, 207
Arthur 105
Barney 105
The Berenstain Bears 105
cartoons 105
Dr. Seuss 105
Fairly Odd Parents 105
Goosebumps series 171
Harry Potter 131, 137–41, 169–71, 169(f), 173

The Hunger Games 173
Jane Austen 173
Junie B. Jones 87, 89, 105, 169–71, 169(f), 207
Khaled Hosseini novels 173
The Simpsons 105
SpongeBob SquarePants 105
Teletubbies 105
specific, social media
Facebook 167–8, 198–9, 213
Goodreads 167, 196
Quora 198–9, 213
Reddit 167–8, 198–9, 208, 213
Snapchat 198–9
Tumblr 87, 137, 167–9, 198–9, 208, 213
ravines, Edmonton. *See* Roman
reading
about 1–2, 28–32, 47–8
as agency 199
being in space 201–3
close reading 30–1, 200
closure vs. open-endedness 4
diversity in cognition 145–6, 147(t), 159–62
embodiment 28–9, 70
emotional responses 144
formats and versions 205–8
forward movement 8, 39, 158–9, 199–201, 204–5
graphic organizer 7–8, 8(f), 209–14, 209(f)
immersive vs. aesthetic response 160–1, 160(f)
initial moods and actions 199–200
invisibility 187–91
key questions 29
metaphor of painting/drawing 200, 208
neurocognitive model 160–2, 160(f)
reader-response theory 8
as reflection 196–9
relationships vs. action 145–6
rereading 149, 164, 199, 205–6, 212
respect for preferences 3, 213
satisficing and making do 151–2, 208
shadow life of 87
situated beings 28–9, 31–2
verbal counterpoint 203–5
See also affect; life spaces and reading spaces; visualization

reading spaces 34–5, 47–8, 164–5
  See also life spaces and reading spaces
Reddit 167–8, 198, 208
  See also online spaces
reflection, reading as 196–9
rereading 149, 164, 199, 205–6, 212
research project
  about 1–2, 47–8
  autotopographical method 44–6, 47
  closure vs. open-endedness 4–5, 195–6, 213–14
  data set 2
  diversity of reading 9, 145–6, 159, 162, 166
  focus on reader vs. text 31–2
  graphic organizer 7–8, 8(f), 209–14, 209(f)
  interdisciplinary approach 32–3, 145–6
  invisibility of reading 187–91
  key questions 29, 162, 195
  layers vs. patterns 2
  limitations 1, 5, 9, 187–9, 194–5, 213–14
  messiness of reading research 1–3, 27–8, 194–5
  metaphor of painting/drawing 195–6, 200, 208
  narrative fiction 29
  time and place 5
  truth and narrative 194–5
  use of present/past tense 4, 195
  See also Mackey, Margaret
research project, interviews
  about 1–2, 5, 213–14
  data set 2
  first and second interviews 1, 5, 213–14
  Harry Potter discussions 126, 128–9, 137–9
  limitations 5, 187–9, 194–5, 213–14
  nostalgia effects 5
  questions on reading processes 5, 146, 210–11
  time and place 1, 5, 213–14
research project, key terms
  about 6, 32–3, 46–8
  autotopography 44–6, 47
  deictic 40–3
  (im)materiality 33–4
  life and reading spaces 34–5
  movement 35–40
  subjunctive 40–3
  See also autotopography; deictic; (im)materiality; life spaces and reading spaces; movement; subjunctive
research project, maps
  about 1–6, 27, 47–8, 194–5
  agency in mapmaking 44
  autotopographical method 44–6, 47
  briefing of participants 4–5, 50
  closure vs. open-endedness 195–6, 213–14
  data set 2
  diversity of 159
  first place 50
  icons and keys 6
  (im)materiality 33–4
  interviews on 47
  key questions 29
  landmarks 6
  limitations 5, 187–9, 194–5
  messiness of reading research 194–5
  metaphor of painting/drawing 195–6
  movement in 36–8
  multiple vs. single 5
  simulation of seeing 36–7
  social and textual fluidity 52
  software programs 2, 3–4, 18–19, 18(f), 84
  trees as landmarks 121
  See also home, first place; research project, interviews
research project, map categories
  about 12, 27
  abstract maps 21, 22(f), 167, 168(f)
  fiction-oriented maps 23, 24(f)–26(f)
  home images 15–17, 16(f)–19(f)
  park areas 19–20, 20(f), 22(f)
  urban maps 13–15, 14(f)–15(f)
research project, participants
  about 1–2, 10, 11(t), 12(t), 213
  academic disciplines 2, 11, 11(t), 12(t), 146, 159
  ages 2, 10, 126
  bicultural perspectives 213
  briefing of 4–5, 50
  cognitive diversity 145–6, 147(t), 159, 162, 166

Index

consent 10
cultural diversity 11, 11(t), 12(t), 146, 159
gender ratio 10
global travel 52, 198-9, 213
Harry Potter generation 126, 128-9, 210
honorarium 2, 4
lists of 11, 11(t), 12(t)
narrative fiction 29
pseudonyms 10
recruitment 2, 4-5, 10, 11, 52
research by 5, 47-8, 196
time and place 5
See also research project, interviews
Riya
  about 19, 19(f)
  family 19, 57, 60, 129, 138
  first place (home in India)
    friends 57, 60
    home in Assam 19, 19(f), 57, 57(f), 60, 73, 114
    literacy places 19, 58
    loss at age twelve (divorce) 19, 57, 60, 72, 73
  friends 86-7
  international student 11, 19, 57
  languages (Assamese, Hindi) 58, 70, 72
  maps
    floor plan of home in India 19, 19(f), 57-60, 57(f)
  moves
    age twelve (to other parts of India) 19, 57
    age eighteen (to Canada) 19
  travels 19, 57, 60
Riya, reading processes
  agency 60, 69, 71, 190
  diversity in cognition 145-6, 147(t), 159
  first place 52-3, 57-60, 72-3
  forests as reading spaces 114, 119, 124, 125
  home range 92, 94(t)
  island imagery 114, 148
  life and reading spaces 60
  lifelong reading spaces 164-5
  multilingual reader 19, 58, 70, 71, 88
  purposes of reading 70-2
  social media 86-7
  texts as cultural translators 87-8, 207-8
  text-to-text 60, 148
  verbal counterpoint 204-5
Riya, visualization
  about 58, 147(t), 148
  characters in Harry Potter 129, 131-2, 137-8
  generic images 58, 71, 148
  make-do visuals 148, 150
  object vision 159
  specific images 148, 152
  text-to-text 58, 148, 150
  white characters 58-9, 72, 148, 190
Riya, texts (Indian)
  about 72, 88
  pirated books 129, 137-8
  Tinkle comics 19, 58, 58(f), 72
Riya, texts (Western)
  about 19, 58, 70, 72
  British and American 19, 58-60
  correctness of images 129, 131-2, 137-8
  fantasy 70
  forests 114, 119, 125
  islands 114, 204-5
  social media 86-7, 138
  specific
    Animal Farm 58
    Archie comics 58
    Enid Blyton's series 55, 58-60, 71, 114, 119, 125, 204-5, 207, 208
    Game of Thrones 70
    Harry Potter 129, 131-2, 137-8, 140-1
    Nancy Drew series 58
    Tom Sawyer 58
Roman
  about 21, 22(f)
  family 21, 174-5
  first place 52
  friends 21, 133
  maps
    path to ravine 132-3, 132(f), 178
    ravine 19-21, 22(f), 174-80, 175(f), 177(f)-9(f)
  travels 46, 119
Roman, lifelong reading spaces
  about 164-6, 174-80, 190-1
  adrenaline rush 166, 177-8, 178(f), 179
  map
    ravine 165-6, 174-80, 175(f), 177(f)-9(f)

nostalgia 166, 175–7
  tree house 178–9, 179(f)
Roman, reading processes
  about 45–6, 165–6
  agency 190
  autotopography 45–6
  diversity in cognition 145–6, 147(t), 159
  forests as reading spaces 118–19, 176
  games based on fiction 21, 87, 133
  home range 91–2, 94(t)
  life and reading spaces 21, 176, 179–80
  paracanons 45–6
  ravine experiences 21, 91–2, 118–19, 132–3, 132(f)
  subjunctive and deictic 42, 45
  threshold experiences 132–3, 132(f)
Roman, visualization
  about 147–8, 147(t), 175, 184
  faces 132
  Harry Potter 132–3, 132(f), 139–41, 178
  object vision 159
  sounds 175, 184
  spatial relationships 132, 147–8, 175
  specific visuals 118–19, 132, 147–8, 152
  visualizing reader 132–3, 132(f), 147–8, 147(t), 175
Roman, texts
  about 45–6
  art books 45, 179
  fantasy and science fiction 118–19, 175–7
  online encyclopedia 179
  science books 45–6, 179
  specific
    Deltora Quest series 176, 177(f), 179
    Eyewitness books 42, 45–6, 179
    Harry Potter 132–3, 132(f), 139–41, 178, 179
    The Lord of the Rings 118–19
    Magic Tree House series 178–9, 179(f)
    Pirates of the Caribbean 87, 133
    Ranger's Apprentice series 176–7, 179
    Red Rising 175
    Young Bond series 178(f), 179
Rosenblatt, Louise 100–1
Ross, Catherine Sheldrick 161
Rowling, J. K. 127
  See also Harry Potter series
Ryan, Marie-Laure 96–7, 99, 102–3

Sartre, Jean-Paul 29–30, 39
Scarry, Elaine 201
Schafer, Lori 102
Schilling, Derek 38–9
Schubotz, Ricarda I. 102–3
Segal, Erwin 41
senses (sight, smell, taste, touch, hearing) 40, 42–3, 80, 175, 183–4, 201
  See also visualization
sensorimotor system 37–8, 40, 145–6, 201
series books
  lifelong reading space 166, 185
  visualization for world-building 147
  See also Alice McKinley series; Blyton, Enid, series; Harry Potter series; Junie B. Jones series
Shephard, Jennifer 157
Simon, H. A. 151
simulationism
  about 36–40, 47–8, 158–9, 202
  agency of reader 39–40
  vs. being in a space 202
  forward movement 39–40, 158–9, 204–5
  improvisation 38–9, 148, 158–9
  sensorimotor simulation 145–6, 158–9
  visualization 36–7, 145–6, 158–9
  See also visualization
Slowik, Mary 103–4
smells 183–4
  See also visualization
social media. *See* online spaces
social spaces
  about 74, 89–90
  grandparents 71
  life and reading spaces 74, 89–90
  online spaces 86–7
  relationships and reading 74, 86–9
  See also home; home, first place; home range, geographic and social; online spaces
sounds 40, 80, 158, 175, 184
  See also visualization
spaces. *See* lifelong reading spaces; life spaces and reading spaces; place and space
sponsors of literacy 54, 75, 79, 81
sports. *See* games

Spufford, Francis 30-1, 122-3
Starr, G. Gabrielle 40
Steinke, Cody 3
Stimpson, Catharine 45-6
stories. *See* fiction; nonfiction
The Story of Holly and Ivy (Godden) 34-5, 185
subjunctive
  about 40-3, 47
  deictic shifts 99
  games 96, 99
  life and reading spaces 96-9
  non-Western cultures 41-2
  physicality of character movement 43
  possibilities vs. certainties 40-1
  shifting into a story 41-2
  See also deictic
Suleman
  about 25-6, 26(f)
  family 25, 75-81
  first place (Pakistan) 51, 75-6
  friends 75, 96, 106
  homes
    Edmonton 25, 76
    Pakistan 25-6
  international student 11, 19, 25, 75, 76
  languages (Urdu) 25, 77, 78-9, 106
  maps
    books and magazines 26(f), 77-8, 78(f)
    cartoons 25, 26(f), 76(f)
Suleman, reading processes
  bilingual reader 77-81
  diversity in cognition 145-6, 147(t), 159
  emotional readiness 87, 89
  forests not mentioned 110
  formats and versions 80-1
  home range 92, 94(t), 105-6
  life and reading spaces 35, 148, 187
  lifelong reading spaces 164-5, 184, 187, 188-9
  literacy sponsors 54, 75, 77, 79-81
  long vs. short texts 81, 106, 129, 139
  reading instruction 77, 81
  shared reading community 188-90
  social spaces 75-81, 89
  text-to-text 148
  texts as cultural translators 87-8, 207-8
  visualization 147(t), 148, 150, 152

Suleman, texts (Urdu)
  about 26, 79-81
  languages 78-9, 106
  social media 80
  specific
    Harry Potter (pirated) 129, 137
    Naunehal (children's magazine) 26, 77-8, 78(f), 80-1, 188-9
    Umro Ayar comic books 26, 79, 81, 213
Suleman, texts (Urdu) cartoons
  about 26, 26(f), 76(f), 79-81, 105-6
  anime 75, 81
  comics 106
  country of origin 79, 106
  family restrictions 75, 79, 101, 105, 106
  list of 79, 196
  pretend games 80, 106, 107
  specific
    Baby Loonie Toons 76(f)
    Beyblade 76(f), 79, 80, 106, 107;
    Bob the Builder 76(f)
    Digimon 76(f)
    Dragon Ball Super 75, 76(f), 81
    Farmville (game) 80
    Pokémon 76(f), 79, 80, 107
    Samurai Jack 107
    Scooby-Doo 76(f), 79
    Swat Kats 76(f)
Suleman, texts (Western)
  about 26, 26(f), 79-81, 89
  business information 35, 75, 89, 187
  comics 26, 75, 106
  magazines 75
  movies 80, 205
  TV series 80-1
  specific
    Black Beauty 26, 77
    Encarta (encyclopedia) 26, 75, 79-80
    Harry Potter 129, 139-41, 205
    Nicholas Sparks's fiction 26, 77, 80
    Oliver Twist 77
    Thirteen Reasons Why 80-1

television 101, 103, 105
  See also cartoons and animations; home range, textual
textual spaces
  graphic organizer 7-8, 8(f), 209-14, 209(f)
  See also forests; Harry Potter series

Thompson, Evan 158
Tolkien, J. R. R. 123
topos 119–20
transnationalism. *See* global connections
trees. *See* forests
Tripp, David 103
Troscianko, Emily 36, 158
Tumblr 87, 137, 167–9, 198, 208
   See also online spaces

University of Alberta 2, 4, 11(t), 12(t), 213
Urdu language. *See* Suleman
Urquhart, Sarah 92

Van Der Meer, Carolyne 194
Vendler, Helen 30–1
verbalizing readers 157–9
versions. *See* formats and versions of texts; Harry Potter series, formats and versions
video games 136, 138, 184, 212
visualization
   about 38–9, 146, 147(t), 157–62, 211
   aphantasia 156
   brain science 145–6, 157–62, 160(f)
   imagery 36, 146, 147(t), 201
   improvisation 149, 158–9
   life and reading spaces 211
   mentalizing 145–6
   movement in 37–40, 158, 201
   nonvisualizing readers 31, 56, 156–9
   object visualizers 147–8, 157–8
   provisional and indefinite 38–9, 211
   satisficing and making do 151–2
   senses (sight, smell, taste, touch, hearing) 40, 42–3, 80, 201
   sensorimotor system 37–8, 40, 201
   simulation of seeing 36–7, 145–6, 158–9
   smells 183–4
   sounds 40, 80, 158, 175, 184
   spatial visualizers 147–8, 157–8
   text-to-text 64, 72, 147, 147(t), 154–6, 155(f)
   verbalizers vs. visualizers 157–9, 211
   See also simulationism
visualization, diversity
   about 146, 147(t), 162, 211

   culturally specific images 147(t), 152–4, 153(f)
   just knowing 147(t), 156
   make-do visuals 147(t), 150–2
   nonvisualizing readers 156–9
   specific visuals 146–9, 147(t)
   text-to-text (movies/TV/books) 147, 147(t), 154–6, 155(f)
   transient visuals 147(t), 149
visualization, participants
   list of 147(t)
   questions on 146, 210–11
   See also Amani, visualization; Amy, visualization; Liang, visualization; Matt, visualization; Rahina, visualization; Riya, visualization; Roman, visualization; Ying Yu, visualization
von Cramon, D. Yves 102–3

Waller, Alison 29, 44–5, 164–5, 185
weather 99–100
   See also atmosphere
Willems, Roel M. 145–6, 158
Wohlwend, Karen E. 3, 52, 106–7
Wolf, Maryanne 211–12

Ying Yu
   about 24, 25(f)
   Edmonton apartments 180–4, 182(f)
   family 24, 180, 184
   languages (Cantonese) 24, 180, 199
   maps
      beaches, oceans, and boats 25(f), 155(f), 180–1, 181(f)
      castles and fortresses 25(f), 180–1, 181(f)
      Edmonton neighborhoods 25(f), 180–2, 181(f), 182(f)
      forests 113(f), 180–1, 181(f)
      Great Wall of China 25(f), 180, 181(f)
   travels 24, 155, 180, 199
Ying Yu, lifelong reading spaces
   about 164–6, 180–4, 190–1
   culturally hybrid images 166, 180–4
   stand-alone vs. series texts 166
   visualization 180–4, 181(f)–3(f)
Ying Yu, reading processes
   about 24, 25(f), 166

bilingual reader 24, 24(f), 180, 199
diversity in cognition 145–6, 147(t), 159
forests as reading spaces 111–13, 113(f), 119, 125, 149, 155
formats (phone) 34, 180
home range 92, 94(t), 102
(im)materiality 34
life and reading spaces 184
series vs. stand-alone texts 166
texts as cultural translators 87–8, 207–8
Ying Yu, visualization
  about 147(t), 149, 152–5, 153(f), 155(f)
  colors 183–4
  culturally hybrid images 24, 25(f), 34, 152–4, 153(f), 166, 180–4, 181(f), 189
  English texts only 180
  flashes of images 149, 152–4, 158–9, 166, 180–4
  forest images 111–13, 113(f), 149, 180
  improvisation 149, 152–4, 153(f), 159, 180
  smells 183–4
  sounds 184
  text-to-text 24, 152, 153–5, 153(f), 155
Ying Yu, texts
  about 24, 25(f)
  Beihai Beach 25(f), 152, 153(f), 180–2

castles and fortresses 25(f), 34, 152–4, 153(f), 155, 180–2, 181(f)
Chinese texts 102, 180
Disney movies 24
Edmonton neighborhoods 24, 25(f)
fantasy 112–13, 152, 155
Great Wall of China 25(f), 34, 152, 181(f), 182, 183(f)
hybrid images 24, 25(f), 152–4, 153(f)
mermaids 182
mystery and journey 25(f)
nature 25(f), 181(f)
oceans and boats 25(f), 155, 155(f), 181(f)
parks 25(f), 181(f), 183
social media 199
TV shows 102, 180
specific
  Finding Nemo 155
  Hannah Montana 24, 25(f), 152, 181–2, 181(f), 207
  Harry Potter movies 129, 139–41
  The Iron Daughter 112
  The Iron King 112
  Morgan Rice 25(f), 34, 180, 181(f), 183
  Scooby-Doo 25(f), 152, 182
  Shrek 24, 25(f), 34, 152, 181–2, 181(f)

www.ingramcontent.com/pod-product-compliance
Lightning Source LLC
Chambersburg PA
CBHW062136300426
44115CB00012BA/1950